The 1998 Training and
Performance Sourcebook

Other McGraw-Hill Titles Edited by Mel Silberman

THE 1998 TEAM AND ORGANIZATION DEVELOPMENT SOURCEBOOK

THE 1997 MCGRAW-HILL TRAINING AND PERFORMANCE SOURCEBOOK

THE 1996 MCGRAW-HILL TRAINING AND PERFORMANCE SOURCEBOOK

THE 1997 MCGRAW-HILL TEAM AND ORGANIZATION DEVELOPMENT SOURCEBOOK

THE 1996 MCGRAW-HILL TEAM AND ORGANIZATION DEVELOPMENT SOURCEBOOK

The 1998 Training and Performance Sourcebook

Mel Silberman, Editor

Assisted by
Patricia Philips

McGraw-Hill

New York   San Francisco   Washington, D.C.   Auckland   Bogotá
Caracas   Lisbon   London   Madrid   Mexico City   Milan
Montreal   New Delhi   San Juan   Singapore
Sydney   Tokyo   Toronto

International Standard Serial Number:
The 1998 Training and Performance Sourcebook
ISSN 1084-1342

McGraw-Hill

A Division of The McGraw·Hill Companies

1 2 3 4 5 6 7 8 9 0   EDW/EDW   9 0 2 1 0 9 8 7 (Paperback)
1 2 3 4 5 6 7 8 9 0   EDW/EDW   9 0 2 1 0 9 8 7 (Looseleaf)

ISBN 0-07-058004-9 (Paperback)
PN 0-07-058063-4
PART OF
ISBN 0-07-058003-0 (Looseleaf)

The sponsoring editor for this book was Richard Narramore, the editing supervisor was Fred Dahl, the designer was Inkwell Publishing Services, and the production supervisor was Sherri Souffrance.

Printed and bound by Edwards Brothers.

CONTENTS

Topical Index   ix

Preface   xiii

TRAINING ACTIVITIES   1

1   Mastery: A Game to Explore Coaching for Skills
     Improvement   5
     Sivasailam (Thiagi) Thiagarajan

2   The Moving Target: A Game about Goal Setting   23
     Bob Pike

3   Delegation with Style: Accommodating Learning
     Preferences   27
     Carol Harvey

4   The Three "M's" of Empowerment: Mission, Milieu, and
     Mind-Sets   39
     Marlene Caroselli

5   The Feedback Toss: Learning about Its Effects on
     Performance   45
     Richard Whelan and Robert Merritt

6   Learning to Drive a Car: Understanding Personality
     Differences   51
     Karen Lawson

7   Taking Charge of Your Career: A Personal SWOT
     Analysis and Environmental Scan   59
     Jane Flagello

8   Political Correctness: A Diversity Opinion Exercise   69
     Hank Karp

9   Fugitive E-Mails: The Challenges of Electronic
    Communication   79
    Peter Garber

10 Alternative Ways to Remember: A Demonstration of
    Five Principles   95
    Brian Kelley

11 Myers-Briggs (MBTI) Preferences: Choosing a Vice
    President for Jetts Fireworks   105
    Nancy Jackson

12 One-to-One Conversations: Receiving High-Quality
    Feedback   115
    Phil Donnison

13 "Play Ball!": Visualizing Productive and Nonproductive
    Communication   118
    Vicki Schneider

14 The New Color Society: Experiencing Stereotyping and
    Classism   133
    Robert Kaeser

15 Stop 'n Jot!: A Versatile Activity to Enhance Learning and
    Transfer   136
    Brenda Gardner and Sharon Korth

    ASSESSMENT INSTRUMENTS   147

16 What Is Your Thinking Style?   149
    Garry Gelade

17 What Is Your Learning Style?   159
    Christopher Hardy and Susan Hardy

18 Are Your Employees Getting the Message?   169
    Janet Winchester-Silbaugh and Caryn Relkin

19 How Consistent Are Your Values with the
    Organization's?   177
    William Harrington and Bob Preziosi

20 What Is My Leadership Style?   187
Deborah Hopen and Laura Gregg

21 Does Your Certification Program Meet Best-Practice Criteria?   202
Susan Barksdale and Teri Lund

22 What Questions Are You Asking During the Employment Interview?   221
Kent Rondeau

23 Is Virtual Reality Training the Right Choice?   229
Nina Adams and Carol Gunther-Mohr

HELPFUL HANDOUTS   239

24 Are You Writing More but Enjoying It Less?   241
Dianna Booher

25 The Magic of Memory- and Mind-Mapping®   251
Jeanne Baer

26 Twenty-Five Tips for Making the Workplace Accessible   257
Sophie Oberstein

27 Sexual Harassment: The Gray Zone   263
Robert Kaeser

28 Four Writing Challenges and What to Do About Them   267
Brooke Broadbent and Lise Froidevaux

29 Sixteen Guidelines for Managing Time in Class   271
Scott Parry

30 Six Principles for Designing Instruction   277
Anne Marrelli

31 Managing Your Communications Web   283
Jacqueline Hall

PRACTICAL GUIDES 289

32 How to Use the Internet and Intranets as Learning and Performance Tools 291
Diane Gayeski

33 How to Be an On-Line Instructor 300
Zane Berge

34 How to Develop a Training Strategy 310
Susan Barksdale and Teri Lund

35 How to Develop Self-Directed Learning Modules 325
Sophie Oberstein

36 How to Design a Workshop 332
Niela Miller

37 How to Make a C.A.S.E. for Problem-Based Learning 337
Rick Rogers

38 How to Teach the Concept of Single- and Double-Loop Learning 345
Diane Stoy and Jennifer Wild

39 How to Develop College Internships 355
Boni Sivi

40 How to Use Meetingware and Facilitators for Effective Meetings 362
Jana Markowitz

TOPICAL INDEX
Find a Tool for Your Specific Topic

In the place of a traditional index is the following classification by topic of the 40 tools found in *The 1998 Training and Performance Sourcebook.*

Alternatives to Classroom Training

23. *Is Virtual Reality Training the Right Choice?*
Assessment Instrument by Nina Adams and Carol Gunther-Mohr

32. *How to Use the Internet and Intranets As Learning and Performance Tools*
Practical Guide by Diane Gayeski

33. *How to Be an On-Line Instructor*
Practical Guide by Zane Berge

40. *How to Use Meetingware and Facilitators for Effective Meetings*
Practical Guide by Jana Markowitz

Career Development

7. *Taking Charge of Your Career: A Personal SWOT Analysis and Environmental Scan*
Training Activity by Jane Flagello

39. *How to Develop College Internships*
Practical Guide by Boni Sivi

Communication Skills

9. *Fugitive E-Mails: The Challenges of Electronic Communication*
Training Activity by Peter Garber

13. *"Play Ball!": Visualizing Productive and Nonproductive Communication*
Training Activity by Vicki Schneider

18. *Are Your Employees Getting the Message?*
Assessment Instrument by Janet Winchester-Silbaugh and Caryn Relkin

24. *Are You Writing More but Enjoying It Less?*
Helpful Handout by Dianna Booher

28. *Four Writing Challenges and What to Do about Them*
Helpful Handout by Brooke Broadbent and Lise Froidevaux

31. *Managing Your Communications Web*
Helpful Handout by Jacqueline Hall

Diversity and Cross-cultural Awareness

8. *Political Correctness: A Diversity Opinion Exercise*
Training Activity by Hank Karp

14. *The New Color Society: Experiencing Stereotyping and Classism*
Training Activity by Robert Kaeser

26. *Twenty-Five Tips for Making the Workplace Accessible*
Helpful Handout by Sophie Oberstein

27. *Sexual Harassment: The Gray Zone*
Helpful Handout by Robert Kaeser

Evaluation

21. *Does Your Certification Program Meet Best-Practice Criteria?*
Assessment Instrument by Susan Barksdale and Teri Lund

Learning and Training Techniques

10. *Alternative Ways to Remember: A Demonstration of Five Principles*
Training Activity by Brian Kelley

15. *Stop 'n Jot!: A Versatile Activity to Enhance Learning and Transfer*
Training Activity by Brenda Gardner and Sharon Korth

17. *What Is Your Learning Style?*
Assessment Instrument by Christopher Hardy and Susan Hardy

25. *The Magic of Memory- and Mind-Mapping*®
Helpful Handout by Jeanne Baer

29. *Sixteen Guidelines for Managing Time in Class*
Helpful Handout by Scott Parry

37. *How to Make a C.A.S.E. for Problem-Based Learning*
Practical Guide by Rick Rogers

38. *How to Teach the Concept of Single- and Double-Loop Learning*
Practical Guide by Diane Stoy and Jennifer Wild

Management Development

1. *Mastery: A Game to Explore Coaching for Skills Improvement*
Training Activity by Sivasailam Thiagarajan

5. *The Feedback Toss: Learning about Its Effects on Performance*
Training Activity by Richard Whelan and Robert Merritt

6. *Learning to Drive a Car: Understanding Personality Differences*
Training Activity by Karen Lawson

20. *What Is My Leadership Style?*
Assessment Instrument by Deborah Hopen and Laura Gregg

22. *What Questions Are You Asking during the Employment Interview?*
Assessment Instrument by Kent Rondeau

Performance Support

2. *The Moving Target: A Game about Goal Setting*
Training Activity by Bob Pike

3. *Delegation with Style: Accommodating Learning Preferences*
Training Activity by Carol Harvey

4. *The Three "M's" of Empowerment: Mission, Milieu, and Mind-Sets*
Training Activity by Marlene Caroselli

12. *One-to-One Conversations: Receiving High-Quality Feedback*
Training Activity by Phil Donnison

Personal Effectiveness

11. *Myers-Briggs (MBTI) Preferences: Choosing a Vice President for Jetts Fireworks*
Training Activity by Nancy Jackson

16. *What Is Your Thinking Style?*
Assessment Instrument by Garry Gelade

19. *How Consistent Are Your Values with the Organization's?*
Assessment Instrument by William Harrington and Bob Preziosi

Training Design

30. *Six Principles for Designing Instruction*
Helpful Handout by Anne Marrelli

34. *How to Develop a Training Strategy*
Practical Guide by Susan Barksdale and Teri Lund

35. *How to Develop Self-Directed Learning Modules*
Practical Guide by Sophie Oberstein

36. *How to Design a Workshop*
Practical Guide by Niela Miller

PREFACE

Welcome to the third year of *The Training and Performance Sourcebook,* a yearly collection of practical tools to develop human resources. *The 1996 Sourcebook* was a huge success. *The 1997 Sourcebook* has another great lineup of resources for your professional use.

Along with its companion, *The Team and Organization Development Sourcebook, The Training and Performance Sourcebook* provides the latest cutting-edge advice and learning aids on topics important to today's public and private sector organizations. While *The Team and Organization Development Sourcebook* emphasizes systemwide issues, *The Training and Performance Sourcebook* focuses on development and support at the individual level of the organization.

The Training and Performance Sourcebook includes discussion of both training and nontraining solutions to performance problems. You will find several materials, prepared by leading experts, that will enhance your efforts as a trainer, instructor, or coach. You will also discover ways to support individual performance through performance technology.

The 1998 Sourcebook contains 40 training activities, assessment instruments, handouts, and practical guides ... creating a ready-to-use toolkit for trainers, HRD consultants, performance support specialists, and subject matter experts. It is also invaluable for managers and other organizational representatives who are interested in coaching, training, learning, and performance development. Best of all, because these tools are reproducible, they can be shared with others.

Here are some of the topics you will find covered in *The 1998 Training and Performance Sourcebook:*

✓ Alternatives to classroom training

✓ Career development

✓ Communication skills

✓ Diversity and cross-cultural awareness

✓ Evaluation

✓ Learning and training techniques

✓ Management development

- ✓ Performance support
- ✓ Personal effectiveness
- ✓ Training design

I hope you will find *The 1998 Training and Performance Sourcebook* to be a one-stop resource you can draw on again and again in your efforts to facilitate learning and support performance improvement.

Mel Silberman
Princeton, New Jersey

TRAINING ACTIVITIES

In this section of *The 1998 Training and Performance Sourcebook,* you will find fifteen training activities. They are designed to:

✓ Introduce training topics
✓ Practice skills
✓ Promote attitude change
✓ Increase knowledge
✓ Stimulate discussion
✓ Foster participation and retention
✓ Enhance concepts

You can use these activities in a variety of settings:

✓ Classroom-based training sessions
✓ Meetings and retreats
✓ One-to-one coaching
✓ Distance learning
✓ Consultations

All of the activities featured here are highly participatory. They are designed with the belief that learning and change best occur through experience and reflection. As opposed to preaching or lecturing, experiential activities place people directly within a concrete situation. Typically, participants are asked to solve a problem, complete an assignment, or communicate information. Often, the task can be quite challenging. Sometimes, it can also be a great deal of fun. The bottom line, however, is that participants become active partners in the learning of new concepts or in the development of new ideas.

The experiences contained in the activities you are about to read can also be of two kinds: simulated and real-world. Although some may find them to be artificial, well-designed simulations can provide an effective analogy to real-world experiences. They also have the advantage of being time-saving shortcuts to longer, drawn-out activities. Sometimes, of course, there is no substitute for real-world experience. Activities that engage teams in actual, ongoing work can serve as a powerful mechanism for change.

Experience, by itself, is not always "the best teacher." Reflecting on the experience, however, can yield wisdom and insight. You will find that the team activities in this section contain helpful guidelines for reflection. Expect a generous selection of questions to process or debrief the actual activities.

All of the activities have been written for ease of use. A concise overview of each activity is provided. You will be guided, step-by-step, through the activity instructions. All of the necessary participant materials are included. For your photocopying convenience, these materials are on separate pages. Any materials you need to prepare in advance have been kept to a minimum. Special equipment or physical arrangements are seldom needed.

Best of all, the activities are designed so that you can easily modify or customize them to your specific requirements. Also, time allocations are readily adaptable. Furthermore, many of the activities are "frame exercises" ... generic activities that can be used for many topics or subject matters. You will find it easy to plug in the content relevant to your team's circumstances.

As you conduct any of these activities, bear in mind that experiential activity is especially successful if you do a good job as facilitator. Here are some common mistakes people make in facilitating experiential activities:

1. *Motivation:* Participants aren't invited to buy into the activity themselves or sold the benefits of joining in. Participants don't know what to expect during the exercise.

2. *Directions:* Instructions are lengthy and unclear. Participants cannot visualize what the facilitator expects from them.

3. *Group Process:* Subgroups are not composed effectively. Group formats are not changed to fit the requirements of each activity. Subgroups are left idle.

4. *Energy:* Activities move too slowly. Participants are sedentary. Activities are long or demanding when they need to be short or relaxed. Participants do not find the activity challenging.

5. *Processing:* Participants are confused and/or overwhelmed by the questions posed to them. There is a poor fit between the facilitator's questions and the goals of the activity. Facilitators share their opinions before first hearing the participants' views.

To avoid these pitfalls, follow these steps:

I. Introduce the activity.

   1. Explain your objectives

   2. Sell the benefits

   3. Convey enthusiasm

4. Connect the activity to previous activities

5. Share personal feelings and express confidence in participants

II. Help participants to know what they are expected to do.
    1. Speak slowly
    2. Use visual backup
    3. Define important terms
    4. Demonstrate the activity

III. Manage the group process.
    1. Form groups in a variety of ways
    2. Vary the number of people in any activity based upon that exercise's specific requirements
    3. Divide participants into teams before giving further directions
    4. Give instructions to groups separately in a multipart activity
    5. Keep people busy
    6. Inform the subgroups about time frames

IV. Keep participants involved.
    1. Keep the activity moving
    2. Challenge the participants
    3. Reinforce participants for their involvement in the activity
    4. Build physical movement into the activity

V. Get participants to reflect on the activity's implications.
    1. Ask relevant questions
    2. Carefully structure the first processing experiences
    3. Observe how participants are reacting to the group processing
    4. Assist a subgroup that is having trouble processing an activity
    5. Hold your own reactions until after hearing from participants

1

MASTERY: A GAME TO EXPLORE COACHING FOR SKILLS IMPROVEMENT

Sivasailam (Thiagi) Thiagarajan

As president of Workshops by Thiagi, **Sivasailam Thiagarajan, Ph.D.** *specializes in designing and delivering training for improving human performance. Thiagi has been the president of the International Society for Performance Improvement (ISPI) and of the North American Simulation and Gaming Association (NASAGA). He is the author of 24 books, 175+ articles, and several hundred games and simulations, including* **Games by Thiagi (HRD Press).** *Thiagi was a contributor to* **The 1996 McGraw-Hill Team and Organization Development Sourcebook** *and* **The 1996 and 1997 McGraw-Hill Training and Performance Sourcebook.**

Contact Information:

Workshops by Thiagi
4423 East Trailridge Road
Bloomington, IN 47408
812-332-1478
www.thiagi.com

Overview   This game explores factors that influence the effectiveness of coaching for skills improvement. You play Mastery in three acts, spaced over a couple of days or weeks. Not all participants will be involved in the game all the time. The total time required of each participant is about 45 minutes. The only time all the participants get together is for the debriefing, which lasts 15 to 30 minutes. During the first act (priming), you teach a few participants how to do a magic trick. During the second act (coaching), these participants recruit and coach other participants, one or two at a time. During the third act (debriefing), you conduct a general session to identify and discuss the factors that influence the effectiveness of coaching for skills improvement.

Mastery requires at least 12 participants. The best game involves 30 or more participants. You can effectively play this game with hundreds of participants.

Suggested Time	*Priming:* Two sessions of 10–20 minutes each.
	Coaching: 10–20 minute sessions, spread over one or more days.
	Debriefing: 15–30 minutes.

Materials Needed

✓ Form A (Let Me Read Your Mind)
✓ Form B (Human Performance Improvement Strategies)
✓ Form C (Blank Matrix)—reproduce on the back of Form B
✓ Form D (Coaching Contest Instruction Sheet)
✓ Form E (Guidelines for Effective Coaching)

Procedure

Preliminary Activities

1. Read through these instructions first. Decide which group you are going to teach. Find out the total number of participants. Select 2, 3, or 4 participants to be trained to become the head coaches for 2 teams. Come up with a schedule for the initial training of the head coaches (two separate sessions of 10 to 20 minutes each), mutual coaching by participants (10- to 20-minute sessions, spread over several days), and the general meeting (15 to 30 minutes). Prepare copies of handouts for the coaching activities and posters to announce the final meeting time and location.

2. Study Form A (Let Me Read Your Mind). Follow the instructions on Form A, using the *Human Performance Improvement Strategies* matrix on Form B. Check out the magic trick. This trick works automatically: It does not matter which rectangle you begin with. You will always end up at the *coaching* rectangle. Test the magic trick by starting at different rectangles. This trick will work only if you give the correct instructions to the spectator. A cheat sheet for recalling the instructions is printed at the bottom of the *Human Performance Improvement Strategies* matrix itself, disguised as a footer. Ignore the date in this footer. This is what the rest of the symbols and letters mean:

   |: "Move your finger up or down until …"

   _: "Move your finger left or right until …"

   / : "Move your finger diagonally until …"

   r: "... you reach a rectangle without any stars."

   s: "... you reach a rectangle with four stars."

3. Mentally rehearse the trick. This is how you do the trick. Carry several copies of the *Human Performance Improvement Strategies* matrix. Find an unsuspecting spectator and give him or her a copy of the matrix. Casually retain the other copies in your hand. Turn your back to the spectator and give the instructions. Begin by asking the spectator to place his or her finger on any rectangle that contains the preferred performance improvement strategy.

Emphasize that you cannot see what the spectator is doing. Ask the spectator to make another choice if his or her original choice is *violence*. Follow with the other instructions, using your hidden job aid as explained in the previous paragraph. At the end of the final instruction, still keep your back turned to the spectator and pretend to read his or her mind. Reveal the strategy on the rectangle with the spectator's finger (which will always be *coaching*). Don't blurt out the answer. Drag it out, using a monologue similar to the one in the last paragraph of Form A.

4. Keep practicing until you can casually glance at the footer and reel off the instructions. Test your ability. Find a live spectator and perform your magic trick.

Priming

1. Select people for priming. If you have fewer than 20 participants, select 4 of them. Two of these selected participants will be head coaches for the Blue Team and the other two will be the head coaches for the Red Team. If you have 20 to 50 participants, select 6 head coaches, 3 each for the 2 teams. If you have more than 50 participants, select 4 head coaches for each team. (With this many participants, spread the coaching act over several days.)

2. Coach the Blue Team head coaches. Meet with the selected participants. Begin by performing the magic trick. Then explain how the trick is done. Ask the head coaches to practice the trick a couple of times and get ready to coach others.

3. Explain the contest to the Blue Team coaches. Tell the head coaches that they should recruit 1 or 2 other participants and coach them to perform the magic trick. (If 2 participants are recruited, they should be coached at the same time.) After the participants learn the trick, they become members of the Blue Team. They receive copies of the matrix and the contest instructions, and coach 1 or 2 other participants. This process is repeated until 5 minutes before the time scheduled for the debriefing. At this time, whichever team has the most members (or coaches) wins the game. Give each coach several copies of the *Human Performance Improvement Strategies* matrix (with the blank matrix on the back) and the *Coaching Contest Instruction Sheet*. Explain that the instruction sheet summarizes the contest rules. Walk the new coaches through these instructions.

4. Read the *Guidelines for Effective Coaching* (Form E). Spend some time getting ready to train the head coaches for the Red Team, using these guidelines. You are now ready to coach the Red Team head coaches. Meet with the selected participants. Begin by performing the magic trick. Then coach the head coaches, incorporating the guidelines for effective coaching. Ask the head coaches to practice the trick several times and get ready to coach the others.

5. Distribute and discuss the guidelines on Form E. Explain that knowing the trick is only one part of becoming an effective coach. The other part is learning how to coach effectively. Explain and discuss each guideline.

6. Explain the contest to the Red Team coaches. Tell the head coaches that they should recruit 1 or 2 other participants and coach them to perform the magic trick. If 2 participants are recruited, they should be coached at the same time. After the participants learn the trick, they become members of the Red Team. They receive the guidelines for effective coaching and discuss how they can incorporate these guidelines in their coaching session. They also receive several copies of the *Human Performance Improvement Strategies* and *Guidelines for Effective Coaching*, and coach 1 or 2 other participants (not only on the magic trick, but also on effective coaching procedures). This process is repeated until 5 minutes before the time scheduled for the debriefing. At this time, whichever team has the most members (or coaches) wins the game. Give each coach several copies of the *Human Performance Improvement Strategies* matrix (with the blank matrix on the back) and the *Coaching Contest Instruction Sheet*. Explain that the instruction sheet summarizes the contest rules. Walk the new coaches through these instructions.

Coaching

1. Coordinate the coaching act. During this act (which is spread over days or weeks), your main task is to coordinate the activity. Make sure that the coaching chain continues with each new coach teaching 1 or 2 others. Newly-taught participants become members of the team of their coach, receive additional copies of the handouts and coach 1 or 2 others. Make sure that no one coaches more than 2 participants, and no participant gets coached more than once.

2. Monitor to see if the Red Team members use the effective coaching guidelines. Help the coaches find additional participants. Remind the participants of the scheduled time for the final debriefing session. During the final stages of this act, some of the newly coached participants may run out of people to coach. Tell these participants that they need not coach others, but they should still count themselves as members of the appropriate teams.

Debriefing

1. Begin the session. Make sure that all the participants attend this session. You should invite the participants who did not get coached on the magic trick, if there are any. Welcome all the participants and tell them that you are going to identify the winning team and discuss some factors associated with effective coaching.

2. **Determine the winning team.** Ask the members of the Blue Team to stand up. Quickly count the number of Blue Team members. Repeat the same procedure with the Red Team. Identify the team with the most members as the winning team and lead a round of applause. In most cases, the Blue Team will be the winning team. Explain that the Red Team coaches spent more time applying a set of effective coaching principles. This could probably account for the difference in the number of participants being coached by the two teams.

3. **Conduct a quick evaluation activity.** Give an index card to each participant. Instruct the participants to write their team color on one side of the index card. Then ask the participants to think back on how *they* were coached (*not* how they coached the others). They should rate the *enjoyment* of this coaching experience on a 5-point scale (5: very enjoyable, 4: enjoyable, 3: fair, 2: slightly unpleasant, and 1: unpleasant) and write this number under the team color. They should then grade the effectiveness of their coach (A: excellent, B: good, C: fair, and D: poor) and write the appropriate letter below the previous number rating. After a suitable pause, collect the index cards and give them to a couple of volunteer statisticians.

4. **Compute the ratings.** Ask the participants to individually write down on a piece of paper two or three lessons they learned about effective coaching from how they were coached and the way they coached the others. While the participants are busy doing this, ask your volunteer statisticians to separate the index cards by team color and calculate the average *enjoyment* rating and *effectiveness* rating. To calculate the effectiveness rating, they should count A's as 4 points, B's as 3, C's as 2, and D's as 1.

5. **Discuss coaching principles.** Ask the participants to share the lessons they learned. Discuss the principles of effective coaching behind each lesson. Here are some of the important principles that you want to get across:

   ✓ Effective coaching requires a time investment.

   ✓ You should take time to prepare for a coaching session.

   ✓ Knowing what to coach is not enough. You should also know how to coach.

   ✓ Different people learn in different ways. An effective coach changes his or her coaching strategy to suit the learner's preference.

   ✓ Most people coach the way they were coached. This may not always be an appropriate strategy.

   ✓ You can personalize your coaching strategy by asking the learner how he or she would like to be coached.

   ✓ Knowing the steps does not guarantee that you will be able to perform the skill.

✓ It is important to practice a new skill.

✓ Learners should have the freedom to experiment with their personal variations.

Feel free to suggest these lessons if the participants do not bring them up. Discuss additional lessons learned by the participants.

6. Distribute the guidelines for effective coaching (Form E) to the members of the Blue Team. Tell them it summarizes many of the principles discussed earlier. Suggest that all participants use these guidelines whenever they have to provide on-the-job coaching to others.

7. Report the results of the ratings computation. Ask your volunteer statistician to report the average enjoyment score for the two teams. The average of the Red Team is usually higher than that of the Blue Team because of the use of the guidelines for effective coaching. Discuss the causes for the difference (or for the lack of difference). Repeat the same procedure with the average effectiveness scores.

8. Evaluate transfer of training. Ask the participants if they performed the magic trick to anyone outside the group, not as a part of their coaching task. Ask the number of Blue Team members who have done so to stand up. Repeat with the Red Team members. Point out that this is the truest test of the effectiveness of coaching. Discuss any differences in the numbers between the two teams.

9. Invite comments and questions from the participants. Respond appropriately. Thank the volunteer statisticians and all the participants. Remind them to keep coaching, using the guidelines for effective coaching.

Look at the figure on Form B. This 3×5 matrix lists 15 different strategies for improving human performance. Some rectangles have four stars and the others don't. For the present, ignore these differences among the rectangles and follow these steps:

1. Quickly review the strategies and decide which one is the most effective and efficient one. Place your finger on the rectangle that contains this strategy.

2. If your finger is on *violence*, please reconsider. *Violence* is not a nice strategy and its use presents several ethical problems. Choose some other strategy and place your finger on the rectangle that contains this strategy.

3. I don't know where your finger is, but let me ask you to move it around. Please move your finger up or down (vertically in the same column) until you come to a rectangle *that does not have any stars*. Place your finger on this rectangle. It does not matter what strategy is listed in this rectangle.

4. Now move your finger left or right (horizontally in the same row) until you reach a rectangle *with four stars*. Place your finger in this rectangle. It does not matter what strategy is listed in the rectangle with stars.

5. Now move your finger diagonally (in any of the four directions: \ / \ /) until you come to a rectangle *that does not have any stars*. Place your finger in this rectangle. It does not matter what strategy is listed in the rectangle.

6. Now move your finger up or down until you come to a rectangle *with four stars*. Place your finger in this rectangle. Read the strategy that is listed in this rectangle. Concentrate your thoughts on this strategy. Visualize mental images of this strategy in action.

7. I am going to do some remote control mind reading. Please focus on the mental images related to the strategy in this rectangle…. I don't know which strategy you selected initially, and I definitely don't know which you ended up with…. But let me catch your mental waves…. Please focus on the strategy in the rectangle…. I can now see the stars…. I see the letters dimly. They are out of focus…. Please concentrate…. I see that the name of the strategy begins with the letter "C"…. I've got it now. The strategy is *coaching*.

HUMAN PERFORMANCE
IMPROVEMENT STRATEGIES

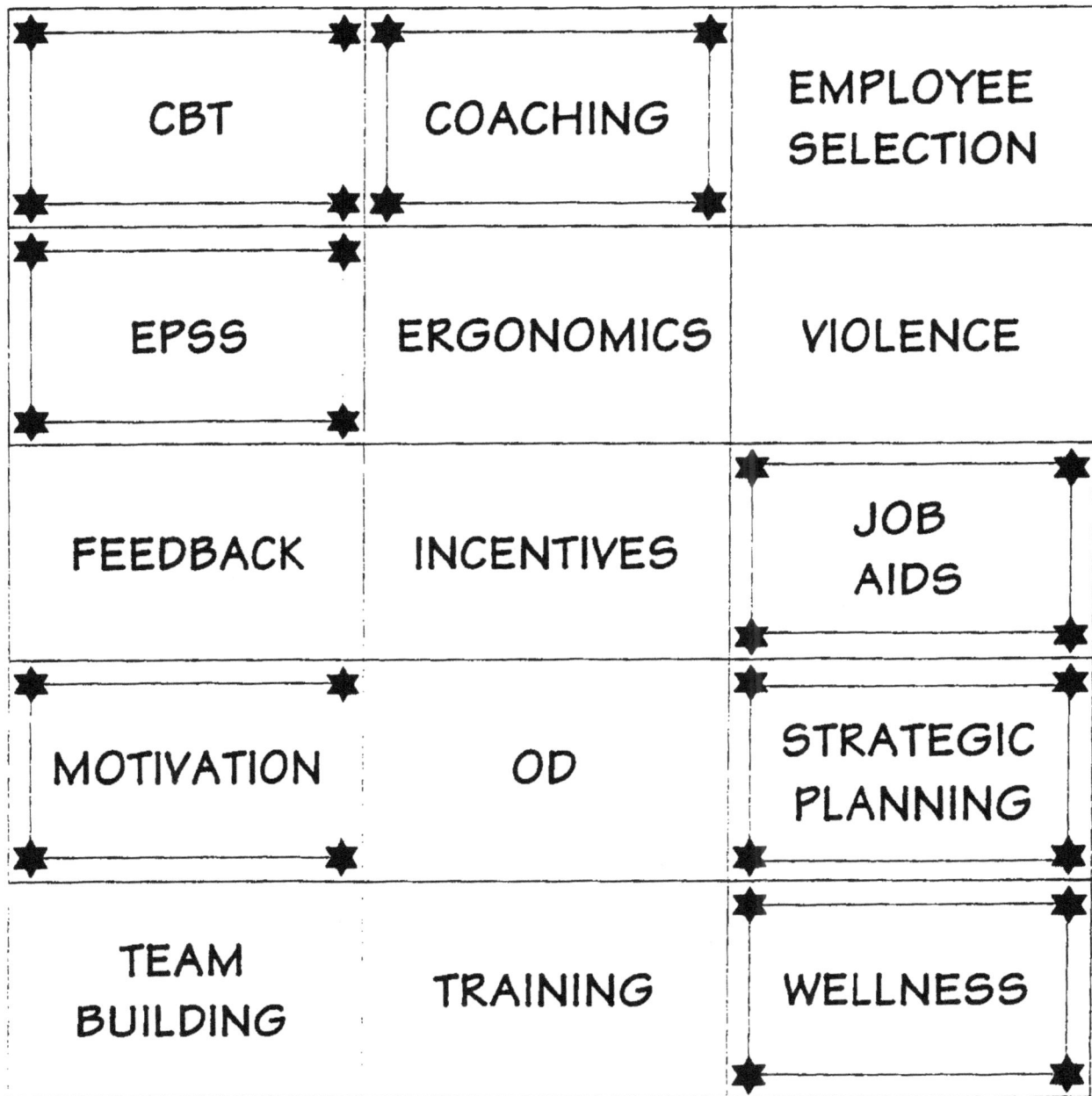

CBT	COACHING	EMPLOYEE SELECTION
EPSS	ERGONOMICS	VIOLENCE
FEEDBACK	INCENTIVES	JOB AIDS
MOTIVATION	OD	STRATEGIC PLANNING
TEAM BUILDING	TRAINING	WELLNESS

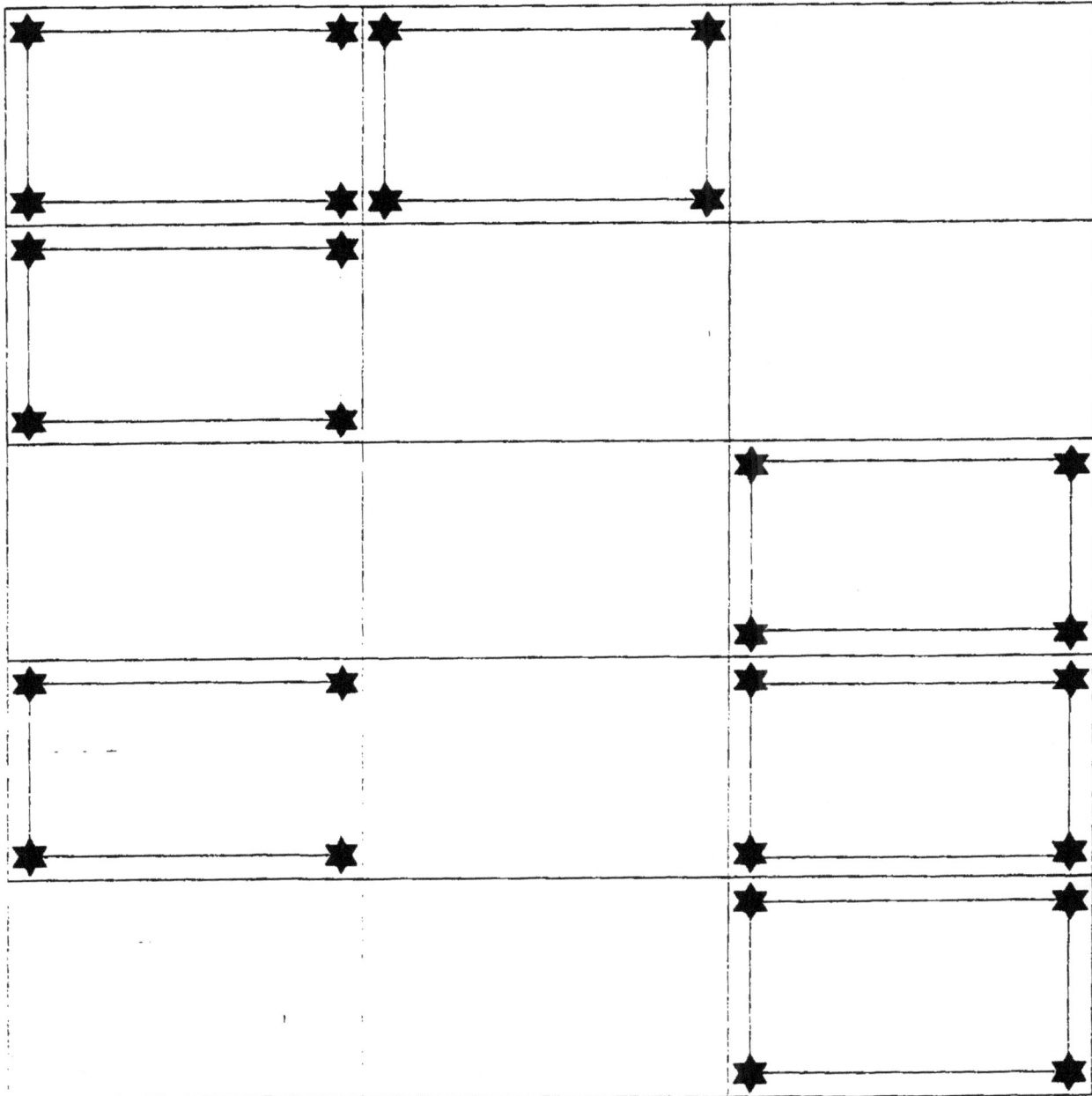

COACHING CONTEST INSTRUCTION SHEET

Congratulations!

Since you have learned how to perform this magic trick, you have become a member of the team to which your coach belongs. Find out from your coach whether you are a member of the *Blue Team* or the *Red Team*.

Your next task is to recruit more people to qualify to become members of your team. Find two people from the group and coach them to perform the magic trick. If you prefer, you may coach just one person. But you may not coach more than two people.

Make sure that the people you are coaching don't already know how to do the trick.

After you have completed your coaching assignment, make the new magicians members of your team. Give them copies of the different handouts. Tell them to find other people and coach them just like you did.

All coaching activities should stop 5 minutes before the start of the general meeting. Find out from your coach the start time for this meeting. Be sure to attend the meeting. Remember, your team will win if it has more members than the other team. So motivate the new coaches to find and coach others.

General guidelines for coaching for any type of skill improvement are given first. Sample applications of these guidelines to the magic trick are printed in *italics*.

1. **Prepare to coach.** Design a job aid to help the learner. Assemble all the necessary materials.

   Prepare a chart of symbols and letters used in the hidden job aid.

2. **Ask the learner how he or she would like to be coached.** This question signals that the learner has to assume control and to take responsibility for mastering the skill.

   Perform your magic trick first. Then ask this question.

3. **Demonstrate the skill at least twice.** First, demonstrate the skills just like you would like the learner to do. Next, demonstrate slowly, explaining and emphasizing critical moves.

   During your slow-motion demonstration, refer to the steps indicated by the hidden job aid.

4. **Get the learner into the practice stage as quickly as possible.** Use a hands-on approach.

   Avoid too many demonstrations and explanations. Let the learner do the trick as quickly as possible.

5. **Encourage flexible variations.** Help the learner modify the activity to suit his or her personal preferences and style.

   Encourage the learner to come up with his or her own line of patter. Also suggest that the learner use the blank matrix to prepare a personalized list of items (of such things as TV shows or favorite vacation destinations) as an alternative to the set of human performance improvement strategies.

6. **Check the performance after a delay.** Ask the learner to repeatedly practice the new skill. Check his or her performance after a few hours or few days. Offer suitable reinforcement and feedback.

   Ask the learner to demonstrate the magic trick to you after a suitable delay.

7. **Two is better than one.** Coach two people at the same time. Encourage them to practice with each other. If you are coaching on an interpersonal skill, encourage them to practice on each other.

   Coach two learners at the same time. Ask them to take turns and practice showing the magic trick to each other.

2

THE MOVING TARGET: A GAME ABOUT GOAL SETTING

Bob Pike

Robert W. Pike *is president of Resources for Organizations, Inc., Creative Training Techniques International, Inc. and the Resources Group, Inc. Bob leads sessions over 150 days per year covering topics of leadership, attitudes, motivation, communication, decision making, problem solving, personal and organizational effectiveness, conflict management, team building, and managerial productivity. He has earned the Certified Speaking Professional (CSP) designation from the National Speakers Association. The author of* **The Creative Training Techniques Handbook** *and* **Dealing with Difficult Participants** *and editor of the* **Creative Training Techniques Newsletter,** *Bob also developed the Creative Training Techniques™ Seminar that now has over 65,000 alumni. His video,* **Creative Training and Presentation Techniques***, won the "Best Business Video" award from the Special Interest Video Association.*

Contact Information:

Creative Training Techniques International, Inc.
7620 West 78th Street
Minneapolis, MN 55439
800-383-9210
www.cttbobpike.com

Overview   Often participants are asked to accomplish tasks without having "what success looks like" defined. People need to know the task, the purpose, and the conditions of satisfaction ("what success looks like") before they begin to maximize motivation, commitment, performance, and communication. This activity demonstrates the importance of setting goals or performance objectives before a team activity or task takes place—not during or after.

Suggested Time   30 minutes.

Materials Needed   ✓ Flip chart and easel
✓ Contrasting color markers (e.g., blue and red)
✓ Copies of Form A (Discussion Questions)

Procedure   1. Ask one person to volunteer. Hand the volunteer one of the markers and have him or her stand about 8 feet from a flip chart. Ask the person to hit the target and gesture to the flip chart. Using the uncapped marker as a dart, the volunteer throws (or uses an underhand toss) the marker at the easel, leaving a colored mark on the paper.

2. Wherever the mark is made, go over to the easel and draw three circles making up a target someplace else. Then say, "You didn't hit the target, but you can try again." Allow the volunteer to make another toss. Once again, wherever they hit, draw the target someplace else. Do the same thing one more time.

3. Then ask small groups of 3–5 to discuss the questions on Form A. Have each group select a group leader to lead the discussion. Allow 5–7 minutes or until you see that most groups have finished two-thirds of the questions. Then give the groups a one-minute warning. After discussion is complete, ask 3 group leaders to volunteer to give one-minute summaries of their groups' discussion.

4. Conclude by rewarding the volunteer for taking a risk and helping to model something that is not very fun in a class setting, but far worse when it happens in real life.

Variation   Allow the volunteer to have someone else take over after the first toss. Do the same with subsequent tosses.

DISCUSSION QUESTIONS

The group leader should read the questions aloud one at a time and lead a discussion on each question before moving to the next.

1. Did you understand the purpose of the game from the beginning? Why or why not? What would you have needed to know to have the object of the game be clear to you?

2. What did it take to "win"? Was winning possible? How do you think the volunteer playing the game felt? How did you feel as you watched?

3. Most of the time when this game is played neither the observers nor the volunteer attempt to clarify the rules, the objectives, or the unfairness of how the game is being played. Was it true for this group? Did anyone attempt to clarify the rules or objectives? What do you think the purpose of the activity was?

4. What lessons learned from this activity could be applied to:
   a) coaching employees?
   b) setting goals?
   c) giving feedback?

5. What other learning points could be drawn from this activity?

3

DELEGATION WITH STYLE: ACCOMMODATING LEARNING PREFERENCES

Carol Harvey

Carol P. Harvey, Ed.D *is an associate professor of management and marketing at Assumption College. A former manager with the Xerox Corporation, she is the coauthor of* **Understanding Diversity: Readings, Cases and Exercises** *(HarperCollins, 1995) and a contributor to* **The 1996 McGraw-Hill Training and Performance Sourcebook** *and* **The 1997 McGraw-Hill Team and Organizational Development Sourcebook.**

Contact Information:

Assumption College
500 Salisbury St., Worcester, MA 01615-0005
508-767-7459
charvey@eve.assumption.edu or COOLIDGEROAD@worldnet.att.net

Overview   Many supervisors and managers find it difficult to successfully delegate tasks to subordinates. However, much of the success of delegation depends on how well people learn to carry out whatever tasks they are being asked to perform. This activity presents a new approach to delegation by utilizing learning theory to teach managers how to improve their delegation success rates. It has been used successfully in supervisory training programs and in time management seminars.

Suggested Time   30 minutes.

Materials Needed
- ✓ Flip chart and markers
- ✓ Form A (What Is Your Style?)
- ✓ Form B (Role Play), cut into sections
- ✓ Form C (Learning Style Guidelines)

Procedure

1. Distribute Form A.

2. Explain that each participant should complete this sheet by choosing the most appropriate answers. There are no right or wrong answers, so participants should choose the answers that *best* describe how they would usually prefer to handle each situation.

3. Instruct the participants to add up their total number of A, B, and C answers.

4. Ask the participants to list their first names and A, B, and C scores on the flip chart.

5. Without explaining what these scores mean, select up to 2 sets of participants with *dissimilar* learning styles and place in dyads. For example, pair the participant with the highest A score with the participant with the lowest A score. This activity works best when you have opposite letter scores between the members of the dyad. For example, pair a person who has an A score of 7 or higher *and* a low B score with someone who has a B score of seven or higher *and* a low A score. Listing the group's scores on the chart pad makes it easier for you to select the 2 pairs with the most striking differences in learning styles.

6. Hand out the *appropriate sections* of Form B to the 4 participants, who will participate in the role play. Give them a few minutes to read their roles as outlined in Form B. Their task is to prepare a 5-minute role play illustrating the situation presented to them. Partners should *not* discuss their roles with each other.

7. Distribute Form C to the rest of the class, who will act as observers.

8. Conduct the role plays.

9. Facilitate a discussion in which you explain that this activity illustrates that how we prefer to learn often influences how we expect others to learn. Write the following on the flip chart: Participants who had

   —more *A* answers prefer to learn by *seeing.*

   —more *B* answers prefer to learn by *hearing.*

   —more *C* answers prefer to learn by *doing.*

   Some participants will have more than one category that are scored particularly high, such as 5 A's, 2 B's, and 5 C's. This means that this person is comfortable learning new information in more than one way.

   When a participant's answers are fairly evenly divided into A's, B's, and C's, this person does not have a strong preference for any one particular style of learning. These participants take in new information by all three processes.

10. Ask the observers for examples of behaviors from the role plays that illustrate each of these learning styles (e.g., people who prefer to learn by seeing often draw diagrams, take notes, use phrases like "see what I mean," etc.). Facilitate a discussion of the added difficulties one encounters when trying to get a person to do an unfamiliar task, if it is taught in a way that makes it more difficult for that person to learn. Ask the group to provide examples from their own experience.

11. Ask the participants what they have learned about: (a) how they learn new information, and (b) how this relates to teaching others new tasks.

For each situation, circle the **one** answer that best represents how you would usually prefer to act.

1. You have just purchased a complicated new piece of electronic equipment in your home. The easiest way for you to learn how to operate it would be to

   A. carefully watch the instructional video that came with the product.

   B. ask your next-door neighbor who has the same model to explain how it works.

   C. just start tinkering with it.

2. You are lost and late for an important meeting. You would be more apt to

   A. ask for directions, write them down, and then follow them.

   B. ask for directions, listen, and then try to follow the directions.

   C. just try to find the site by driving around.

3. Your company has purchased new equipment that is important to performing your job. You have your choice of how to learn it. You would tend to prefer to

   A. go to a class, take notes, and use the manual.

   B. go to a class, listen to what the instructor has to say, but take hardly any notes

   C. skip the class and try to learn by using it.

4. You are trying to improve your ability to remember names. In a meeting with several new clients you

   A. keep glancing at their business cards.

   B. listen to the names that they call each other.

   C. try to use their names more in the conversation.

5. You are having trouble with a piece of machinery at your work site that you need to master ASAP. The first action that you usually take is to

   A. consult the instruction manual.

   B. call the manufacturer's toll-free help line.

   C. fiddle with it and try to get it working by yourself.

6. If you had to master a new foreign language for an overseas assignment, the easiest way for you to do that would be to

   A. read the text and/or take lots of notes in class.

   B. listen to others speak it and/or listen to tapes.

   C. practice speaking the language.

7. You are in a phone booth and call information for a phone number. You usually

   A. write it down immediately as the operator gives it to you.

   B. don't write it down but repeat it out loud to yourself, as you dial.

   C. just dial it.

8. You have to memorize a speech. The easiest way for you to do that would be to

   A. keep reading it over and over.

   B. put it on tape and listen to it over and over.

   C. keep saying it out loud.

9. You want to learn the latest dance craze. The easiest way for you to learn it would be to

   A. watch someone do it.

   B. listen to directions on how to do it.

   C. just try to do it.

10. You feel more comfortable in a class when the instructor begins by saying:

    A. "Here are some handouts that outline what I am going to do."

    B. "There is no need to take notes, just listen to what I am going to tell you."

    C. "This is a hands-on class."

11. Which do you tend to remember best?

    A. What you have seen.

    B. What you have heard.

    C. What you have done.

12. How do you think that you usually learn best?

    A. By watching someone do something

    B. By listening to someone tell you how to do something

    C. By doing it yourself

Add up your total number of A's, B's, and C's.

    Number of A's _____

    Number of B's _____

    Number of C's _____

ROLE PLAY FOR HIGH A, B, OR C SCORERS

Assume that you are going on a four-week cruise vacation. Your boss has made it clear that in order to get so much time off, you must show your assistant how to do your job in your absence. In a five-minute role play, go over a task that he or she will be performing for the first time in your absence. You may choose to teach any relevant task, such as how to complete a report, run a machine, etc. Your goal is to teach this employee how to perform any task that will be delegated to him or her in your absence. You may do this any way that is comfortable for you.

CUT HERE

ROLE PLAY FOR LOW A, B, OR C SCORERS

Assume that your boss is going on a four-week cruise vacation during which you will need to do the job in his or her absence. In a five-minute role play you and your partner will go over some of the tasks that you will be performing for the first time in his or her absence. Remember, this is your *only* opportunity to learn how to do this work. So your goal is to understand the instructions. Be sure that you are clear about what you will need to do in his or her absence.

Most people tend to prefer one way of taking in information over others. Some people need to learn by seeing, or through hearing, or through doing, or a combination of these. All three ways are equally valid. However, we tend to teach other people new tasks using the methods that *we prefer* to use to acquire new information, which may be the hardest way for them to learn. This is particularly important to be aware of when we try to delegate unfamiliar tasks to others. If people are unsure of what to do or how to proceed, they will be less successful at learning the delegated task. Sometimes what we perceive as an unwillingness to accept delegation is just a colleague's inability to learn the task the way we are teaching it. This problem develops when there is a mismatch between learning styles.

Since you have been provided with the scores of those involved in the role plays, you are to watch for examples of how people in these role plays instruct another person in an unfamiliar task in the way that they prefer to learn.

Jot down observations that illustrate this behavior. For example,

—High A scorers use words and phrases that indicate learning through *seeing* such as "watch how I do this," etc. They tend to provide written instructions, draw diagrams, and refer the learner to the manual, etc.

—High B scorers encourage *listening* to the instructions rather than doing, showing, or providing written instructions about how to accomplish a task. They often discourage others from taking notes or trying to do the task.

—High C scorers teach by actually *doing* a task with the learner.

OBSERVATION NOTES:

4

THE THREE "M'S" OF EMPOWERMENT: MISSION, MILIEU, AND MIND-SETS

Marlene Caroselli

Marlene Caroselli, Ed.D. *is the author of* **Quality Games for Trainers** *(McGraw-Hill, 1996) and two dozen other books dealing with business issues. She is also a frequent contributor to the* **International Customer Service Association Journal,** *the* **National Business Employment Weekly,** *and Stephen Covey's* **Executive Excellence.** *In addition to directing the Center for Professional Development in Rochester, New York, she conducts training programs for corporate, government, and academic organizations, both nationally and internationally. Her clients include federal agencies, Fortune 500 firms, small businesses, academic institutions, and professional organizations on both the national and international levels.*

Contact information:

Center for Professional Development
324 Latona Road; Suite 1600
Rochester, NY 14626
716-227-6512
mccpd@aol.com

Overview   Author Paul Hersey believes the empowerment experience, for many people, is like "having had fairy dust sprinkled on them with the expectation that they would go forward and be more productive." True empowerment policies involve much more than wishful thinking. They involve vision and planning and learning and even courage. They also involve big-picture thinking: that awareness of mission is the guiding force behind all endeavors.

This activity deals with the three "M's" of empowerment— *Mission, Milieu, Mind-sets*—and explores their interconnectedness.

Suggested time   25 minutes.

Materials needed   ✓ Flip chart and markers
✓ Form A (Participant Instructions)

Procedure

1. Begin with a brief capsule of the rationale behind the empowerment offshoot of the quality movement. Explain that numerous benefits accrue to the organization (in terms of increased productivity, for example), to the managers (in terms of more time to do the work for which they were hired), and to the individual worker (in terms of reduced stress resulting from having greater control over his or her own work).

2. Distribute Form A. On the top half, ask participants to write (anonymously) a number from 1 (low) to 5 (high) that reflects the degree of empowerment they believe they currently have on the job .

3. Direct attention to the second half of Form A. Ask participants to write a three- or four-word sentence that captures a message their supervisors often repeat, such as "support the team," "make a profit," or "satisfy our customers." Encourage participants to state this in language that accurately reflects a persistent message commonly heard, rather than some lofty statement no one really believes in. Collect the papers.

4. Next, divide the group as follows: Have all the "3's" assemble outside the room and await your arrival. Quickly, form two groups with the remaining participants so that each group has at least two people who wrote a "1" or "2" and at least two people who indicated a "4" or "5" for their empowerment assessment.

5. Ask these two groups to prepare a report detailing what barriers to and what positive forces for empowerment exist in the work environment that justify their ratings.

6. The "3's" have a two-part assignment: First, they will use the collected papers to obtain an average of the empowerment figures for the whole group. Second, they will analyze the short supervisory statements to determine the underlying forces shaping the workplace culture. This second assignment may give them trouble, as the comments may, at first, reveal few definable trends. Read one or two of the comments and give a sample interpretation. For example, these are actual supervisory declarations: "Don't rock the boat." "Do whatever it takes." "Don't embarrass me or the company." "I don't want any surprises." "Handle it to the best of your ability."

   It would seem that two distinct messages are being conveyed here: (1) Some supervisors seem more concerned with their personal positions than with the organizational mission. (2) Others seem to trust their employees to do the best work they can. Tell the group they, too, will make a brief report to the larger group in about 10 minutes.

7. Call on each group to share their observations. Record the barriers and the positive factors from these reports on flip chart paper.

8. Lead a discussion touching upon some of these questions:

✓ What is our mission?

✓ To what extent is that mission driving our efforts?

✓ Some experts feel an empowered culture is not a new set of rules but rather a new set of rule makers. Tell why you agree or disagree with the statement.

✓ Other experts posit that in an empowered workplace, the mission becomes the "boss." How close does your own organization come to having such bosses?

✓ Based on your own experience in this organization, can you relate to the definition(s) of the existing culture provided by the "3's" group? Explain.

✓ What empowerment messages do employees need to hear?

✓ What empowerment messages do managers need to hear?

✓ What empowerment messages does senior management need to hear?

Variation   The format of this activity could be applied to virtually any training session. To illustrate, if the topic were leadership development, participants could be asked, "On a scale of 1 (low) to 5 (high), how would you rate your own leadership abilities?" The second question would read, "In one or two sentences, assess our organizational leaders."

On a scale of 1 (low) to 5 (high), indicate the degree of empowerment you have on your job.

1   2   3   4   5

What is a message your immediate supervisor often conveys to you and others in your work unit? (Aim for a 3- or 4-word sentence.)

_____

_____

5

THE FEEDBACK TOSS: LEARNING ABOUT ITS EFFECTS ON PERFORMANCE

Richard Whelan and Robert Merritt

Richard Whelan *is director of Associated Consultants for Training &
Education, a part of The Westminster Group. He designs, develops, and delivers training programs—to be used in conventional classroom settings, as well
as computer-based and distance learning formats—pertaining to human
resource and mental health issues for organizations in both the public and private sectors. Rich was a contributor to* **The 1997 McGraw-Hill Training
and Performance Sourcebook** *and* **The 1997 McGraw-Hill Team and
Organization Development Sourcebook.**

Contact information:

Associated Consultants for Training and Education
P.O. Box 5312
Deptford, NJ 08096
609-227-4273
AssocCnslt@aol.com

Robert Merritt, Ph.D *is director of Organization Effectiveness Resources. He
works with companies to achieve business results by developing effective operational environments. The practice focuses on organizational development,
training, process design, systems analysis, and training. His clients include
organizations and agencies in both the public and private sectors. Robert's
work has been published in numerous human resource development sourcebooks. Robert was a contributor to* **The 1997 McGraw-Hill Training and
Performance** *Sourcebook and* **The 1997 McGraw-Hill Team and
Organization Development Sourcebook.**

Contact information:

Organization Effectiveness Resources
28 St. George Terrace
Bear, DE 19701
302-324-0347
RMMerritt@aol.com

Overview   This activity is designed to have participants learn four forms of feedback and the usefulness and drawbacks of each. Through the experience of a simple activity, participants will learn the effects of feedback on performance.

Suggested Time   30–40 minutes.

Materials Needed   ✓ 1 chair
✓ 6 Nerf™ or Koosh™ balls (or any soft, spongy ball)
✓ 1 box with no lid (at least 18″ × 18″)
✓ Flip chart, pad, and markers
✓ Form A (Feedback Styles)

Procedure   1. Before the activity begins, have the four sets of instructions from Form A, "Feedback Styles" written on four separate flip chart pages (one instruction per page).

2. Keep these four sheets covered until it is time to reveal them to the participants later in the activity.

3. Evenly divide the participants into four groups. This can be done through a standard "counting off" method.

4. Have each group choose one member of the group who will be asked to stand outside the room with the "electees" from the other three groups.

5. Place the chair in the center of the room, with the empty box at least 10 feet behind it. (As you continue to use this exercise, you may feel the need to move the box farther away or closer to the chair based on your participants and experience; however, don't change the distance during the activity itself.) Place the 6 balls near the chair.

6. Give the remaining participants (who are still in their groups) the following instructions:

"Your selected team members will be attempting, one at a time, to throw these six balls over their shoulders and into the empty box. Your job, as teammates, is to provide feedback on their performance. The form and method of feedback each team will be using will be listed on the flip chart. It is crucial that you follow the instructions on the flip chart. Only a participant's teammates can provide the feedback, all others are silent observers." Ask if there are any questions, and if not, proceed to the next step.

7. Randomly select one of the groups to go first. Show them the flip chart page with the label and instructions for "Positive Feedback." Read the instructions to them, ask if there are any questions, cover the instructions, and then bring that team's designee back into the room. Sit the designee in the chair and hand him or her the 6

balls. Instruct the person to throw the balls, one at a time, over his or her shoulder and into the box. At no time can the person look over the shoulder to see how he or she is doing or exactly where the box is. (Often, participants fear the box is being moved on them. Assure them it remains in the same spot they observed when they entered the room). Tell the person, also, that teammates will help by giving feedback on his or her attempts.

8. After the 6 balls have been tossed, have the designee join his or her teammates and prepare for the next person, following the same procedure as in Step 7, but uncovering the second feedback label and instructions, "Technical Feedback." There is no discussion, at this time, on how any particular person or team did. Once one team finishes, the next one proceeds. This same process continues for both "Critical Feedback" and "Passive Feedback."

9. When all four teams have finished, ask the designees the following questions:

   ✓ How did you do?

   ✓ How helpful were your teammates in helping you to succeed in your task?

   ✓ Would you have wanted them to do anything else? Why? Why not?

10. Show the four flip chart pages so the designees know what instructions their teammates had. Then ask the individual teams what it was like for them to give the feedback they were assigned and what would they have liked to do instead.

11. Finally, as a general question, ask the group what they have learned about feedback and the importance it plays in a person's performance.

12. At the close, you may want to give a short lecturette on the principles of good feedback.

Variation If you are working with a very large group, you can still use four teams of six or seven members each and have the other participants be observers. In this case, you might first ask them what they observed, getting their responses, and then ask the team members.

Flip Chart Page "A":

> **SUPPORTIVE FEEDBACK:** Provide your teammate with as much support, encouragement, instruction, and positive direction as you can.

Flip Chart Page "B":

> **TECHNICAL FEEDBACK:** Provide your teammate only with specific, "technical" feedback and suggestions to help him or her complete the task successfully.

Flip Chart Page "C":

> **CRITICAL FEEDBACK:** Provide your teammate with nonproductive criticism any time he or she has not succeeded.

Flip Chart Page "D":

> **PASSIVE FEEDBACK:** Remain relatively silent and passive throughout the activity, giving little verbal or nonverbal feedback.

6

LEARNING TO DRIVE A CAR: UNDERSTANDING PERSONALITY DIFFERENCES

Karen Lawson

Karen Lawson, Ph.D. *is president of the Lawson Consulting Group, an organization and management development consulting firm. She has over 20 years of experience in the fields of management, training, consulting, and education across a wide range of industries. Karen is the author of* **The Art of Influencing** *(Kendall/Hunt, 1996),* **Improving Workplace Performance through Coaching** *(American Media, 1996), and* **Improving On-the-Job Training and Coaching** *(American Society for Training and Development, 1997). Karen was also coauthor of* **101 Ways to Make Training Active** *(Pfeiffer, 1995) and a contributor to* **The 1997 McGraw-Hill Team and Organization Development Sourcebook.**

Contact Information:

Lawson Consulting Group
1365 Gwynedale Way
Lansdale, PA 19446
215-368-9465
www.lawsoncg.com

Overview This activity is very effective in communications or management development programs to show the importance of recognizing and adjusting to various style differences.

Suggested Time 45 minutes.

Materials Needed ✓ Form A (Personality Profile)
✓ 4 flip chart pages and 4 markers

Procedure 1. Distribute the personality assessment instrument (Form A) and ask participants to complete the assessment according to the written instructions. Walk around and check to make sure participants are completing the instrument correctly. Assist participants in scoring the instrument.

2. Next, group participants according to their styles: *Candid; Persuasive; Logical; Reflective.* Provide participants with these further descriptions of their styles:

Candid: dominant, driving, direct

Persuasive: amiable, influencing, expressive

Logical: steady, systematic, thinking

Reflective: conscientious, considerate, amiable

3. Give each group a flip chart page and marker and ask them to make a list of how they would like to learn how to drive a stick-shift car and the attributes they would most want in an instructor. Further explain that if they already know how to drive stick-shift, they should not think about how they learned because how they were taught and how they would like to have been taught might not be the same.

4. Ask each group to post its list on the wall. Ask participants to compare the lists, noting the major differences as well as similarities.

5. Expect the following outcomes:

   ✓ *Candid*—List will be short and to the point; action-oriented

   ✓ *Persuasive*—List will be slightly longer than that of Candid; list will not be in any order and will emphasize importance of having a friendly instructor; will reflect social aspect of the experience

   ✓ *Logical*—List will reflect step-by-step procedure; need for structure and detail; may want to read manual and learn how everything works

   ✓ *Reflective*—List will be similar to that of *Logical* but will reflect a more cautious approach (and lots of opportunities to practice in a parking lot) as well as a need for a patient, caring instructor

6. Ask participants to give examples of how these style differences can be seen in the workplace or in their personal lives.

7. Conduct a discussion about the importance of communicating in the other person's style, not yours, in order to be more effective in both professional and personal relationships.

8. Point out the following strategies in communicating with each style:

   ✓ *Candid:* Get to the point quickly; emphasize big picture and bottom line; avoid details

   ✓ *Persuasive:* Emphasize the human element; express enthusiasm; socialize, establish relationship

   ✓ *Logical:* Provide details and approach the subject logically and systematically

   ✓ *Reflective:* Exercise caution and reservation; don't try to push for action; reflect and acknowledge emotions

9. Ask each participant to think about an individual with whom they have had difficulty communicating. Ask each person to speculate as to the other person's style. Then ask them to think about a typical scenario or interaction they might experience with this individual and write down how they might modify their approach to communicate in that person's style. Invite a few participants to share their strategies with the entire group.

Variation Instead of using Form A, you may choose to use another assessment instrument. Be sure to use a personality/communication style assessment instrument that identifies four different personality profiles. Some suggested profiles:

I Speak Your Language (Drake Beam Morin)
Personality Profile System (Carlson Learning)
What's My Style? (HRDQ)
Behavior Profiles (Jossey-Bass/Pfeiffer)

To get a flavor for style differences, read each of the following statements and circle the ending that is most like you.

1. When I am in a learning situation, I like to …
   a. be involved in doing something.
   b. work with people in groups.
   c. read about the information.
   d. watch and listen to what is going on.

2. When I am working in a group, I like to …
   a. direct the discussion and activity.
   b. find out what other people think and feel.
   c. remain somewhat detached from the rest of the group.
   d. go along with the majority.

3. When faced with a conflict situation, I prefer to …
   a. confront the situation head on and try to win.
   b. work with the other person to arrive at an amicable resolution.
   c. present my position by using logic and reason.
   d. not make waves.

4. In a conversation, I tend to …
   a. come straight to the point.
   b. draw others into the conversation.
   c. listen to what others have to say, then offer an objective opinion.
   d. agree with what others say.

5. When making a decision, I tend to …
   a. make a decision quickly and then move on.
   b. consider how the outcome will affect others.
   c. take time to gather facts and data.
   d. consider all possible outcomes and proceed with caution.

*Adapted from **The Art of Influencing.** Karen Lawson, Ph.D. Dubuque, IA: Kendall-Hunt Publishing Company, 1996.

6. I am seen by others as someone who …
  a. gets results.
  b. is fun to be with.
  c. is logical and rational.
  d. is a calming influence.

7. In a work environment, I prefer …
  a. to work alone.
  b. to work with others.
  c. structure and organization.
  d. a peaceful atmosphere.

Now count the number of times you circled each letter. The letter with the most circles indicates your preferred style:

a=Candid; b=Persuasive; c=Logical; d=Reflective.

7

TAKING CHARGE OF YOUR CAREER: A PERSONAL SWOT ANALYSIS AND ENVIRONMENTAL SCAN

Jane Flagello

Jane R. Flagello, Ed.D. *is president of Direction Dynamics, Inc. a coaching, training, and consulting firm that specializes in providing coaching services in the areas of management and leadership development, career management, and personal growth. Jane is also a professor of management and leadership at DeVry Institute of Technology, DuPage campus. Her writing projects and speaking engagements specifically focus on coaching people to take charge of their own lives and careers.*

Contact Information:

Direction Dynamics, Inc.
P. O. Box 2463
Naperville, IL 60567-2463
630-637-3318
drjane@xnet.com
www.xnet.com / ~drjane

Overview   This activity provides rich information about how to take charge of one's career and, more importantly, one's life. So many of us make lifetime career decisions with less information than we use to buy a new tie or change our hairstyles! It's time to stop this madness, take a step back and a deep breath, and really examine how our skills, our talents, and our current personal desires all mesh to enable us to create the life we want to be living, now and in the future.

Suggested Time   45–60 minutes.

Materials Needed
- ✓ Form A (Personal SWOT Analysis)
- ✓ Form B (Environmental Scan)
- ✓ Form C (Key Action Steps)

Note: You should make several copies of each form for participants so they can "play" with different scenarios.

Procedure

1. Give each participant at least two copies of each form.

2. Tell them that the exercises they are about to participate in are related to the types of activities that organizations do when they engage in strategic planning. It will give them a strategic picture of "possible" career futures. This is empowering for them and will give them insights into how to achieve their desired career goals.

3. Inquire if anyone knows what a SWOT is. Ask if they know how an organization would use a SWOT analysis in their strategic planning activities.

   A SWOT is an assessment of strengths, weaknesses, opportunities, and threats. Organizations use SWOT analyses to help them strategize how to best position products and services in the marketplace, utilize resources effectively, and enhance their profit potential.

4. Inquire if anyone knows what an environmental scan is. Ask if they know how an organization would use an environmental scan in their strategic planning activities.

   An Environmental Scan is used to examine factors and forces that are outside of the direct control of an organization, but have the potential to impact that organization. This might include the economy, technological changes, political issues, global issues, demographics, etc.

5. Tell participants to work on the Personal SWOT Analysis (Form A) first.

   a) Explain that a personal SWOT analysis is an assessment of one's *strengths, weaknesses, opportunities,* and *threats.*

   b) Tell them to put the specific title or responsibilities that they would like to have in a job in the center circle on the SWOT Analysis form.

   c) Then request that participants look at the top two boxes, strengths and weaknesses. With respect to the job duties or title that they wrote in the center circle, ask them to list the specific strengths that they have right now that would enable them to perform that job effectively. Then ask them to list the areas where they are weak. These are skills and abilities that would prevent them from getting the job they want. Remember to tell them that strengths and weaknesses are all about **them**—they are in **their** control to **do** something about.

   d) Now tell them to move to the other two boxes, *opportunities* and *threats.* Tell them that opportunities and threats are external to them. They exist in the world around them. They happen and impact them, but are usually not directly in their control. Have them focus their attention on these boxes.

Here are some questions you can use to help guide their thinking:

- ✓ Is this a growing or declining industry?
- ✓ Are the jobs I want in my geographical area?
- ✓ How is my immediate support network affected by my career goals?
- ✓ Is specialized training available locally?
- ✓ Can I afford it?

6. Tell them to move on to work on the Environmental Scan (Form B).

   a) Explain that an Environmental Scan is another management strategy tool. Businesses use these all the time as they look for new opportunities in the marketplace for their products and services.

   b) Remind participants that no one (outside of themselves) is going to be responsible for their careers. It is up to them to continually scan the environment, looking at what is really happening that may have an impact (positive or negative) on them and their careers.

   c) Ask participants to copy the information from the SWOT center circle into the center circle on Form B.

   d) Tell them to think about each of the issues in each box and ask themselves how this "force" is impacting the job market. Here are some thought-provoking questions to ask participants to engage their thinking:

   - ✓ How is the economy affecting the job tasks that you want?
   - ✓ How does a changing population picture impact you? How do an aging population, increased minorities, and a skilled or unskilled labor force impact your career goals?
   - ✓ How does the current political climate impact the industries that employ people in the type of job you want?
   - ✓ How does technology change your industry? Will it wipe out the job you want? How soon?
   - ✓ What is going on globally that impacts the type of career goals you have? Where is the marketplace? Where is the labor pool?
   - ✓ What regulations impact the career job you want?
   - ✓ Who is the competition? Where is the competition? How strong is the competition? How hard is it for a new player in town to become competition?

   e) Ask participants to take each factor in turn and ask themselves, "How does this factor impact this industry / career / product / service?" "Will this factor hamper growth in this area?" "Will this factor encourage growth?" "What new opportunities will be realized as a result of this factor being in play?"

7. Tell participants that now that they have completed a possible scenario for themselves, it is time to do a reality check. Have them sit back and think about the pictures that have appeared in their SWOT boxes and as a result of their examination of the environment.

8. Give participants the Key Action Steps sheet (Form C). Tell them that Key Action Steps are steps that a person can begin to take right now to make the desired future come closer to reality. Tell participants to brainstorm three specific actions that they can take starting right now to bring them closer to their goals.

   If time permits, break the participants into dyads or triads so they can share their thoughts and brainstorm together.

9. To end the session, tell the participants that they now have a road map to guide their careers in the direction they want to go. Tell them to try a second or third career scenario on the blank forms they have been given, and to review their maps every six months.

Variation   If a participant would like to start a business, this tool is very useful. Have the participant put the business in the center circles of Form A and Form B. Then do the SWOT and Environmental Scan based on the business venture. Form C will list the action steps that make the dream come to life!

PERSONAL SWOT ANALYSIS

Job Title / Position

Strengths

Weaknesses

Opportunities

Threats

ENVIRONMENTAL SCAN ANALYSIS

Environmental   *Political*

Business / Industry

Economy   *Competition*

Demographics   *Technology*

Global Trends   *Legal / Regulatory*

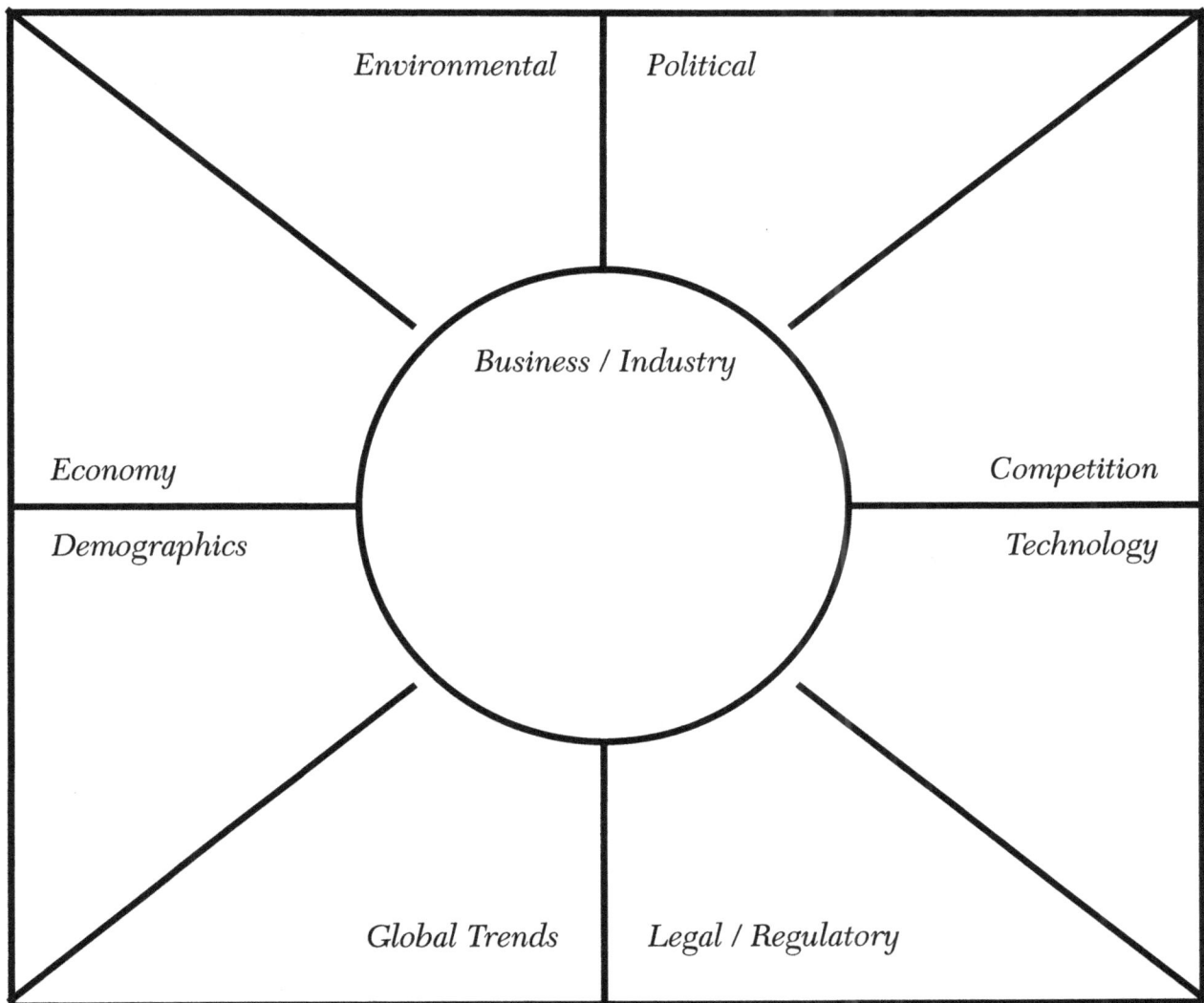

Factor Analysis Questions

How does this factor impact this industry/ career/ product/ service?

Will this factor hamper growth in this area?

Will this factor encourage growth in this area?

What new opportunities will be realized as a result of this factor?

KEY ACTION STEPS

To be most effective, Key Action Steps must be specific and have target dates for completion.

Only fill in the first three lines of this worksheet. List three Key Action Steps that you are really going to take and target dates for each one. When you complete a Key Action Step, put a big red check in the "done" box and then add another Key Action Step on line #4. Keep going until you have reached your goals.

STEP	ACTION ITEM	TARGET DATE	DONE!
1			☐
2			☐
3			☐
4			☐
5			☐
6			☐
7			☐
8			☐
9			☐
10			☐
11			☐
12			☐
13			☐
14			☐
15			☐
16			☐
17			☐

8

POLITICAL CORRECTNESS: A DIVERSITY OPINION EXERCISE

Hank Karp

H.B. Karp, Ph.D. *is currently on the faculty of management at Christopher Newport University, and is also the owner of Personal Growth Systems, a consulting firm that has offered training, team-building consultation, and executive development to large corporations and government agencies, such as the Smithsonian Institution, General Dynamics, and Chaparral Steel, for the past 18 years. He is author of over 50 publications including the recent books,* **Personal Power** *(Gardner Press, 1995) and* **The Change Leader** *(Pfeiffer,1996). He has presented at many international conferences and is currently working on his next book,* **Difficult People: The Hidden Resource.** *Hank was also a contributor to* **The 1996** *and* **The 1997 McGraw-Hill Training and Performance Sourcebooks.**

Contact Information:

Personal Growth Systems
4217 Hawksley Drive
Chesapeake, VA 23321
(757) 483-9327
PGSHank@aol.com

Overview This exercise is particularly suited for participants who are about to participate in a longer diversity training program. Participants who make up training groups in diversity are as diverse a group of people as any other, particularly in regard to assumptions about this type of training. Before undertaking any diversity training program, the trainer needs to consider the nature of the group and then make and test certain assumptions about the people who make it up. One of the most critical areas to assess is the group's receptivity toward "Political Correctness," or similar values that might be underlying the program content. If the trainer holds a markedly different set of values regarding PC than the group holds, the probability of alienating the group and increasing its resistance to the program content is greatly increased. The underlying assumption of this exercise is that the less "politically correct" a diversity program is, the higher are its chances for yielding cooperative and positive results.

The exercise allows the group to start interactively by getting clear about where they are on some of the issues that define the politically correct set of values. This not only provides an opportunity for participation early in the program, it forces the participants to become clear about where each one is personally in regard to these issues, *before* being exposed to the program content or the trainer's values. This provides the probability for a much more active and involved program.

Suggested Time 40 minutes.

Materials Needed ✓ Form A (Diversity Opinion Exercise)
✓ Form B (Preferred Answers)

Procedure 1. Divide the total group into subgroups of 3 to 6 people.

2. Distribute Form A to the participants. Ask them to answer the 10 questions individually. When everyone in the subgroup has completed this, ask the subgroups to attempt to reach consensus on each of the 10 items within 15 minutes.

3. If consensus is not possible on an item, they are to put a "?" by that item and continue on.

4. When all subgroups are finished or time has expired, distribute Form B and discuss the "preferred" answer to each question. Ask for differing opinions and open discussion to the entire group. If the discussion gets active, use a "call-on-the-next-speaker" format in which the current speaker selects the next person to speak, rather than using the facilitator for this function.

Instructions:

Below are ten statements that pertain to diversity training. If you basically agree with each statement, place an "A" under the *Individual* column next to it. If you partially agree, or disagree, respond with a "D." When you have finished, see if you can reach consensus on the answers within your small group. Record these answers under the *Group* column. If you cannot come to a quick consensus for an item, place a "?" next to it and keep going. *This is an opinion survey; there are no right or wrong answers!*

	Individual	*Group*
1. Only people who belong to a minority are really qualified to conduct diversity training.	_____	_____
2. Using phrases such as *vertically challenged* rather than *short* indicates a real concern for the sensitivity of the affected person.	_____	_____
3. The key to effective diversity training is to get the SWAM (Straight White American Male) to modify his attitude and behavior toward other groups.	_____	_____
4. Diversity and discrimination are best addressed as societal issues, rather than as issues of individual accountability.	_____	_____
5. No headway can be made in changing group relationships until accountability has been assigned for past injustice.	_____	_____
6. Because some people have benefited from injustice committed by others, they are also responsible for those injustices.	_____	_____
7. It is always the speaker's responsibility to be sure that the language being used has no possibility of offending the sensibility of the listener.	_____	_____

8. Only the SWAM can be held accountable for the social oppression of others.

     _____   _____

9. To be effective, the major focus of diversity training should be on assessing causes from the past and planning for the future, rather than attending to current issues.

     _____   _____

10. The more time we spend attempting to understand *why* people are the way they are, the more information we will have available to make needed changes.

     _____   _____

[The "preferred" answers to these 10 questions are drawn from: Karp & Sutton, "Where Diversity Training Goes Wrong." *Training*, July, 1993; and Karp, "Choices in Diversity Training." *Training*, August, 1994. Both articles can also be found in *The Cultural Diversity Sourcebook*, Abramms and Simons, Eds., ODT, Inc. 1996.]

1. **Only people who belong to a minority are really qualified to conduct diversity training.**

   While it is true that many minority trainers and group leaders can more closely relate to minority issues, it is just as important, if not more so, that they understand and relate just as well to the people who are there to be trained. A concern with both elements is essential.

2. **Using phrases such as *vertically challenged* rather than *short* indicates a real concern for the sensitivity of the affected person.**

   While politically correct language may be taken as sensitive, it can just as easily be seen as patronizing. Recent research indicates that a great majority of the group prefer the term "black" to "African-American."

3. **The key to effective diversity training is to get the SWAM (Straight White American Male) to modify his attitude and behavior toward other groups.**

   The major thrust of most all diversity training has been to have the majority group (SWAMs) develop a more open and nonjudgmental view of other groups. However, prejudice and discrimination are not the sole property of this group.

4. **Diversity and discrimination are best addressed as societal issues, rather than as issues of individual accountability.**

   As long as we hold with the view that "Society is at fault" nobody has to hold themselves accountable for their actions. Effective diversity training needs to be geared to each *individual* taking responsibility for his or her own perceptions, regardless of background or identity.

5. **No headway can be made in changing group relationships until accountability has been assigned for past injustice.**

   Past injustice needs to be recognized, acknowledged, and then put behind us! The more time we spend in wallowing in the past, the more self-pitying victims we become. The truth is that nobody in the training program is personally responsible for anyone being enslaved, beaten, or murdered because of their ethnic status! We need to spend the time finding ways of dealing with *present* injustice and ways to work better together.

6. **Because some people have benefited from injustices committed by others, they are also responsible for those injustices.**

   You are going to have a hard time convincing people that they should feel guilty about something that they had no direct hand in. This condition exists *within* ethnicities as well as between them. For example, it makes little difference, in terms of justice, if you lay me off, instead of your brother, because he is your brother, or because you are prejudiced against my ethnic group.

7. **It is always the speaker's responsibility to be sure that the language being used has no possibility of offending the sensibility of the listener.**

   Speakers are unquestionably responsible for what they say and should be held accountable for it. They are *never* accountable, however, for how listeners feel. If a speaker inadvertently says something the listener finds offensive, *it is the listener's responsibility to make the speaker aware of it.*

8. **Only the SWAM can be held accountable for the social oppression of others.**

   This is a purely biased political perspective. Regardless of your view on this, if this point is verbalized in a training function you are going to totally alienate the very group you are trying to win over.

9. **To be effective, the major focus of diversity training should be on assessing causes from the past and planning for the future, rather than attending to current issues.**

   Both the past and the future deserve a brief acknowledgment and a "tip of the hat." Change is going to occur only when we deal with current issues!

10. **The more time we spend attempting to understand *why* people are the way they are, the more information we will have available to make needed changes.**

    It makes practically no difference at all *why* people are the way they are, mainly because there is nothing you can do about it. Time is much better spent assessing *what* people want from each other, and *how* they might be stopping themselves from getting it.

9

FUGITIVE E-MAILS: THE CHALLENGES OF ELECTRONIC COMMUNICATION

Peter Garber

Peter R. Garber *is Manager of Teamwork Development for PPG Industries, Inc., Pittsburgh, Pa. He is the author of nine books on a variety of human resource and business-related topics including:* **Coaching, Self-Directed Workteams, Don't Shoot the Messenger, The Paradox of Business Ethics, Team Skill Builders,** *and* **25 Customer Service Activities.** *He has also been a contributing author in a number of other collections of works including* **The 1998 Team and Organization Development Sourcebook.**

Contact Information:

PPG Industries
One PPG Place
Pittsburgh, PA 15272
412-434-3417
garber@ppg.com

Overview This activity illustrates many of the challenges that the new ways of communicating electronically are creating in the workplace.

Suggested Time 60 minutes.

Materials Needed ✓ Form A (Introduction)
✓ Form B (Fugitive E-Mail Exercise)

Procedure 1. Distribute Form A to participants and give them an opportunity to read it. Or, give a brief presentation based on Form A. Briefly discuss any comments participants may have concerning their experiences of communicating via E-mail.

2. Distribute Form B to each participant.

3. Have each person read the first E-mail message from Ken Richardson to J. Smith and then answer the questions that follow. Do not have participants read the next E-mail messages until you have discussed the group's responses to these questions. Again, solicit any similar problems participants may have had themselves sending E-mail messages.

4. Have the group read the E-mail from Joan Smith to John Smith. Discuss problems of E-mail addresses that participants may have experienced.

5. Participants should next read John Smith's E-Mail to Jerry Cramton, Henry Tailbor, Karen Rogers, Cliff Harring, and Sarah Platt and then answer the five questions that follow. Make sure participants understand that the date and time of the meeting are still unclear. Highlight the fact that John Smith listed the subject of the message as: "Dinner meeting next Tuesday?" Ask participants what they think is the significance of the question mark at the end of this sentence. Ask, "Will the recipients of this message even see this question mark and understand its significance?"

6. Have participants continue on to Karen Rogers's E-mail message to Frank Blackburn. Have the group answer the questions that follow. Review the concepts of Fugitive E-Mails and discuss in some detail the answer to the last question, "What might be the consequences of this now Fugitive E-Mail?"

7. Ask the group to read the message from Frank Blackburn to William Weston and answer the questions that follow. Encourage participants to predict what Mr. Weston's reaction might be and the consequences that could result.

8. Conclude the exercise by having participants read William Weston's message to Ken Richardson with copies to Frank Blackburn and John Smith. Discuss as a group the two questions that follow this message.

9. Emphasize the need for and importance of sending clear and accurate messages to those you communicate with electronically.

Variations
1. Have participants complete the entire exercise first and then discuss the problems created during the journeys of these messages and their responses to the questions.

2. As a pre-work assignment, have participants bring examples of recent E-mail messages they have received that they can share with the group to critique.

3. As a follow-up, have participants send each other E-mails and give feedback to the senders on the quality of their messages, based on what they learned in this exercise.

Electronic mail or E-mail is dramatically changing the ways in which we communicate with one another. No longer is it necessary to draft a letter, have it typed, put in an envelope, stamped, mailed, and delivered to the receiver days or even weeks later. Today, through E-mail, this same process can be completed instantaneously, thus saving many steps. Messages can be simultaneously sent to virtually unlimited networked recipients. E-mails can be delivered, read, and filed for future reference without a single piece of paper being involved. E-Mail is making us more efficient, productive, and organized. Or is it? E-mail and other forms of electronic communication may indeed be the wave of the future, but they are not without their problems.

One of the challenges of E-mail is that it has created a whole new form of communication, E-talk. E-talk is how we send information to one another via E-mail. The difference between E-talk and other messages we send is that it is neither truly written or truly verbal in its nature. At first glance, messages sent by E-mail might appear to be totally written forms of communication. But are they? Do we always write messages to be sent through E-mail the same way we would when creating a memo or letter?

E-talk is a hybrid of written and verbal communications. We have a tendency to try to be as casual and conversational as possible when sending an E-mail message (other than when transmitting a formal letter or document electronically). We are much less concerned about grammar, format, style, spelling, etc. in an E-mail message than in other forms of written communication. We are, in many ways, trying to talk with one another through our computers. Unfortunately, in this form of electronic conversation there are none of the voice inflections and nonverbal communication that are such an important part of the face-to-face verbal communications we receive. We miss much of the "real" message when all we see are words on a computer screen.

Computers also allow us to be tied electronically to many people with a single keystroke. Some of these people may be as close as the office next door, others are across the country or even the world. E-mail has also redefined the concept of cc's, or what at one time were known as carbon copies (in the days when that was the only way to conveniently create a copy of the document). With E-mail there is no need for that annoying carbon paper that used to rub off on everything and caused making corrections a nightmare! It is almost effortless to copy as many people as you want to on an E-mail throughout the computer network. You don't have to look up street addresses or spelling of cities or find out zip codes. A push of a button and the message is sent and delivered.

The problem is that with this ease of access to people, the messages we send are sometimes confusing. You may not always understand why you were included in the delivery of the message. Making things even more unclear are the "passages" E-mail messages go through from their creation to their final destinations. A single E-mail message may pass through many "stops" in its travels. At each stop it may grow in content and distribution. Recipients being included in the later stages of the message may feel that they are being included in the E-mail only as an afterthought.

Sometimes E-mails are sent to places they were never meant to travel! These E-mails might be called "Fugitive E-Mails." Fugitive E-mails are messages that escape into cyberspace. They get into the hands of people they were never intended for. To prevent the release of Fugitive E-mails, think carefully before sending out an E-mail message. Ask yourself, "Is there anything in this message that I would be concerned about if other people on the computer network saw it?" If the answer to this question is "yes," then you should not send the E-mail without revising its content. Keep in mind that your E-mail can be redirected to anyone else on the network. Don't say anything in the message that you would be embarrassed about if everyone on the network was sent a copy.

E-mail provides us with many new and better ways to communicate with one another. However, to maximize the benefits of this powerful communication tool we must use E-mail in the most efficient manner and follow the same basic rules we would for other forms of written communication. We need to be clear in our electronic messages and remember that we are actually still writing business letters or memos when sending E-mail to other people at work. Copy your E-mail only to those people who have a legitimate need for and interest in receiving the information.

FUGITIVE E-MAIL EXERCISE

Read the following E-mail and answer the questions that follow concerning your understanding of the true intent and meaning of this message.

From: Ken Richardson
Date: Tuesday, May 6, 1997
To: J. Smith
Subject: Big Meeting

I just got a message from Weston. The big meeting is back on! It has been moved up to Tuesday at 7. Can you believe the time? I guess he thinks we work the same kind of weird hours that he does! You need to make sure that you have everything ready for the presentation. Be sure to bring all the latest numbers. I think the boss will be interested in that new data. Maybe that will put him in a better mood! If you need a hand let me know. I'll be out most of the time between now and the meeting but will be checking my messages. Let the others know of the change in the meeting time. Talk to you later. By the way- when are we going to play some golf again? You still owe me five bucks from last time!

Questions:

✓ Could there be more than one J. Smith on this computer network?

✓ What did Ken Richardson mean by "the meeting is back on"? Was it canceled or postponed at one time?

✓ Which Tuesday is the meeting scheduled for?

✓ Is it scheduled for 7:00 a.m. or 7:00 p.m.?

✓ What does J. Smith need to get ready for the meeting?

✓ What numbers should J. Smith be bringing?

✓ Where will Ken Richardson be until the meeting—on vacation, where he can't be reached, or on business if Smith needs to get in touch with him?

✓ What kind of assistance is Ken Richardson offering?

✓ What kind of message will Richardson be checking for—E-mail, VMX, fax, etc.?

Now let's follow this E-mail as it begins its journeys into cyberspace.

From: Joan Smith
Date: May 6, 1997
To: John Smith
cc: Ken Richardson
Subject: Wrong mailbox address

I received another one of your E-mails. Please ask Ken again to be sure to use your full first name when sending you messages.

Repeat prior message

From: John Smith
Date: May 7, 1997
To: Jerry Cramton, Henry Tailbor, Karen Rogers, Cliff Harring, Sarah Platt
cc: Roy Robinson
Subject: Dinner meeting next Tuesday ?

Attached is a message from Ken about the big meeting. I assume from his message that it got canceled and then rescheduled again, I didn't hear about any changes but I never seem to hear from anyone anymore unless it is across a computer screen! I think one day we should all just log on to our computers and have a meeting via E-mail! It would sure cut down on travel costs. The "old man" would sure like that! Anyway, according to Ken's E-mail I assume that the meeting is going to be on Tuesday but I'm not sure which one? It looks like its going to be another long meeting. Dinner meetings usually mean that they want to "soften" us up with a few drinks before laying a lot of bad news on us. I wonder what it is this time?

Let your people who will need to be there know that this is coming up. I'll have to get back to you about the time and date after I hear from Ken again with more details. Let me know if I left anyone out in this message or just send them a copy of this one. Roy-I'm also copying you on this message even though I know you won't be able to go to the meeting. You lucky dog!

Previous Messages

Questions:

✓ What new communication problems may have been created in this message from John Smith to those who received this message?

✓ What assumptions did John Smith make that he wasn't really sure about?

✓ What problems might be created for John Smith if this message gets into the "wrong hands"?

✓ What did he say that he might be sorry about at a later time?

✓ How is saying these things in person or even over the telephone (other than on a recorded message system) different from sending them out in an E-mail message?

From: Karen Rogers
Date: May 7, 1997
To: Frank Blackburn
cc:
Subject: Meeting conflict

Hi Boss. I just picked up this message from John Smith about a meeting I am supposed to go to. As you know, I'm going to be on that special assignment for the next four months and will not be able to attend this meeting. Do you want to send someone else in my place? You might want to call John to get more details on when and where the meeting will be. I don't know anything more than what is in this message.

Previous Messages

Questions:

✓ How could clearer previous E-mail messages have prevented the need for Frank Blackburn to have to contact John Smith for details on the meeting?

✓ Why do you think that Karen suggested that Frank *call* John Smith?

Frank Blackburn is on the same level in the organization as Richardson and Smith's boss.

✓ Do you think that Richardson and Smith expected this message to be sent to Frank Blackburn?

✓ What might be the consequences of this now *Fugitive E-Mail*?

From: Frank Blackburn
Date: May 8, 1997
To: William Weston
Subject: Your meeting

Bill, I thought I should check directly with you. I thought you were going to hold your meeting in the morning rather than the evening? Didn't you mention that in our staff meeting the other day? Have your plans changed? If your meeting is going to be next Tuesday evening, several of the people that I see included in the attached messages are scheduled for another dinner meeting with a big customer who will be in town that evening. This may be the only chance we have to make a presentation to this customer and I don't want to miss the opportunity. Can you reschedule your meeting to another night?

Previous Messages

Questions:

✓ What further problems have developed from the original E-mail.

✓ How many more times do you think this message will become a *Fugitive E-Mail*?

✓ How do you think William Weston will react to this message?

From: William Weston
Date: May 9, 1997
To: Ken Richardson
cc: Frank Blackburn, John Smith

The meeting that you and Smith have been referring to in your E-mail messages is to be held Tuesday, May 20th at 7:00 am. I called the meeting at this "weird" hour so we could all play a round of golf afterward. I thought it might put me in a "better mood" as you had hoped. Perhaps you should spend that time, instead of playing golf, reviewing your budget proposals. I just looked at them and think that they need a lot of work before I will accept them. Sounds like the two of you have already gotten a lot of golf in lately, so it won't hurt you to miss a round or two. By the way, gambling is against our company's policies so you should forget about that five dollars that Smith owes you.

Please send a clear message to everyone with a copy to me with the correct time and date for the meeting and that they should bring their golf clubs. I'll be looking forward to seeing your revised budget proposals.

Smith, this is to you- Let's have dinner soon before I get any older. I have something I want to break to you after I "soften" you up with a few drinks. You lucky dog!

Both of you need to be more careful what you send out in your E-mail messages.

Previous Messages

Questions:

- ✓ What were some of the consequences and long-term implications of this *Fugitive E-Mail*?
- ✓ How can you prevent *your* messages from becoming *Fugitive E-Mails*?

10

ALTERNATIVE WAYS TO REMEMBER: A DEMONSTRATION OF FIVE PRINCIPLES

Brian Kelley

Brian G. Kelley *is a consultant and trainer specializing in communication and training skills. Brian has been conducting workshops and seminars on management and communication skills since 1979. He develops workshops that integrate the information, materials, and activities for precise outcomes. He is a doctoral candidate in Educational Psychology at the University of Northern Colorado and owns a private consulting firm in New Orleans, Louisiana.*

Contact Information:

1125 St. Michael
Harvey, LA 70058
504-328-8927
gaelican@earthlink.net

Overview   This exercise is designed to help participants identify their usual ways of remembering information and introduce them to alternative ways to remember.

Suggested Time   40 minutes.

Materials Needed   ✓ Form A (Word List)
✓ Form B (Answer Sheet)
✓ Form C (Five Principles to Remember)

Procedure   1. Give each person Forms A and B and give them the following instructions:

"This is a simple one-minute test to help you learn how you can improve the way you remember new information. Look at the list of words on Form A for one minute. Study the list so you can remember the words. At the end of one minute, write the words you remember on the answer sheet, Form B. If a word is repeated, write it down once. Begin studying."

2. At the end of the minute, ask participants to remove Form A from sight and instruct them to write down as many words as they can remember on Form B.

3. Allow one minute for completing the answers and then have participants check on Form A how many words were recalled.

4. Distribute Form C and invite participants to read it. Form study groups (of any size) to discuss the five principles and have them apply the principles to the words on Form A.

5. Reconvene the entire group and answer questions about Form C.

6. Give participants one minute to study the words on Form A once again. Encourage them to use the five principles. Give them another opportunity to recall the words. Have them compare the results to the first time they were tested. Obtain comments and reactions.

primacy

rode

of

and

bike

the

books

and

home

of

repetitive

and

the

associative

class

pen

of

paper

the

yesterday

red

while

of

wind

notes

two

wind

quiet

plate

blue

flew

six

kite

dinner

high

Christmas Tree

yellow

bread

ant

of

watch

and

television

oval

walk

and

program

dog

the

recency

1.

2.

3.

4.

5.

6.

7.

8.

9

10.

11.

12.

13.

14.

15.

16.

17.

18.

FIVE PRINCIPLES TO REMEMBER

Five principles are involved in remembering material: Recency, Primacy, Distinctiveness, Repetition, and Association. Let's look at each one of them.

Recency

How many of you wrote down the last word that you saw as the first word of your answer sheet? Recency is the reason for that. Recency is the memory principle that says we tend to remember the last item best. You can take advantage of the recency principle by finishing each learning session with a summary.

Primacy

How many of you wrote down the word *primacy*? The memory principle associated with that word is primacy. In addition to remembering the last item best, we also tend to remember the first item. You can take advantage of the primacy principle by constructing a short overview before you begin any learning experience.

Distinctiveness

Did anybody write down the phrase *Christmas Tree*? The reason for that is that *Christmas Tree* stands out from all the rest and that is the distinctiveness principle involved in memory. It is distinctive: it consists of two words; it has capital letters; and it is often associated with good feelings. You can use the distinctiveness principle by creating a distinctive representation of new material that you are learning. Could you make that overview of the material distinctive and take advantage of both the primacy and distinctiveness principles? Could you also make your summary of what you have learned distinctive and tie it to the recency principle?

Repetition

How many of you have the words *and, of,* or *the*? Why do you think that happened? (Somebody will say they were repeated.) That is correct! All those words were repeated many times on the list, and that is the repetition principle of memory. The more we hear, see, or do something, the more apt we are to remember it. If you had a distinctive overview of the material, and repeated your overview with a distinctive summary of new material, do you think you would be more apt to remember it?

Association How many of you had any of the words *paper, pen,* or *notes*? What about *walk, dog,* or *street*? Or maybe *plate, dinner,* and *bread*? All of these words are involved in the association principle of memory. One of the easiest ways to remember items is to associate those items with other items that are easy to remember. The primacy and recency principles are easy to remember. They become even easier to remember when you associate something distinctive with them in an overview or review and you repeat the message.

These five principles of memory, Recency, Primacy, Distinctiveness, Repetition, and Association are all tools for you to use in improving your memory. If you apply these five principles to the material you are learning today, you will surprise yourself with the results.

11

MYERS-BRIGGS (MBTI) PREFERENCES: CHOOSING A VICE PRESIDENT FOR JETTS FIREWORKS

Nancy Jackson

Nancy Jackson, Ph.D. *is an educator, mediator, and consultant in communication, teams, leadership, and problem solving. She is currently writing a book,* **Portable Skills,** *that focuses on the essential skills for workplace effectiveness, and has published articles in several training journals. Nancy teaches leadership and workplace communication as an adjunct professor and has over 15 years of experience designing and presenting communication-related programs in organizations. She is a member of the American Society for Training and Development, the International Society for Performance Improvement, the International Association of Facilitators, and the Colorado Council of Mediators.*

Contact Information:

592 S. Victor Way
Aurora, CO 80012
303-363-1930
nansolo@aol.com

Overview
This activity will help those already familiar with the Myers-Briggs Type Indicator (MBTI) to further their understanding of the concepts and of the strength of their own preferences. A role-play exercise asks participants to choose one candidate for a promotion. Discussion can center around how preferences influence decisions and interpersonal relationships. (The activity is not meant to take the place of a qualified MBTI trainer, the inventory itself, nor of a thorough explanation of the theory.)

The MBTI is based on Jung's theories and is an assessment that has withstood testing of millions of people and translation into several languages. The theory rests on four key concepts or preferences. As we live our lives, we perceive our environment and make choices. We tend to have preferences (which Jung states are inborn) in the way we perceive and make decisions. These preferences can be described by four dimensions:

- ✓ You can focus your attention either inwardly, or outwardly (**I or E**).
- ✓ You can collect data through your senses, or gather it intuitively (**S or N**).
- ✓ You can base decisions on thinking or feeling (**T or F**).
- ✓ You can keep an open mind and be spontaneous, or you can live a planned, orderly life (**P or J**).

This activity is for any number of subgroups of 4 to 5 people. If the role-playing variation is used, a group of 8 role players with a larger observer group will be needed.

Suggested Time   Approximately 60 minutes.

Materials Needed   ✓ Form A (Candidates for the VP of Jetts Fireworks)

Procedure
1. Introduce the activity by reviewing MBTI preferences and how preferences might shape choices and interactions with others.

2. Distribute Form A and ask participants to read the descriptions of the candidates for the vice presidency of Jetts Fireworks.

3. Place participants into small groups to discuss the merits of each candidate and select one to recommend as the best vice presidential candidate to the whole group. A spokesperson for the small group should give the group's reasons for the selection. Each candidate represents one of the dimensions of the MBTI preferences:

Pat....Extroverted	Chris....Introverted
Sandy....Sensing	Leslie....Intuiting
Lee....Thinking	Terry....Feeling
C.R....Orderly	Brooke....Spontaneous

4. Invite the whole group to discuss the selection process and reasons for selection. Use the following questions as a guide:
   - ✓ Which of these candidates would be the best new vice president? Why or why not?
   - ✓ What would each of the individuals have to do or learn to qualify? How would you suggest they learn it?
   - ✓ Which dimension do you believe would be most important in a work situation? Why or why not?
   - ✓ What does your selection say about your own preferences and values?
   - ✓ Which preferences seem to be most prevalent where you work?
   - ✓ How do you solve the conflicts that arise because of preferences?

✓ If you could select a committee, or a combination of styles, what would you choose?

✓ What problems might arise due to characterizing people by only one preference?

Variation Select 8 participants to role play each of the candidates. Ask the remaining participants to interview the candidates and make a selection.

CANDIDATES FOR VP OF JETTS FIREWORKS

Jetts Fireworks, Displays, and Design has an opening for a new vice president in charge of national marketing. The eight individuals below have been approached as possible candidates. Each candidate has the education and experience to do the job, but as you will see, all have different modes of operating. The position will require meeting with new accounts, convincing clients of the ability of the company to solve their problems, and motivating and managing the sales force. As the consultant hired to help with this decision, what are your recommendations?

Candidates:

Pat is on the charities committee and the softball team, and is trying to organize a card game for lunchtime players. Pat loves to be with people, to be doing things, and to be involved. Although Pat is not necessarily the life of the party, Pat does enjoy a good time. Pat excels in marketing and sales. Everyone Pat meets feels like a potential friend. Pat tends to say whatever comes to mind, and then think about how it sounds. Pat may occasionally be heard to say, "Yes, I said it, but I didn't mean it!"

Chris is also in sales. Chris takes pride in a thorough knowledge of the product and troubleshooting abilities. Whenever there's a problem, you can E-mail Chris for a quick solution. Chris prefers to do sales and troubleshooting work from the computer, which Chris says is much more efficient. That way, Chris can meet with people from all over the world, without having to move from the office. When Chris does take a lunch break, Chris can be seen with one or two best friends in the office. Although Chris is friendly, gives generously to the charities campaign, and can be outspoken at times, Chris projects an "I want to be alone" image.

Sandy has been called a "number cruncher." Sandy has been heard to say, "You can trust your eyes, ears, and sense of touch. Let me feel it and count it. I know what's real that way!" Sandy is a manager whose hobby is collecting coins. Sandy likes the shine and feel of the cool metal and the history that they represent. Sandy also likes the look and speed of new computers and software, although change is hard to adapt to. Sandy notices when things are out of place in the office and likes to keep an accurate count of employees' sick days, vacation days, and comp time. Employees see Sandy as strict, a bit fussy on details, but fair.

Leslie is the head of the marketing department and constantly amazes coworkers with creative ideas for the company's products. Leslie's work in graphic design has won several awards, although the marketing department's budget doesn't always balance. "That's what accountants are for," responds Leslie. The people who work for Leslie sense a commitment to them and appreciate how much freedom they're given to work on their own. Leslie once said "I just didn't notice," when someone at a meeting pointed out that Leslie's stockings didn't match.

Lee started working for the company years ago as a clerk, and now, as administrative assistant to the Vice President of Operations, Lee takes the job very seriously. Lee is constantly asked for advice from the younger support staff, and helps them by relying on two pillars—tradition and the policy book. "You're either right or wrong, and it's up to me to discover which!" Whenever a knotty problem arises, Lee thinks back on how the old founder would have responded, then consults the policy book. If there isn't a policy, Lee initiates the procedures for implementing a new policy—so there won't be any confusion the next time the issue comes up. Rain or shine, Lee makes sure that things are clearly defined and run fairly. "I have no favorites," Lee frequently claims, "everyone knows exactly where I stand."

Terry, who prefers to make decisions by taking "the human element" into account, runs the human resource department. "Well, I don't really run it," Terry laughs, "it runs me, is more like it. Even though we have policies for human resources, you really have to use your heart. Just because someone's late a few times—heck, they might have a sick kid or something! I really think Lee is a little rough on folks sometimes—but I understand that Lee feels that's the job." Terry has been in charge of human resources for ten years. The employees there have high morale and the department has had the lowest turnover of any in the company. Terry rarely misses a day—except once for ulcer surgery, which occurred after a small downsizing had to be managed.

C.R.'s performance appraisals are a dream. C.R. is well-organized, conscientious, and consistently exceeds standards. CR's system is to use a day planner correctly. C.R. writes lists and then gets an enormous sense of satisfaction out of scratching things off when they are completed. C.R. schedules appointments for the sales crew and makes arrangements for the periodic sales fairs that the company sponsors. Any written work is always neat and complete—on time, every time. C.R.'s biggest problem is that the sales force don't appreciate that work. C.R. has to get on their cases when they don't follow the schedules, or when they forget to do something that C.R. has asked them to do. "They're children, really," C.R. often says.

Brooke resents C.R.'s condescension. "Who says that life runs according to your schedule? Sometimes I have to wait for a client, sometimes we decide to go out for lunch. Not everything can be planned—and besides, it takes the fun out of life!" Indeed, Brooke's flexibility has been a great asset to the company as new technology has demanded changes in the products. Brooke outsells every other salesperson in the company, but is constantly late for meetings and cannot be pinned down for planning long-term goals. "Hey! We'll see how it looks when we get there!" Brooke replies with a wink.

12

ONE-TO-ONE CONVERSATIONS: RECEIVING HIGH-QUALITY FEEDBACK

Phil Donnison

Philip Donnison *is a course director and training consultant at Brathay Development Training, providing training programs for senior managers and strategic teams. He currently specializes in outdoor management development, experiential learning, and the facilitation of senior teams. Phil is a Chartered Occupational Psychologist. He was a contributor to* **The 1997 McGraw-Hill Training and Performance Sourcebook.**

Contact Information:

Brathay Development Training
Brathay Hall, Ambleside, Cumbria, LA22 0HP, England, UK.
(+44) 015394 33041
brathay@brathay.org.uk
www.brathay.org.uk

Overview   This exercise provides a practical forum for participants who may be worried about exchanging feedback, perhaps because of a bad experience with it in the past. It should be used during a training event when people have spent a number of days together, as a supplement to feedback from a psychometric instrument, or as part of a meeting of a team during everyday work.

The phrase "Let me give you some feedback" often has negative connotations. However, high-quality feedback is often associated with rapid improvements in performance and can be a powerful tool for bringing about changes in behavior. By focusing on receiving feedback, one-to-one conversations allow participants to feel they have control of the exercise to receive individual feedback on a specific area. This increases the chances that they will be receptive to the information they get.

Suggested Time   Approximately 50 minutes (for a group of 10 people)

Materials Needed   ✓ Chairs, set up in pairs with enough room between pairs to allow private conversation.

Procedure

1. Introduce the session by explaining that you will be asking participants to have a short, one-to-one conversation with one other person. Explain that it does not matter who they choose because they will have a chance to have a conversation with everybody in the room.

2. Explain that the conversation is to allow them to exchange perceptions and observations with each other. If you wish, you do not even have to use the word "feedback." Emphasize that specific observations of action and behaviors is the subject of the conversation, rather than general opinions and reactions.

3. Tell person A to spend 2 minutes talking to person B about the way he or she (person A) is operating as a member of the group and any behavioral changes he or she would like to make. This 2-minute period is also person A's opportunity to compare notes with person B about how he or she comes across. During the 2 minutes, person A has a chance to check out the way person B sees him or her. A typical conversation might start: "The way I see myself operating in this team is …"

4. At the end of the 2 minutes, ask each pair to switch roles so that person B now has 2 minutes to talk to person A and ask him or her for feedback.

5. At the end of the 4 minutes, ask person A and B to start a new round by moving on to new partners to have the same conversation with them. For example, person A will now talk to person C and person B will talk to person D. During this new round, they will repeat the process set out in steps 3 and 4.

6. Steps 3 and 4 are repeated, each time with a new partner, until each participant has had a chance to have a one-to-one conversation with everybody.

7. It is important that participants find a new partner during each round and that they do not have a second conversation with the same person. If there is an odd number of people, ask a different individual to sit out each time, perhaps filling the role of timekeeper for a round of conversations.

8. About halfway through the exercise, ask participants to change the focus of the conversation. By this stage, they will be starting to hear similar things from each person. Ask participants to tell their partners what they have heard so far and what common themes have emerged. They can then ask the other person to agree or disagree with this feedback and to add to what has been said so far. A typical statement might start, "Something I've heard a lot from other people is…."

9. Toward the last couple of rounds of the exercise, it is important to make sure that everyone is sitting down with someone they have not talked to yet. During the last round, participants can bounce ideas off their partners. Notice that this is not asking for advice, but giving them a chance to use the partner as a sounding board to see what their next steps sound like. Typically, this might start with the phrase, "This leads me to think that...."

10. At the end of the last round, explain that what have been exchanged are perceptions and observations, which should not necessarily be treated as the truth. They are just perceptions of the truth—they may or may not be true. On this basis each person is free to accept or reject anything. If the comments that have been made are treated as if they were gifts, the recipient can decide whether to accept them, reject them, or just put them away and forget about them. Use the analogy of obtaining a gift from a highly regarded store. If you return the gift to the store, no questions are asked and the giver does not even need to know that you have done so.

Variation If the participants work together in the same team or department, parties in the one-to-one conversations can share what each expects of the other. Typically, this might start with the phrase, "I need you to _____ in order to get my own work done effectively." The conversation could also be focused on the well-known "stop-start-continue" model. Typically, this might start with the phrase, "I wish you would stop _____, start _____, and continue _____," inserting specific behaviors you would like the other person to stop, start, or continue doing.

13

"PLAY BALL!": VISUALIZING PRODUCTIVE AND NONPRODUCTIVE COMMUNICATION

Vicki Schneider

Vicki Schneider, *founder and principal consultant of Vantage Solutions, has been helping public and private sector organizations and businesses for more than 20 years. Vicki specializes in designing and delivering customized training systems that improve job performance, change behaviors, and increase profitability. Her programs concentrate on interpersonal and organizational skills, including effective communications, team functioning, trainer development, customer focus, change management, and conflict resolution. Vicki is also director and adjunct faculty of the Key Manager's Program at the Center for Entrepreneurship at Canisius College.*

Contact information:

Vantage Solutions
4434 Waveland Court
Hamburg, NY 14075-2003
716-627-1265
vicki.schneider@astd.noli.com

Overview   For oral communication to be effective, it must be interactive and reciprocal, involving the sender of the message and the receiver of the message. By using the analogy of a game of catch, "Play Ball!" gets the group to visualize the characteristics of productive and nonproductive verbal exchanges. The group creates a shared vocabulary that they use to classify common communication problems and distinguish between effective and ineffective communications. The role play gets the group to act out each communication model using on-the-job situations. The debriefing questions help the group identify practical ways to improve communications.

The four models that this activity demonstrates are:

1. "Brick Wall"—The sender throws a message to the receiver, but the receiver does not catch it. This model illustrates a communication breakdown that occurs for a variety of reasons, such as the sender

hasn't ensured that the receiver was ready to hear the message, the sender sent the message in a way that was difficult or impossible for the receiver to "catch," the receiver wasn't interested in catching the message, or the receiver didn't have the skills to catch the message.

2. "Ricochet"—The sender throws the message to the receiver, but instead of catching the message, the receiver bats it away with the words "Okay, but...." In this model, the sender has succeeded in getting the receiver's attention, but the receiver discounts the message. It helps to illustrate how "killer comments" end productive communication.

3. "Passing Ships"—Both members throw their messages to each other simultaneously, and neither member catches the other person's message. This model illustrates people who talk "at" each other, not "to" each other. What appears to be a conversation is really a series of parallel monologues. In this model, each person sticks to his or her own agenda, despite what the other person says or does.

4. "The Loop"—One person throws the message to the other, who catches the message and throws it back. This round illustrates a successful communication loop. Each person throws his or her message in such a way that the other person can (and does) catch it. Both members take responsibility for the communication's success.

Suggested Time 45–60 minutes.

Materials Needed
✓ Form A (Play Ball worksheet) and overhead transparency of Form A
✓ Form B (Thespians Wanted worksheet)
✓ Form C (Players' Guide—Player 1)
✓ Form D (Players' Guide—Player 2)
✓ Form E (Script Cards)
✓ 2 balls per pair of volunteers (Koosh balls or sponge balls preferred), maximum 6 balls
✓ Colored markers for overhead transparency (or flip chart)
✓ Overhead projector and screen (or flip chart and easel)

Procedure
1. Give each participant a copy of Form A and Form B.
2. Depending on the size of the group, select 2 to 6 volunteers to be "players." (If you have a large group, use all 6 volunteers.)
3. Have the players pair off and line up in front of the room facing their partners.
4. Tell the participants that the game will have four rounds. After each round participants will be asked to diagram (draw) what they saw as if it were a sport play. Participants will draw their diagrams on Form A in the box corresponding to the round that was just played.

5. Give players 1, 3, and 5 the four cards cut from Form C. Give players 2, 4, and 6 the four cards cut from Form D. Instruct the players not to read the cards or show them to anyone at this time.

6. Give players 1, 3, and 5 one ball each.

7. Ask each player to silently read the card that contains instructions for Round 1. Have the players put their cards face down on the floor and tell players 1 and 2 to begin. Then tell players 3 and 4 to begin, followed by players 5 and 6.

8. Tell the seated group to draw the "play" they saw on Form A.

9. Have players retrieve the balls and repeat steps 6 to 8 for Round 2.

10. Have players retrieve the balls. Give one ball to each player and complete Round 3 (following steps 6 to 8.)

11. Have players retrieve the balls. Give one ball each to players 1, 3, and 5. Complete Round 4.

12. Ask for a round of applause for the players and have them return to their seats.

13. Ask a group member to come up to the overhead projector (or flip chart) and diagram Round 1 on the acetate copy of Form A (or on a flip chart replica of Form A). Ask the group member to describe what he or she saw and why he or she drew the round in that particular way. (If the diagram is inaccurate, ask if anyone else had a different diagram.) Repeat the procedure for Rounds 2 to 4.

14. Label each round on the Form A overhead as follows and have the group write the labels on their copies of Form A:

    Round 1 = Brick Wall (Ask how the label suits what happened in the round.)

    Round 2 = Ricochet (Ask how the label suits what happened in the round.)

    Round 3 = Passing Ships (Ask how the label suits what happened in the round.)

    Round 4 = The Loop (Ask how the label suits what happened in the round.)

15. Divide the group into 4 smaller groups. Have everyone read the Thespians Wanted worksheet. Hold out the 4 Script Cards from Form E face down and have someone from each group select a card. They are not to tell the other groups which card they selected. The card describes the communications model each group will act out in a brief role play.

16. Give each group 15 minutes to prepare a 3-minute skit enacting their model.

17. After each skit, have participants jot down which model they think the role play demonstrated. When all 4 skits have been completed, ask each group which model was enacted in each skit. Then ask how they knew, and what the characteristics were that led them to their decision.

18. Confirm accuracy by asking each group which model they enacted.

19. Discussion questions:

   ✓ Which communication model is most effective? Why?

   ✓ Why don't we always use The Loop when we talk to each other?

   ✓ What problems occur with the other models?

   ✓ What can you do to ensure that you are closing the loop when you talk? (Examples: make sure it's a convenient time for the other person, make sure you use language the other person is familiar with, ask the other person to reflect back (repeat) what she or he heard you say.)

   ✓ How will you use what you learned today to improve communications on the job?

Play Ball!

Directions: There will be 4 rounds. After each round, diagram what you saw (as if it were a sports play). The "X" and the "O" represent the two players.

Round 1:		Round 2:	
X	O	X	O
Round 3:		**Round 4:**	
X	O	X	O

THESPIANS WANTED

Directions: Select a card to determine which communications model your group will act out. Write a 3-minute script that illustrates the model. Base your skit on an incident that occurred (or could have occurred) at your work site. After you perform your skit, we will guess which model you demonstrated.

Round 2

Toss a ball to your partner.

Player 1

Round 1

Toss a ball to your partner.

Player 1

Round 4

Toss a ball to your partner.
Catch the ball your partner tosses to you and toss it back to your partner again.

Player 1

Round 3

Toss a ball to your partner.
Make **no** attempt to catch the ball your partner tosses to you.

Player 1

Round 2

> When your partner tosses a ball to you, bat it aside while saying "Okay, but …"

Player 2

Round 4

> Toss a ball to your partner. Catch the ball your partner tosses to you and toss it back to your partner again.

Player 2

Round 1

> Make **no** attempt to catch the ball your partner tosses to you.

Player 2

Round 3

> Toss a ball to your partner. Make **no** attempt to catch the ball your partner tosses to you.

Player 2

"Ricochet"

"The Loop"

"Brick Wall"

"Passing Ships"

14

THE NEW COLOR SOCIETY: EXPERIENCING STEREOTYPING AND CLASSISM

Robert Kaeser

Robert M. Kaeser, Ph.D., *is president of RMK Associates, a training and consulting group. Bob has over 20 years of human resource development, consulting, and training experience in a wide variety of organizational settings. He has created and presented workshops for individual clients as well as presenting at local and national conferences. Areas of expertise include: cultural diversity, sexual harassment prevention, change management, management development, and team building.*

Contact Information:

RMK Associates
1919 Chestnut Street
Suite 1918
Philadelphia, PA 19103
215-568-1338

Overview This activity can be used in a cultural diversity workshop setting. It is highly interactive, and will enable participants to experience the effects of stereotyping and classism in a safe learning environment. An emerging issue in cultural diversity training is the effect of economic, educational, or birthright differences. These differences can create new categories that separate people not by race and gender, but by some form of perceived social status. This activity can be used to illustrate how we react to classism, and the role that it plays in organizations and society. Designed for groups of 15 to 25 participants, this activity can be effectively used with highly diverse or relatively homogeneous groups.

Suggested Time Approximately 60–90 minutes.

Materials Needed ✓ Blue, green, and orange index cards
✓ Opaque envelopes

✓ Markers

✓ Three flip charts

✓ Chairs and tables

Procedure

1. Tell the group that they are going to experience an activity called "The New Color Society."

2. Divide the group into teams of 5 to 7 members (counting off is a good way to create diverse teams).

3. Instruct the teams to imagine a world in which there are only three types of people:

   a. True Blue

   b. Odd Orange

   c. Average Green

   With no further explanation about these categories, tell the teams that they are to brainstorm a list of the characteristics of the three types based only on the category names. Provide flip chart paper and markers and instruct each team to select a team reporter. Give them 5 to 10 minutes for this task.

4. When the time is up, ask each group to give a summary of what they have brainstormed. These summaries should be recorded on flip charts by the trainer, starting with **Odd Orange,** then **Average Green,** and finally **True Blue.** Each color identity should have its own flip chart, so that the characteristics of all three will be visible throughout the rest of the activity. While all groups are different, some patterns will most likely emerge. Typical characteristics for **Odd Orange** include: eccentric, artistic, off-beat, creative, strangely attired, different drummer, and so forth. Typical characteristics for **Average Green** include: hardworking, middle-class, boring, dependable, traditional, in a rut, and so forth. Typical responses for **True Blue** include: privileged, high-class, wealthy, patrician, ethical, socially connected, and so forth. Engage the entire group in a discussion of the characteristics:

   ✓ How did they develop the characteristics?

   ✓ Are there similarities or differences among the groups?

   ✓ Was their process similar to the way in which stereotypes emerge in the "real world"?

5. Next distribute a sealed envelope to each participant. The envelopes should each contain a colored index card; there should be about the same number of each color. Tell participants to hold the envelopes carefully, as they contain their new identity. Instruct them not to open the envelopes until instructed to do so. Explain to them that they are now members of the **True Color Society.** Ask them to think about which color they would like to be, and

how they feel about having such an identity assigned to them. Ask the group for some reactions to having an identity assigned randomly to them. Tell them that they are free to exchange their envelopes with someone else in the room if they wish, and if they can find someone willing to switch with them. (People will generally not switch.) Make the point that this is not unlike the way in which many of our identities are assigned to us at birth, but that we are not given the opportunity to "switch envelopes" or to make any change in these identities.

6. Tell the group that the "moment of truth" is at hand. Ask them to open and peek into their envelopes, without taking the cards out of the envelopes, or sharing the contents with anyone elses. Ask how they are feeling now that they know their new identities, but no one else does.

7. Ask participants to form groups according to their colors. In their color groups, they are to discuss the positive aspects of their identities, and the validity or lack of validity of the characteristics that were brainstormed about their color identity earlier. Give the groups 10 to 15 minutes to do this. They will record their findings on flip chart paper. Next have each group present its results to the large group.

8. Announce that anyone from the three identity groups is now free to change groups if they want to do so. Typically no one will change groups. Process this by asking why people were willing or unwilling to change groups.

9. Instruct participants to say "goodbye" to their color identity groups and return to their original teams. In these teams, ask them to process the entire activity, by considering such questions as the following:

   ✓ How did it feel to be in such a structured society?

   ✓ How much was it like or unlike the real world?

   ✓ Why was it so easy to stereotype? What was the effect of stereotyping?

   ✓ Did one of the identities seem more favored by the larger society? Why?

   ✓ Did one seem less favored? Why?

   ✓ What role did classism play?

   ✓ Does classism have a negative or positive effect in our society?

10. Ask the group for any final thoughts about the activity.

15

STOP 'N JOT!: A VERSATILE ACTIVITY TO ENHANCE LEARNING AND TRANSFER

Brenda Gardner and Sharon Korth

Brenda S. Gardner, Ph.D. *is an assistant professor and director of the Executive Human Resource Development Graduate Program at Xavier University. She is on the board of the Academy of Human Resource Development and has extensive experience in training and organization development in public and private organizations.*

Sharon J. Korth, Ed.D. *is an assistant professor of HRD at Xavier University. She has chapters in* **In Action: Conducting Needs Assessment,** *edited by Jack Phillips and Elwood Holton, Alexandria, VA: ASTD, 1995, and in* **ASTD Toolkit: More Needs Assessment Instruments,** *edited by John Wilcox, Alexandria, VA: ASTD, 1994.*

Sharon and Brenda were contributors to **The 1996 and 1997 McGraw-Hill Team and Organization Development Sourcebooks** *and* **The 1997 McGraw-Hill Training and Performance Sourcebooks.**

Contact information:

Xavier University
3800 Victory Parkway
Cincinnati, OH 45207-6521
513-745-4287
gardner@xavier.xu.edu
www.xu.edu/depts/hrd
513-745-4276
korth@xavier.xu.edu

Overview Trainers often feel pressured to cover a certain amount of material in a session. While knowing that just because they "said it" does not mean that the participants "learned it" and can "apply it," trainers are sometimes reluctant to slow down and find out what is being learned by the participants. If they wait until the end of the session to appraise the participants' learning, valuable time has been wasted and it may be too late!

Stop 'n Jot is a framework for a number of quick learning assessment activities that can be used by a trainer to find out "how things are going" and to "check for understanding" throughout the training. It provides answers from participants to the following questions:

✓ What am I learning?

✓ How can the trainer help my learning?

✓ How can I enhance my own learning?

✓ How can I apply what I'm learning?

With the knowledge gained by the Stop 'n Jot activity, trainers and trainees can make adjustments that will strengthen participants' learning as well as their ability to transfer the knowledge and skills back on the job.

The trainer may employ Stop 'n Jot several times throughout a session. Depending on the participant feedback and the follow-up by the trainer, it may be helpful to repeat one or more of the questions later in the session to see if the adjustment has helped the learning or transfer.

Suggested Time Variable. If the training is one or more days, invest 15–30 minutes for the initial assessment and 5 minutes for follow-ups. If the training is less than a day in length, the trainer may want to select one or two of the forms with questions that seem the most appropriate for the group and limit the time spent to 5–10 minutes for the initial assessment.

Materials Needed ✓ Form A (What Am I Learning?)

✓ Form B (How Can the Trainer Help My Learning?)

✓ Form C (How Can I Enhance My Own Learning?)

✓ Form D (How Can I Apply What I'm Learning?)

Procedure 1. At the time you have selected for the intervention, ideally at the end of a training segment, before a break, or before lunch, stop your instruction and explain to the participants that they will be involved in a quick activity to see "how things are going" and to "check for understanding" so that adjustments can be made in the training to maximize learning and transfer. Describe how the process will work, including their role in providing input and your joint responsibility in enhancing learning.

2. Distribute Forms A, B, C, and D and ask the participants to answer the questions on the forms.

3. Have participants Sit 'n Share, discussing their responses in dyads or triads.

4. Have some of the participants Stand 'n Shout, explaining their responses and insights to the large group. Facilitate a discussion with the large group so that you get a sense of common issues raised by their answers. For example, you may learn that a majority of participants are having difficulty understanding how they can apply the learning to their work situations.

5. Extend the discussion to focus on what you and the participants can do to address some of these issues. To follow up on the previous example, you could ask participants what might help them make the connection to their work situations or ask them if more examples of workplace applications would be helpful.

6. Then, jointly come up with a follow-up plan, such as you agreeing to include more examples and participants agreeing to ask for examples when the transfer is not clearly evident. Also establish a process to check up on the plan, such as asking participants before the next break if they are better able to apply the learning to their work situations.

7. Complete the follow-up plan, such as asking again before the next break, and repeat the previous steps as necessary.

Variations
1. Use only one form for the entire session. You may want to focus on just one element during the session, such as Form C: How Can I Enhance My Own Learning? Follow the above procedure using only one form.

2. Use the forms separately through the training. Instead of distributing all four forms at once, hand out one form at a time, interspersing and focusing the discussion on one element at a time.

3. Collect the completed forms instead of having participants discuss them in dyads or triads. Compile and consolidate the information during lunch, a break, or at the end of the day of a multi-day session. Report your findings back to the group as part of step 4 of the procedure and continue with steps 5, 6, and 7.

✓ List three things that have changed during this training (your knowledge, skill, or beliefs).

1.

2.

3.

✓ Using 20–25 words, describe the most important thing you have learned.

_____

_____

_____

_____

_____

_____

_____

HOW CAN THE TRAINER HELP MY LEARNING?   FORM B

✓ How is the pace of the session for me?

✓ How appropriate is the technical level of the content for me?

✓ How effective are the learning activities for me?

✓ How effective are the trainer's communication skills?

✓ How conducive is the environment (room, logistics, etc.) for learning?

✓ What questions do I have about the training content?

✓ What could the trainer do to enhance my learning?

HOW CAN I ENHANCE MY OWN LEARNING?   FORM C

✓ How well am I concentrating during the training?

✓ How well am I understanding the material?

✓ What factors within my control may be inhibiting my learning?

✓ How can I apply what I know about my own learning style and preferences to this situation?

✓ What can I do to help my own learning and processing of information?

HOW CAN I APPLY WHAT I'M LEARNING?

✓ How important is this material to me?

✓ What did I expect to learn that I could transfer to other situations?

✓ What connections do I see between what I'm learning and future applications?

✓ What could help me better apply what I'm learning (things I could do, things the trainer could do)?

✓ How confident am I in applying my learning to other settings?

✓ What is one thing I can do to ensure that I make use of my learning?

ASSESSMENT INSTRUMENTS

In this section of *The 1998 Training and Performance Sourcebook,* you will find eight assessment instruments. With these instruments, you will be able to answer these questions:

✓ What is your thinking style?

✓ What is your learning style?

✓ Are your employees getting the message?

✓ How consistent are your values with the organization?

✓ What is my leadership style?

✓ Does your certification program meet best-practice criteria?

✓ What questions are you asking during the employment interview?

✓ Is virtual reality training the right choice?

The instruments are designed both to evaluate training/performance issues and to suggest areas for improvement. Most are not for research purposes. Instead, they are intended to build awareness, provide feedback about your own specific situation, and promote group reflection.

In selecting instruments for publication, a premium was placed on questionnaires or survey forms that are easy to understand and quick to complete. Preceding each instrument is an overview that contains the key questions to be assessed. The instrument itself is on a separate page(s) to make reproduction more convenient. All of the instruments are scorable and may contain guidelines for scoring interpretation. Some include questions for follow-up discussion.

Many of these instruments are ideal to utilize as activities in training sessions. Participants can complete the instrument you have selected prior to or during the session. After completion, ask participants to score and interpret their own results. Then, have them compare outcomes with other participants, either in pairs or in larger groupings. Be careful, however, to stress that the data from these instruments are not "hard." They *suggest* rather than *demonstrate* facts about people or situations. Ask participants to compare scores to their own perceptions. If they do not match, urge them to consider why. In some cases, the discrepancy may be due to the crudeness of the measurement device. In others, the discrepancy may result from distorted self-perceptions. Urge participants to open themselves to new feedback and awareness.

Other instruments will help you and others to assess future training needs. Again, it would be useful to show and discuss the data that emerges with others involved in the area under evaluation.

You may also wish to use some instruments as a basis for planning retreats or staff meetings. Have participants complete the instruments prior to the session. Then, summarize the results and open them up to team discussion.

If you choose this option, be sure to state the process clearly to respondents. You might want to use the following text:

We are planning to get together soon to identify issues that need to be worked through in order to maximize our future effectiveness. An excellent way to begin doing some of this work is to collect information through a questionnaire and to feed back that information for group discussion.

I would like you to join with your colleagues in filling out the attached questionnaire. Your honest responses will enable us to have a clear, objective view of our situation.

Your participation will be totally anonymous. My job will be to summarize the results and report them to the group for reaction.

You can also share the instruments with others in your organization who might find them useful for their own purposes. In some cases, merely reading through the questions is a valuable exercise in self- and group reflection.

16

WHAT IS YOUR THINKING STYLE?

Garry Gelade

Garry A. Gelade, Ph.D. *holds a master's degree in Psychology from Cambridge University and a doctorate from the University of Nottingham. He spent four years at Oxford University conducting research in cognitive psychology, and has held senior management positions in American Express and Lloyds Bank. He is a charter member of the British Psychological Society, and an associate of the Centre for Research in Applied Creativity. He works as an independent consultant and trainer in the area of corporate creativity and innovation, and has published a number of scientific papers on cognitive psychology and creative thinking.*

Contact Information:

Business Analytic Ltd.
1, Circus Lodge, Circus Road, London
NW8 9JL, UK
0171 289 6305 (International +44 171 289 6305)
simplex@compuserve.com
http://www.ourworld.compuserve.com/homepages/simplex

Overview   Just as people have different physiques and different personalities, they have different thinking styles. This questionnaire infers a person's preferred thinking style from some related behavioral and personality characteristics. It is *not* a test of intelligence; different thinking styles are equally valuable in work and ordinary life.

However, individuals who have a strong preference for one particular style may find they can solve problems better if they consciously try to balance their thinking by "stepping into" the opposite style from time to time. Use of the nonpreferred style will improve with practice.

Teams that consist of individuals with all the same style are likely to have difficulties in solving problems effectively. This questionnaire can also be used to rapidly diagnose the thinking style of a team.

THE FIRECRACKER AND TREE QUESTIONNAIRE

ADMINISTERING THE QUESTIONNAIRE

Hand out the questionnaire on page 153, but not the Scoring Instructions or Scoring Interpretation. Then read the following instructions to participants:

"The questionnaire you are about to complete will help you to understand your own thinking style. It is not a test of intelligence; different thinking styles are equally valuable in work and ordinary life, but knowing your own preferred style and how you differ from your colleagues will help you to be more effective in individual and team problem solving. The results will help you understand what types of task will be easier and more enjoyable for you to work on, and what types of task will be less so. For the results to be of value to you, it is essential you answer the questions as honestly as possible.

In the questionnaire you are about to complete, the items are arranged in pairs labeled 'A' and 'B.' You are asked to compare the statements in each pair and decide how well each statement describes you. Then distribute 5 points between the two statements, giving more points to the statement that describes you better, and giving the rest of the 5 points to the other statement in the pair. For example, if you think the 'A' statement in a pair describes you extremely well, and the 'B' statement describes you very poorly, you would give all 5 points to statement 'A' and no points to statement 'B.' If the two statements are both somewhat descriptive of you, you would split the 5 points more evenly. The points in a pair can be split 5 and 0, 4 and 1, or 3 and 2, but you are not allowed to use fractions. In all cases, the scores for the two statements in each pair must add up to 5. Score every statement, and do not spend too long on any one question—your first response is usually your true judgment.

Example: 1A. I enjoy doing crosswords. **2**
1B. I enjoy listening to music. **3**

Make sure everyone understands the instructions, and answer any questions. Then give them about 10 minutes to fill in the questionnaire. While they are working, it is a good idea to go around the room to check that everyone has understood the instructions correctly, and to assist anyone who is having difficulty.

After everyone has finished, hand out the Scoring Instructions and have the participants score their results.

Next hand out the Scoring Interpretation sheet and give participants time to digest the information.

(Optional: If all participants are willing to share their results with the whole group, record the results on a flip chart. If the participants belong to work teams, work out the average score for each team.)

Begin a group discussion by asking those with strong preferences to say what kinds of problems and tasks they find easy, and what kinds they find difficult. Try to bring out the contrast between the two different styles, and the difficulties and advantages of people with opposing styles working together. Pose the following question to the group: Where do you think your own work team fits on this measure of thinking style, and what might be done to improve its thinking and decision making?

THE FIRECRACKER AND TREE QUESTIONNAIRE

Distribute 5 points between each pair of statements, giving more points to the statement in each pair that describes you better.

		Score			Score
1A	I rarely waste any time before getting down to work.		1B	I often find it difficult to get down to work right away.	
2A	I often have to search for things I've misplaced.		2B	I mostly know where everything is.	
3A	I am a realist and stick to the facts.		3B	I enjoy indulging in flights of fancy.	
4A	I'm prone to overindulge in some things.		4B	I rarely let myself overindulge in things.	
5A	I like to work through things methodically.		5B	I tend to approach things in a hit-or-miss way.	
6A	Self-discipline is one of my main strengths.		6B	I admit to lacking a strong sense of self-discipline.	
7A	I rather enjoy being shocked or scared by films or TV programs.		7B	I avoid watching films or TV programs that are disturbing.	
8A	I often let myself drift off into daydreams or fantasy.		8B	I usually manage to keep my mind firmly on the job at hand.	
9A	I take trouble to keep my personal work area neat and tidy.		9B	My personal work area gets in a bit of a mess at times.	
10A	I prefer using tried and tested ways that I am confident will work.		10B	I enjoy the risk of doing things differently.	
11A	I think of myself as a down-to-earth person.		11B	I have a vivid imagination.	
12A	Curious things like strange-sounding names can sometimes evoke strong feelings in me.		12B	Rarely, if ever, do I experience strange or inexplicable moods.	
13A	I have trouble getting myself organized.		13B	I can work at a steady pace so as to finish on time.	
14A	I believe in sticking to a plan.		14B	I believe in "going with the flow."	

THE FIRECRACKER AND TREE QUESTIONNAIRE

Transfer your scores from the questionnaire above to the blank spaces below. Be sure to write the A and B scores for each pair in the correct column. Then add the numbers in each column to obtain the two column totals. If correct, the two column totals should add up to 70.

Question number	Tree	Firecracker
1	A _____	B _____
2	B _____	A _____
3	A _____	B _____
4	B _____	A _____
5	A _____	B _____
6	A _____	B _____
7	B _____	A _____
8	B _____	A _____
9	A _____	B _____
10	A _____	B _____
11	A _____	B _____
12	B _____	A _____
13	B _____	A _____
14	A _____	B _____
Total for *Tree*	☐	**Total for** *Firecracker* ☐

Check: Total for Tree + Total for Firecracker = 70

THE FIRECRACKER AND TREE QUESTIONNAIRE

Everyone's thinking style is a blend of FireCracker and Tree, but most people naturally incline more strongly to one style of thinking than the other. The strength of your preference for each style is reflected by the total scores in each. The higher your score for a particular style, the stronger your preference for it. If your two scores are equal or nearly so, there is no need to worry. It simply indicates you have a well-balanced pattern of thinking, and are equally at home in both styles.

If your score for Tree is higher than your score for FireCracker, you have a preference for Tree-style thinking. Trees are logical and systematic, and their thinking is firmly rooted in hard fact. Tree-style thinking proceeds on a step-by-step basis, and like the branches of a tree, each thought grows out of a previous one, and has a recognizable connection to it. Trees are good at analyzing situations by marshaling all the facts, seeing relationships between them, and drawing rational conclusions based on sound arguments. Trees are objective, cautious in their judgements and decision making, and like to base their conclusions on solid evidence. The main problems Trees face are fence-sitting, when they feel they have too little information to form a conclusion, and paralysis by analysis, when they feel they have too much information to understand all the implications.

If your score for FireCracker is higher than your score for Tree, you have a preference for FireCracker thinking. FireCracker thinking is speedy and intuitive, and like a lit firecracker, often proceeds in unpredictable jumps between seemingly unrelated concepts. FireCrackers are often good at thinking up unusual new ideas or different ways of doing things. They tend to base their judgments and conclusions on what subjectively feels right rather than on analysis of the objective evidence. They tend to decide on a general direction, and not worry too much about the details. FireCrackers are good at making decisions in situations where there are few facts available, or when there are so many facts it is difficult to analyze all the possibilities in the time available. The main weaknesses of FireCracker thinking are the tendency to jump to premature conclusions and the inability to really think through all the implications of an idea.

When working together, Trees often mistrust the more intuitive FireCrackers, while FireCrackers often see the Trees as slow and obsessed with unnecessary details. However, a good team should have a blend of both thinking types. Without any FireCrackers, a team may find it hard to come up with anything radical. It may also find itself permanently stuck at the data-collecting stage, without ever seeming to have enough evidence to come to a decision. Without any Trees on the other hand, a team might, like Don Quixote, simply "leap on its horse and gallop off in all directions at once."

17

WHAT IS YOUR LEARNING STYLE?

Christopher Hardy and Susan Hardy

Christopher R. Hardy, Ph.D., and Susan Hardy *are professional educators and combined their experience and expertise to develop a reliable and valid cognitive adult learning style instrument. Susan Hardy provided 20 years of educational and curriculum experience in assisting in the format of HELP's profile. Chris Hardy designed, developed, tested, and validated the instrument's method of measurement and its conceptualization using multivariate analyses. Dr. Hardy holds degrees from Virginia Tech and Auburn University, and Susan Hardy from Old Dominion and Norfolk State University. Psychometric and technical information (item and scale factor structures and reliability data) are available upon request.*

Contact Information:

P.O. Box 436
Occoquan, VA 22125
Chrishardy@aol.com

Overview The Hardy Educational Learning Profile is an adult cognitive learning style instrument. The HELP is written at an eighth-grade reading level. It is comprised of three scales of ten semantic descriptors representing and measuring cognitive learning style constructs. The HELP is a paper and pencil, self-administered, and self-scored instrument. It is an economical and efficient diagnostic educational and training tool—with an average administration time of 7 minutes for the worksheet and 10 minutes to score.

Its theoretical conceptualization is derived from the theories of Jung, Osgood, Ashcraft, and Vygotsky, all of which are incorporated within an easy-to-understand, modern cognitive psychology information-processing framework:

✓ Attention to the learning situation or source of information, inner or outer focus;

✓ Acquire information with a concrete or abstract perception;

✓ Processing information with objective or subjective decision-based function.

The HELP is one of the most reliable and valid instruments available. It has undergone in-depth psychometrics and multivariate analysis. This means that the HELP measures what it is intended to measure and that you can have confidence in the accuracy of your profile.

HARDY EDUCATIONAL LEARNING PROFILE (HELP)
ESPECIALLY FOR ADULT LEARNERS

What is HELP? The HELP was developed for your use as an accurate, efficient, economical, and effective cognitive learning style instrument by a cognitive motivational learning specialist and a master teacher. For ease of interpretation and understanding, it uses a modern information-processing frame of reference. It measures your interaction or approach to learning situations and how you prefer to acquire and process information. Your profile will indicate your general cognitive preference pattern for the way you like to learn, understand, and make sense of things based on your total scores. It can be very useful for teachers, facilitators, educators, and students to understand individual differences in how we like to learn.

The HELP is designed to be self-administered and self-scored. It is comprised of a cover sheet, a worksheet, a score sheet, and description HELP profiles. The HELP consists of three sets of ten paired word choices. Participants select between word choices according to their preferences. There are no right or wrong answers or profiles. Discovering your profile, or unique style of learning, and sharing your results can be rewarding in many learning settings. Please take a few minutes to fill out and score this instrument.

HARDY EDUCATIONAL LEARNING PROFILE (HELP) WORKSHEET

Circle the appropriate block between each word pair based on your preference.
Consider each pair carefully. Think of the meaning (not the sound).

Example:

FAR	a	b	c	d	e	f	CLOSE

(The closer to the word, the stronger your preference and vice versa.)

A) INTERACTION. Your preferences for words or meaning which best describe your approach to interaction to most situations:

ACTION	a	b	c	d	e	f	REFLECTION
OUTGOING	g	h	i	j	k	l	RESERVED
CALM	m	n	o	p	q	r	ACTIVE
HASTY	s	t	u	v	w	x	HESITANT
ALONE	y	z	aa	ab	ac	ad	CROWD
VERBAL	ae	af	ag	ah	ai	aj	NONVERBAL
DOING	ak	al	am	an	ao	ap	REHEARSING
LISTENING	aq	ar	as	at	au	av	TALKING
OUTWARD	aw	ax	ay	az	ba	bb	INWARD
ACTING	bc	bd	be	bf	bg	bh	WATCHING

B) GATHER INFORMATION: Your preferences for words or meanings which best describe how you like to gather information or perceive things:

FACTS	a	b	c	d	e	f	THEORIES
HORIZON	g	h	i	j	k	l	NEARBY
REAL	m	n	o	p	q	r	IMAGINATION
DETAIL	s	t	u	v	w	x	GLOBAL
CONCEPTUAL	y	z	aa	ab	ac	ad	FACTUAL
LITERAL	ae	af	ag	ah	ai	aj	FIGURATIVE
SPECIFICS	ak	al	am	an	ao	ap	POSSIBILITIES
ESTIMATE	aq	ar	as	at	au	av	PRECISE
PRESENT	aw	ax	ay	az	ba	bb	FUTURE
ABSTRACT	bc	bd	be	bf	bg	bh	CONCRETE

C) PROCESS INFORMATION: Your preferences for words or meanings which best describe how you like to process information or make decisions:

LOGIC	a	b	c	d	e	f	VALUES
RATIONAL	g	h	i	j	k	l	COMPASSION
SENTIMENT	m	n	o	p	q	r	PRAGMATIC
ANALYTIC	s	t	u	v	w	x	CONSIDERATE
PERSONAL	y	z	aa	ab	ac	ad	IMPERSONAL
THOUGHTFUL	ae	af	ag	ah	ai	aj	PRACTICAL
HELPFUL	ak	al	am	an	ao	ap	SENSIBLE
EVIDENCE	aq	ar	as	at	au	av	FAITH
REASONS	aw	ax	ay	az	ba	bb	FEELINGS
BELIEF	bc	bd	be	bf	bg	bh	PROOF

Step 1. On the previous page (worksheet) look at the small letters in the blocks you circled. Then, find the corresponding small letters in each of the three columns below, and circle the numbers or values next to these small letters.

For example: If you circled the block "a" in the first section, A), on the HELP worksheet, you would mark or circle the value "6" next to the "a" in the column 'A) below.

| a | ⑥ | ae | 6 |
| b | 5 | ae | 5 |

(Within each column A), B), and C) below, you should finish with 10 values in each circled.)

A) INTERACTION

Block #	Value	Block #	Value
a	6	ae	6
b	5	af	5
c	4	ag	4
d	3	ah	3
e	2	ai	2
f	1	aj	1
g	6	ak	6
h	5	al	5
i	4	am	4
j	3	an	3
k	2	ao	2
l	1	ap	1
m	1	aq	1
n	2	ar	2
o	3	as	3
p	4	at	4
q	5	au	5
r	6	av	6
s	6	aw	6
t	5	ax	5
u	4	ay	4
v	3	az	3
w	2	ba	2
x	1	bb	1
y	1	bc	1
z	2	bd	2
aa	3	be	3
ab	4	bf	4
ac	5	bg	5
ad	6	bh	6

B) GATHER INFORMATION

Block #	Value	Block #	Value
a	6	ae	6
b	5	af	5
c	4	ag	4
d	3	ah	3
e	2	ai	2
f	1	aj	1
g	6	ak	6
h	5	al	5
i	4	am	4
j	3	an	3
k	2	ao	2
l	1	ap	1
m	1	aq	1
n	2	ar	2
o	3	as	3
p	4	at	4
q	5	au	5
r	6	av	6
s	6	aw	6
t	5	ax	5
u	4	ay	4
v	3	az	3
w	2	ba	2
x	1	bb	1
y	1	bc	1
z	2	bd	2
aa	3	be	3
ab	4	bf	4
ac	5	bg	5
ad	6	bh	6

C) PROCESS INFORMATION

Block #	Value	Block #	Value
a	6	ae	1
b	5	af	2
c	4	ag	3
d	3	ah	4
e	2	ai	5
f	1	aj	6
g	6	ak	1
h	5	al	5
i	4	am	3
j	3	an	4
k	2	ao	5
l	1	ap	6
m	1	aq	6
n	2	ar	5
o	3	as	3
p	4	at	3
q	5	au	2
r	6	av	1
s	6	aw	6
t	5	ax	5
u	4	ay	4
v	3	az	3
w	2	ba	2
x	1	bb	1
y	1	bc	1
z	2	bd	2
aa	3	be	3
ab	4	bf	4
ac	5	bg	5
ad	6	bh	6

Step 2. After circling all your associated values, total them as instructed below.

A) Total the 10 circled values above to obtain the "Outer" score.

Outer =

Subtract "Outer" total from 70.
(70 – total = "Inner" score)

Inner =

B) Total the 10 circled values above to obtain the "Concrete" score.

Concrete =

Subtract "Concrete" total from 70.
(70 – total = "Abstract" score)

Abstract =

C) Total the 10 circled values above to obtain the "Objective" score.

Objective =

Subtract "Objective" total from 70.
(70 – total = "Subjective" score)

Subjective =

Step 3. To determine your Learning Profile, plot the bar graphs in A), B), and C). See example for A) below.

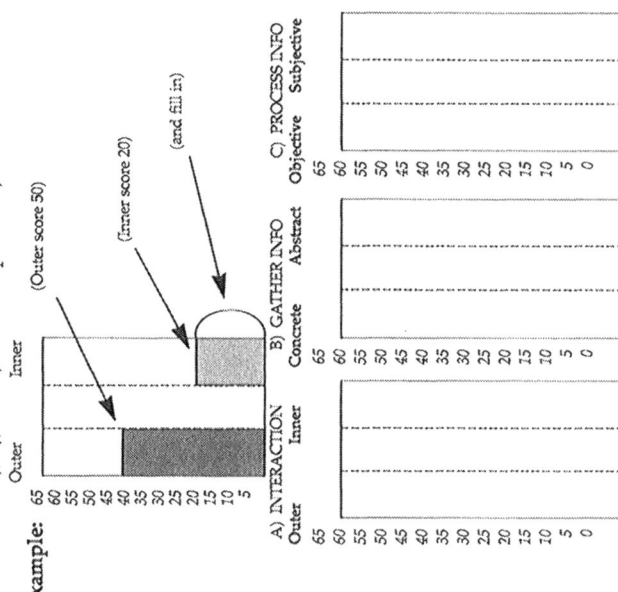

Example: Outer / Inner

(Outer score 50)
(Inner score 20)
(and fill in)

65 60 55 50 45 40 35 30 25 20 15 10 5

A) INTERACTION
Outer / Inner

B) GATHER INFO
Concrete / Abstract

C) PROCESS INFO
Objective / Subjective

65 60 55 50 45 40 35 30 25 20 15 10 5 0

Step 4. Next, in the box below, write the word which represents the larger score from each graph.

For example:

A) INTERACTION	B) GATHER INFO	C) PROCESS INFO
Write: *Outer*	*Abstract*	*Objective*

(Or whichever in each pair is larger; for ties write both words.)

A) INTERACTION	B) GATHER INFO	C) PROCESS INFO
_____	/	_____

This (above) is your learning profile.
Go to the next page to learn more about it.

HELP FOR LEARNING

Directions:

First: Look at the box with your learning profile from the HELP scoring sheet.
Then: Match the word or words from your profile to the profile descriptions in
A), B), and C) below.
Easy as ABC!

A) Interaction, approach, or information source for learning:

Outer:
Social and open
You are observably
outgoing and verbal.
You like to discuss and
debate. Action and
doing with others
describe your learning
preferences.

◄ - ►

Inner:
Introspective and
contemplative. You are
observably reserved and
nonverbal. You like to
reflect and listen.
Watching and reflecting
describe your learning
preferences.

B) and C) Gathering and processing information during learning activities:

Abstract-Objective

Description: You prefer gathering information through
seeing the whole picture or conceptual framework: both
global and theoretical. You also like to connect
information to your conceptional perspective seeing its
relationships and possibilities. In processing or making
decisions, you seek solutions; in doing so, you are
strategic, practical, rational, analytic, and impersonal.
Your perspective is generally long-ranged. In a learning
activity, you have a need to understand the overall
purpose, its relevance to your worldview, and its
significance. You are curious and conceptually associative.
You prefer reason and logic in explanations and are
analytic and deliberate in expressing your final decisions.

Abstract-Subjective

Description: You prefer to gather information, seeking
possibilities and seeing conceptual aspects and patterns.
You relate to information that is figurative, abstract, and
interpretable for its future possibilities. Your decisions are
based on empathetic insight, compassion, and
consideration. Your perspective is conceptual and global.
In a learning activity, you require and seek new, potentially
rewarding, and exciting information. You prefer helping,
coaching, and cooperating. In making important decisions,
you are steadfast and committed to your ideas and values
in consideration of others and self for the common good.
Learning should be in a harmonious setting and be seen as
applicable to your personal goals and as a benefit to others.

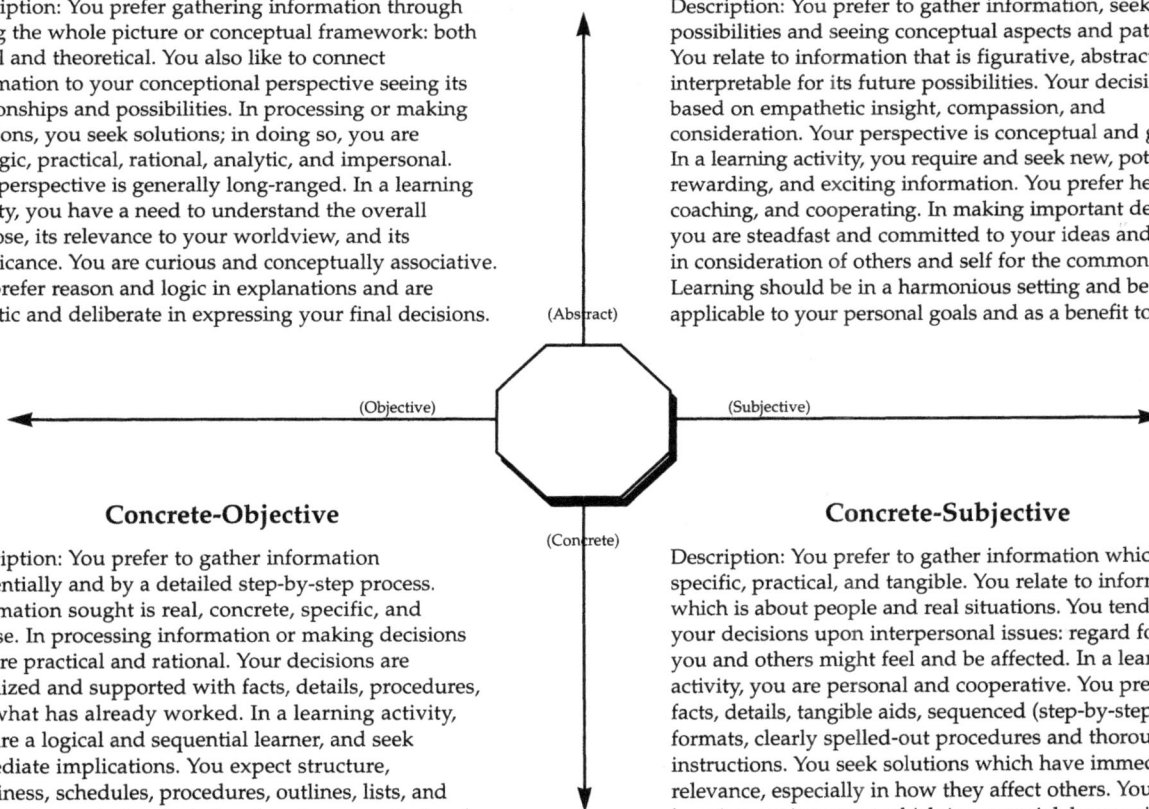

(Abstract)

(Objective) ◄————————————————————————————————————► (Subjective)

(Concrete)

Concrete-Objective

Description: You prefer to gather information
sequentially and by a detailed step-by-step process.
Information sought is real, concrete, specific, and
precise. In processing information or making decisions
you are practical and rational. Your decisions are
organized and supported with facts, details, procedures,
and what has already worked. In a learning activity,
you are a logical and sequential learner, and seek
immediate implications. You expect structure,
timeliness, schedules, procedures, outlines, lists, and
details. You are task oriented and prefer a practical and
orderly environment. Final solutions must be useful,
functional, substantial, definite, and tangible.

Concrete-Subjective

Description: You prefer to gather information which is
specific, practical, and tangible. You relate to information
which is about people and real situations. You tend to base
your decisions upon interpersonal issues: regard for how
you and others might feel and be affected. In a learning
activity, you are personal and cooperative. You prefer
facts, details, tangible aids, sequenced (step-by-step) lesson
formats, clearly spelled-out procedures and thorough
instructions. You seek solutions which have immediate
relevance, especially in how they affect others. You need a
learning environment which is congenial, harmonious,
and focused on clear, present, and personal outcomes.

18

ARE YOUR EMPLOYEES GETTING THE MESSAGE?

Janet Winchester-Silbaugh and Caryn Relkin

Janet Winchester-Silbaugh *is a member of The Synergy Group Limited, an organization development consulting group in Albuquerque, New Mexico which helps organizations design strategic plans and organizational structures and understand organizational dynamics so they can reach their goals.*

Caryn Relkin *is the vice president of Human Resources and Organizational Development for the St. Joseph Healthcare System in Albuquerque, New Mexico. She has been involved in human resources and organizational development for 20 years, working in retail, banking, and the healthcare industry for the last 15 years.*

Contact Information:

The Synergy Group Limited
732 Wellesley Drive NE
Albuquerque, NM 87106
505-266-3104
505-286-2210
silbaugh@ccvp.com - Janet
carynr@sjhs.org - Caryn

Overview Why don't your employees get it? You've repeatedly explained your strategy. You've asked for their support of an important new initiative. Your employees listen politely, but then nothing changes. What is going on here? The *Communication System Assessment—Are Your Employees Getting the Message?* is designed to help you understand your organization's communications better. It should help you see opportunities for using untapped channels of communication and give your messages more staying power.

Organizations are complex adaptive systems. Systems: Almost every part of the organization has an effect on every other part. Complex: There are many relationships among different parts of the system. Adaptive: Each part of the system is constantly taking in new information, making decisions, and changing to fit the environment. Every person in the organization and every department is thinking, aware, and taking action. With a complex, adaptive system, good communication is a key factor in keeping all the parts working toward the same goals.

Your first job is to know what you want to say. Can you write a list of the four or five key messages that all employees must understand for your organization to be successful? If you can't write it, chances are that your employees can't hear it, either.

Your second job is to identify all the channels of communication available to you. People usually think of the formal communication channels: employee newsletters, team meetings, memos, and bulletin boards. But there are many more informal channels. The grapevine is usually interesting and very effective, based on its impact and how fast it permeates the organization. You may not even realize the power of many informal channels of communication, but they include: which departments get the best offices, whose ideas are listened to, which jobs get paid the most, which ideas get increased budget allocations, and who gets promoted. Each channel has its own flavor, level of credibility, and potential to contribute to your goals. Recognizing these informal channels of communication is important if you want to make them work for you.

This assessment tool is designed to help you paint a picture of your organization's communication. It will give you ideas about what might not be working. You can use this assessment to understand just what your employees are hearing, and whether it leads to action or whether it is a jumble of confusing messages. If you fix the problems you see through this assessment, employees just may "get it" in the future.

Communications Survey

Setting up the group. This assessment can be done individually, but is more effective if done in a group of up to 10 people, with different perspectives on the organization. It will take about 90 minutes, including discussion and summarization time. The participants do not have to do any preparation beforehand.

Instructing the group in how to fill it out. A blank assessment is included for you to copy. There is also a sample assessment, so you can see how it might look after it has been completed.

In the boxes at the top of the assessment, write the 4 to 7 key messages your employees have to understand if your organization is going to succeed. Check them against your organization's vision and long-term strategy to make sure you've got them right. The last column is reserved for "all other," information that you have to send out, but doesn't seem connected to one of your key messages.

Down the left-hand side, write the important places employees get their information. They should include the formal channels, such as the employee newsletter, bulletin boards, and meetings. Then list the informal channels. You should have as many informal channels as formal channels of communication. Make sure you include the ones that cause you the most problems. And don't forget the grapevine.

After you are comfortable that you have listed the key messages and have figured out most of the places people get information, then fill out the grid with your candid assessment of how effectively each channel of communication carries each message.

Message not mentioned	leave blank
Message infrequently mentioned	I
Message moderately discussed	II
Message heavily discussed	III

When you fill out the grid, consider the number of times the message is mentioned, how eye-catching the message is, whether employees hear it the way you intend it, and whether they talk about it. You can do this off the top of your head, survey employees, or count data from the actual source.

Look at the assessment once you have filled out the top part. If it is like most organizations, there will be trivial information in the "all other" column that gets lots of attention, and important information that doesn't get mentioned at all. Often the formal channels carry the "facts" and the informal channels carry powerful interpretations of what the facts mean to employees. Take a moment to write your first, off-the-cuff impressions.

Now that you have filled out the basic data on the top part of the evaluation, answer the 7 questions on the lines at the bottom. You can answer these questions using as much input as you want, from relying on your own impression, to talking to people in the elevator, to asking managers to do a poll of employees. Do what is effective for you. Review the sample of a completed evaluation form to give you an idea of what it might look like.

Figure 18.1 Sample: Are Your Employees Getting the Message?
Communication System Assessment

	new quality initiative	organizational structure change	salary bonuses	mail room cost-reduction procedures
all-employee quarterly meeting	III	II		
weekly employee newsletter		I	II	III
talk around the coffee machine	III	III		
budget allocations	III		I	II
What percentage of the potential sources were used?	50%	75%	75%	50%
What message did you want to send?	The new strategy is critical to our survival, and this initiative is part of the action to get there. Support it.	The new structure is also part of the strategy. Support it.	The bonus rewards people for smart, hard work which supports the organization's goals.	Cost control is important. Follow the new procedures.
What message did employees hear?	Yet another new program the boss wants.	I have a new boss.	How much is my check? Was it calculated correctly? Who got more than I did?	Cost control is important. Follow the new procedures. If not, someone will yell at me.
Did employees hear it right?	No. Employees barely understand the program. They don't really support it.	They got part of the message. Employees understand the facts, but not why. They see it politically.	They got part of the message. Employees focused on their payout and the details of how it was calculated. They missed the point.	Yes
Did all sources give the same message?	No	No	Maybe	Yes
Was the "volume" appropriate?	Too quiet	Ok	Ok	Too loud
Did the message result in effective actions?	No action defined.	No, reorganization seen as political, not seen as strategic.	Produced some focus on important actions, but some harmful side effects.	Yes, most employees changed to new procedure.

ARE YOUR EMPLOYEES GETTING THE MESSAGE? COMMUNICATION SYSTEM ASSESSMENT

⇓ Channels of Communication	Messages ⇒					

What percentage of the potential sources were used?						
What message did you want to send?						
What message did employees hear?						
Did employees hear it right?						
Did all sources give the same message?						
Was the "volume" appropriate?						
Did the message result in effective actions?						

INTERPRETATION

Understanding the results.

1. Can people hear the important messages? Is there too much noise?

2. Does each type of message get the right level of attention? Are unimportant messages drowning out important ones?

3. Do your messages include a mix of strategy (what is important to do and why), operational performance (are we succeeding), and operational instructions (how to do it)?

4. Do your topics include unfavorable information (such as bad publicity, regulatory scrutiny, financial losses)? Are you giving employees a way to get accurate information on unfavorable events, and providing them with possible ways of thinking about it?

5. Do all your sources say the same thing? Is there one version or many of the same events?

6. Is there a gap between what information you think you send out and what employees receive?

7. Do employees add interpretation or information from other sources onto messages you send?

8. Do employees leave out important parts of the messages when they remember them?

9. If you look at the messages you were trying to send a year ago, do they makes sense in relation to what you're saying now, or has the shift been extreme? Is there a logical path from last year's communications to this year's? Are you laying a foundation for next year's messages?

10. Do you use all channels of communication?

11. Do the informal sources of communication support or hinder the formal sources?

Information overload is rampant in organizations. The noise level is very high. One way of getting important information across is to increase its noise level compared to other information. The important things can simply be talked about more often and in more noticeable ways. Another way for employees to make sense out of all this information is to give it structure, to put it into categories. To use the noise analogy, it's hard to make sense of a bunch of noises all jumbled together. It's easier to remember the melody and harmony of an interesting song.

19

HOW CONSISTENT ARE YOUR VALUES WITH THE ORGANIZATION'S?

William Harrington and Robert Preziosi

William J. Harrington, *Ed.D. is an associate professor and director of the Institute for Family Business at Nova Southeastern University School of Business and Entrepreneurship. He has over 25 years of experience as a human resource executive, principally in the banking sector. He was a senior vice president of HRM with a leading banking group. He has been a consultant to business and not-for-profit organizations. In addition to teaching HRM and HRD courses at the graduate level, he teaches a course in values-based leadership.*

Robert C. Preziosi, *D.P.A. is a professor of management education for Nova Southeastern University. He has been a leadership training administrator, line manager, HR executive, business school dean, and vice president of management development and training at a Fortune 50 company. He has been a consultant to business, government, and academia. His areas of research and teaching at the graduate level include adult learning, productivity management, team building, and values-based leadership.*

Contact Information:

William Harrington
Nova Southeastern University School of Business and Entrepreneurship
3301 College Avenue
Fort Lauderdale, FL 33314
954-262-5088

Robert Preziosi
Nova Southeastern University
3301 College Avenue
Fort Lauderdale, FL 33314
954-262-5111
preziosi@sbe.nova.edu
www.she.nova.edu

Overview The purpose of this instrument is to help individuals determine how aligned their personal values are with the values of the organization. The degree to which there is alignment or consistency between the two sets of values is a major factor in how effective an individual's performance is likely to be.

The Value Analysis Worksheet is a tool that allows an individual to determine the relationship between individual and organizational values. It uses a commonly accepted set of values to allow for the analysis. The individual who uses this tool will better understand how "in synch" she or he is with the organization. This will result in better individual decision making regarding (1) the acceptance of values, (2) possible adoption of a new values set, or (3) finding an organization with different values.

VALUE ANALYSIS WORKSHEET

VALUE	Consistently—4	Often—3	Occasionally—2	Never—1
Loyalty—Faithful to allegiance and binding to something	Self Org.	Self Org.	Self Org.	Self Org.
Integrity—A firm adherence to a code of moral values	Self Org.	Self Org.	Self Org.	Self Org.
Honesty—A sense of fairness and straightforwardness	Self Org.	Self Org.	Self Org.	Self Org.
Respect—To consider someone worthy of high regard	Self Org.	Self Org.	Self Org.	Self Org.
Supportiveness—To encourage another person during a difficult period	Self Org.	Self Org.	Self Org.	Self Org.
Communication—To openly express ideas effectively	Self Org.	Self Org.	Self Org.	Self Org.
Commitment to Quality—To seek a distinguished level of excellence	Self Org.	Self Org.	Self Org.	Self Org.
Career Enhancement—A pursuit of progressive personal achievement	Self Org.	Self Org.	Self Org.	Self Org.
Diversity—Strive to achieve a sensitivity to cultures in the workplace	Self Org.	Self Org.	Self Org.	Self Org.
Clarity of Progress—Being clear on continuous organization operations	Self Org.	Self Org.	Self Org.	Self Org.

VALUE	Consistently—4	Often—3	Occasionally—2	Never—1
Reliability to Stakeholders— Dependability toward all connected with the organization	Self Org.	Self Org.	Self Org.	Self Org.
Sense of Humor— Capability to laugh at one's self during absurd issues	Self Org.	Self Org.	Self Org.	Self Org.
Trust—Assured reliance on the character, ability, and truth of someone	Self Org.	Self Org.	Self Org.	Self Org.
Fairness & Equity—Freedom from bias to enable one to do what is right and proper	Self Org.	Self Org.	Self Org.	Self Org.
Security—Freedom from fear of ill-conceived organizational issues	Self Org.	Self Org.	Self Org.	Self Org.
Belief in High Performance— Effectively achieve at high quality levels	Self Org.	Self Org.	Self Org.	Self Org.
Openness to Creativity—High degree of receptivity to creativity of organization and people	Self Org.	Self Org.	Self Org.	Self Org.
Fact-Based Decision Making— Objectively deciding on solutions	Self Org.	Self Org.	Self Org.	Self Org.
Swiftness in Learning— Capacity for one to learn at an accelerated pace	Self Org.	Self Org.	Self Org.	Self Org.

VALUE	Consistently—4	Often—3	Occasionally—2	Never—1
Feedback System—Capacity to receive correct information and act on it	Self Org.	Self Org.	Self Org.	Self Org.
Optimism—Inclination to anticipate the best possible outcome	Self Org.	Self Org.	Self Org.	Self Org.
Willing to Help Others—Gaining satisfaction by assisting other people	Self Org.	Self Org.	Self Org.	Self Org.
Belief in Cross-Functional Mode—Functions effectively working together	Self Org.	Self Org.	Self Org.	Self Org.

SCORING INFORMATION

Transfer the scores for each value as indicated below. Then subtract the individual score from the organization score for each value to determine the perceived difference.

SCORES

VALUE	INDIVIDUAL	ORGANIZATION	"DIFFERENCE"
1. Loyalty			
2. Integrity			
3. Honesty			
4. Respect			
5. Supportiveness			
6. Communication			
7. Commitment to Quality			
8. Career Enhancement			
9. Diversity			
10. Clarity of Process			
11. Reliability to Stakeholders			
12. Sense of Humor			
13. Trust			
14. Fairness & Equity			
15. Security			
16. Belief in High Performance			
17. Openness to Creativity			
18. Fact-Based Decision Making			
19. Swiftness in Learning			
20. Feedback System			
21. Optimism			
22. Willing to Help Others			
23. Belief in Cross-Functional Mode			

Interpreting the Value Analysis Worksheet

The ranges below indicate the degree of consistency that your values have with those of your organization.

If you have a difference of two or more points in:	You have
0-3 values	High Consistency
4-7 values	Good Consistency
8-11 values	Poor Consistency
12 or more values	Severe Value Clash

20

WHAT IS MY LEADERSHIP STYLE?

Deborah Hopen and Laura Gregg

Deborah Hopen *has over 20 years of experience in total quality management. She has served as a senior executive with Fortune and Inc. 500 companies and was the 1996-97 Chairman of the Board of the American Society for Quality Control. She currently consults for Xerox Quality Services.* **Laura Gregg** *owns Wizard Textware. She specializes in the instructional design of quality training. She is currently developing structured on-the-job training and certification programs for telecommunications technicians.*

Contract Information:

Deborah Hopen
6400 Southcenter Boulevard
Tukwila, WA 98188
253-927-1759
debhopen@aol.com

Laura Gregg
10445 NE 15th Street
Bellevue, WA 98004
425-453-7210
wizeljay@aol.com

Overview The leader role requires a diverse set of skills. No individual is naturally skilled in all of the required areas, so it's a good idea to assess your strengths and develop an improvement plan. This exercise will help you identify your interests and talents.

The self-assessment lists 16 characteristics that are generally considered desirable for leaders. The list comes from *Management Audits* by Allan J. Sayle. For each characteristic, the authors show statements that describe how you might respond in different situations. The choices range between two possible behaviors. The statement on the left more closely matches the dictionary definition of the behavior associated with that characteristic.

As you complete the assessment, think about each description and develop specific criteria for determining when it would be appropriate to exhibit the behavior described by the statement on the left and when it would be appropriate to exhibit the behavior described by the statement on the right.

The interpretations were developed by the authors after discussions with representative people who lead at different levels in a variety of organizations.

LEADERSHIP STYLE SELF-ASSESSMENT

Look over each of the following statements carefully. Which point on the scale best reflects your day-to-day behaviors and beliefs about leadership? There are no "right" answers to this questionnaire, so don't put down answers you think are best. Be prepared to share situations where each end of the continuum applies.

1. I usually make decisions based on

facts and data	❶	❷	❸	❹	❺	feelings and opinions

2. To meet a specific objective, I believe that it's best to

be open to a variety of processes	❶	❷	❸	❹	❺	rely on a standardized process

3. When I encounter a setback, I usually

focus my attention on finding alternatives	❶	❷	❸	❹	❺	shift my attention to a more fruitful area

4. When making a point, I intend for my words to

improve the relationship	❶	❷	❸	❹	❺	improve the outcome

5. When I am faced with goals and deadlines, I believe it's more important to

keep on schedule and follow the plan	❶	❷	❸	❹	❺	sense the environment and make necessary adjustments

6. Other people would characterize my style during tense situations as

restrained	❶	❷	❸	❹	❺	expressive

7. I believe that my communications should be candid and forthright

regardless of the situation	❶	❷	❸	❹	❺	unless the situation will generate conflict or hurt relationships

8. When listening attentively to another person, I usually

disregard time	❶	❷	❸	❹	❺	keep an eye on the time

9. I get to know new contacts

quickly by "stepping into their shoes"	❶	❷	❸	❹	❺	steadily by "building the castle one brick at a time"

10. When I'm trying to learn about a new topic, I'm more inclined to

diligently gather details, tolerate delays, and build a complete picture	❶	❷	❸	❹	❺	quickly gather information, plow through delays, and extrapolate my findings

11. Those who work with me would say that I'm

always at work, like the "busy beaver"	❶	❷	❸	❹	❺	a deep thinker, like the "wise owl"

12. I'd like to be remembered as

a specialist—a person who mastered the concepts and tools in my field	❶	❷	❸	❹	❺	a generalist—a person who integrated the concepts and tools from many fields

13. Learning new subjects is worth my time if I believe that I'll be able to

increase my overall knowledge	❶	❷	❸	❹	❺	apply the information in the near future

14. It's natural for me to

be curious and ask a lot of questions	❶	❷	❸	❹	❺	be circumspect and listen for information

15. Give me some information and I'll

break it down to find its essential features	❶	❷	❸	❹	❺	pull it together to find its essential self

16. When I speak, my "umm…" factor is

less than 10%—I've always got words on the tip of my tongue	❶	❷	❸	❹	❺	over 10%—I sometimes have to pull my words together as I speak

17. My language arts skills, such as public speaking and writing, are

fine-honed; I take great pleasure in using the best words in well-structured sentences	❶	❷	❸	❹	❺	competent; I focus on making my point

18. Fairness and equality can be achieved most easily by

the consistent application of rules and guidelines	❶	❷	❸	❹	❺	careful analysis of the situation and application of customized solutions

SCORING THE LEADERSHIP STYLE SELF-ASSESSMENT

Count the number of times you selected each of the following ratings.				
❶	❷	❸	❹	❺

Use the following key to match the statements with desirable characteristics for leaders.				
Characteristic	**Statement(s)**		**Characteristic**	**Statement(s)**
Good judgment	1		Patient	10
Open-minded	2		Industrious	11
Resilient	3		Professional	12
Diplomatic	4		Interested	13
Self-disciplined	5 and 6		Inquiring mind	14
Honest	7		Analytical	15
Good listener	8		Articulate	16 and 17
Relational	9		Egalitarian	18

Good Judgment

A key tenet of leadership is that decisions are based on facts and data, which helps you improve your judgment. Under normal circumstances and whenever possible, you should rely on observable, objective evidence.

You may on occasion, however, need to tap into your feelings and opinions to help you interpret your observations. Almost every decision made in life is based on comparisons to other circumstances you have encountered previously. Opinions and the feelings associated with specific situations are based on these earlier experiences.

Open-minded

Leaders need to be open to a variety of processes, or they become too prescriptive. This is particularly true when they are pressed to accomplish goals in different locations or work groups within a short time.

On the other hand, it's usually a good idea for some processes to be standardized within a particular location and, if possible, between different locations of the same work group. In this case, if you observe variations, you may want to point them out without insisting that all the processes be conducted in the same way. Remember, there often is more than one road that will get you to your intended destination!

Resilient

When a leader is unable to gather the necessary information to determine performance in a particular area, he or she will usually search for alternative sources of data.

Time management may become an issue if the leader spends too much effort trying to track down information about one of many processes. That's why leaders frequently seem to be jumping from one area of investigation to another. You might think of this as the best combination of both approaches.

Diplomatic

Words are powerful tools for building relationships and achieving outcomes. All too often words are chosen without thoughtful consideration of their potential effect.

When acting in a leadership role, maintaining and improving the relationships are key concerns. That's why it's better to suggest than to demand. That's also why when an associate irritates you, you need to ask yourself if silence or confrontation will most effectively achieve the goal *and* build the relationship.

If diplomacy will put the success of the work at risk, however, you need to choose careful words that will assert your requirements without damaging the relationship.

Self-disciplined

Keeping on schedule and following the action plan are critical requirements for successful leaders. These outcomes require a great deal of discipline because it's easy to become distracted and get off track.

Being too pushy is not a good idea, though. To build relationships, you must show care and concern for each associate's situation—everyone knows that Murphy's law is a reality of life. This means that you may have to adjust your action plan on occasion, but you should do this without sacrificing the quality of the desired outcome.

Responding to conflict also requires self-discipline. All too often the natural tendency is to become quite verbal and to accent one's opinions with strong body language. This rarely will be effective for leaders unless they are being physically harassed.

Restraint allows you to remain in control. When you become too expressive or agitated, the other person gains control. Leaders really want to control the process without being autocratic.

Honest

Honesty is always the best policy. There are many situations, however, in which silence is golden! That is really the choice you must make. Nit-picking and word-smithing are very counterproductive behaviors.

Never lie. If asked a direct question that has an unpleasant answer, choose your words carefully but speak the truth. If the goal truly will be at risk if you don't mention your concerns, bring them up for discussion—but set the stage by emphasizing that you are confident your associate has a good reason for the existing situation or is unaware of its importance to you.

Good Listening

Although questioning and listening are the two primary skills of successful leaders, neither can be done without a focus on time. Most work efforts require that much be accomplished in a short period. Time pressure sometimes causes leaders to be abrupt or to convey a subliminal message that the associate's input is not valued or necessary, which can hurt relationships and hinder progress toward your goals.

Relational

You have all met the person who approaches you directly, begins to talk with you in a comfortable way, and makes you feel as if you've been friendly acquaintances for years. To an associate who is struggling with his or her assignment, this may convert fear and trepidation to comfort and sharing.

You've also met people who are more aloof when they meet strangers. They start by discussing the weather, moving into more serious subjects slowly over time. Although well-intentioned, this can leave the impression that you are withholding comment or are dissatisfied, which can increase the other person's anxiety about the situation. If you're not naturally outgoing, work with a trusted peer to practice warm introductions and questioning styles.

Patient

Patience is a virtue in almost every job, and leadership is no exception. Under normal conditions, you should remember that "slow and steady" wins the race. Certainly, you should be able to explain your decisions by showing solid facts and data that support them most of the time.

Occasionally, however, you may be forced to move forward with insufficient information and to extrapolate findings. In this case, you always should note that you have less confidence in your findings and explain why you took this approach.

Industrious

There's no doubt that leadership is a high-activity task. Sometimes you will feel like the "busy beaver" or a hamster on the treadmill. It's important that you stop on a regular basis to assimilate your findings, develop hypotheses, and determine what additional information you need to collect.

Professional

The word "professional" and the concept of "professionalism" are changing. Today businesses are encouraging employees to increase scope and take over more generalized job tasks. This increases flexibility for the organization and enriches the job for the employee.

Leaders, however, must be knowledgeable about any process they are evaluating. This is clearly more of a specialist's task. This demand for expertise is one of the reasons that leadership teams are more effective than individual leaders—they make it possible for each person to investigate a few processes for which he or she has more in-depth knowledge and experience.

Interested

It's tough to be a good leader if you're not naturally curious! If you can consider your mind to be a database, the processes and approaches you observe can be archived for permanent use. What you learn today may be invaluable to you under the same or a different circumstance years later.

This is quite different from the "just in time" approach to learning, which relies on the concept of "use it or lose it." Although much of what you observe will be useful for evaluating a given process, you should not ignore any information because it isn't relevant to the current situation—it usually will come in handy in the future!

Inquiring Mind

This characteristic usually brings a chuckle because of the famous (or infamous, depending on how you look at these things) advertising associated with the phrase! As described above, curiosity and a zest for learning are great attributes for leaders.

There are two exceptions, however. First, never let your interest make your mouth start moving when your ears should be listening. Second, never listen to gossip or ask about confidential personal information.

Analytical

To maximize trust and increase the effectiveness of your leadership, you need to focus on learning whatever process you are evaluating. This may require you to rise above more mundane details and to accept some work procedures without a thorough analysis. For example, if all the lower-level procedures seem to work together effectively, you might not need to stop to investigate them individually.

In many ways, this leaves the impression that you are trying to understand the approach, rather than to pick it apart. For leaders who are naturally analytical this may be quite difficult. In the end, there must be an appropriate balance between being sure that the parts do fit together well and being sure that the outcomes are being achieved as desired.

Articulate

Leaders need to be able to listen carefully, think quickly, and respond with questions that help them interpret and verify their observations. People who have trouble maintaining a continuous flow of conversation may find discovery interviewing very difficult.

Beware of focusing on developing your next question while a person is still answering the first one. This is a typical communication style that decreases understanding and shows a lack of respect for the other person's viewpoint.

The ability to be clear and concise in questioning, presenting findings, and writing final reports is invaluable to a leader. In fact, successful leaders often take continuing education courses to improve these skills.

Egalitarian

This is the trickiest characteristic on the list, and it's one that you'll rarely get right from an associate's perspective.

The dictionary defines fairness and equality in terms of consistency in applying rules and guidelines. On the surface, this sounds like a good approach, but think about the many atypical situations that occur in life. Is it really fair to apply the same rules the same way in every case? Doesn't good judgment require that you use "common sense" and work out an alternative approach? If you do that in one case, however, you must ask yourself if you've been fair in all the other cases when you've required adherence to the rules.

As you can see, this is a circular discussion that might best be left to philosophers. Unfortunately, it's a serious factor for leaders, too. You should try to be consistent without being rigid about a process or an individual's approach—try to use the same decision-making process and criteria.

This may mean that you consistently require processes and job performance to adhere exactly to your requirements for one system because it is critical to the achievement of a particular goal. You might be much more lenient in another area because the risks are lower. Clear definitions of what constitute deviations can help you in this troublesome area.

21

DOES YOUR CERTIFICATION PROGRAM MEET BEST-PRACTICE CRITERIA?

Susan Barksdale and Teri Lund

Susan Barksdale *is the founder of Front Line Evaluators, a training consulting firm specializing in evaluating training effectiveness. Susan provides return on investment evaluations for performance improvement initiatives and certification programs. She was a contributor to* **The 1997 McGraw-Hill Training and Performance Sourcebook. Teri Lund** *is a partner in the firm Baldwin & Lund Services, which provides consultation in performance improvement methodologies and certification processes. Teri conducts return on investment evaluations and develops evaluation strategies. She also contributed to* **The 1997 McGraw-Hill Training and Performance Sourcebook.** *Susan and Teri have recently formed Strategic Assessment and Evaluation Associates, LLC, a business entity through which they offer licensing agreements for their various methods and tools.*

Contact Information:

Susan Barksdale
Front Line Evaluators
25 NW 23rd Place #6-412
Portland, OR 97210
503-223-7721
sbbfle@msn.com

Teri Lund
Baldwin & Lund Services
4534 SW Tarlow Court
Portland, OR 97221
503-245-9020
tlund_bls@msn.com

Overview This assessment, the Certification Audit Matrix, assists in determining whether a certification program meets "best-practice" criteria. The authors identified these best practices as a result of research with over 100 companies that offer employee or customer certification programs. The industries represented include high-tech, manufacturing, medical, and retail, as well as professional associations.

This matrix has been used by certification managers, training managers, instructional designers, and those who contract with external providers of certification components, as well as those who evaluate certification program effectiveness.

The Certification Audit Matrix has been used as a tool to evaluate the effectiveness of certification programs after they have been developed and implemented and also has been used as a guideline for developing certification programs.

Specific Uses of the Matrix

Strategic Planning for Certification

Certification audits have been conducted as a way to determine the strengths, weaknesses, and gaps of existing programs. The findings are compared to the organization's current business needs and objectives and it is then decided if the program will be maintained as is, modified, changed, or discontinued.

Setting Standards for Certification Program Development

Another use for the Certification Audit Matrix is to identify and/or maintain program development and implementation standards. These standards can be used both internally within the certification department and externally with vendors or with others in the organization who support the certification program.

Identifying and Designing Certification Program Components

The Certification Audit Matrix has been used to identify the most critical components of a certification program and prioritize design of those components to meet the business objectives.

Validating Certification Needs Assessment Findings

Certification audits have been conducted to validate the findings of needs assessments to pinpoint areas within the program that no longer meet the business need driving the certification program or no longer meet the audience need.

Evaluating Certification Programs

Comparing the results of an audit of a certification program using this matrix will assist in evaluating its effectiveness as compared with best-practice organizations.

Identification of Certification Resources

The Certification Audit Matrix has been used as a guide in identifying the resources that will be needed for designing and implementing a certification program.

Developing a Certification Maintenance Strategy

Continuously monitoring the effectiveness of the certification program development and implementation and comparing the findings with current business and audience needs helps develop a realistic and meaningful maintenance strategy.

CERTIFICATION AUDIT MATRIX

Directions: The Certification Audit Matrix consists of seven categories, each representing an important aspect of certification programs. These categories are:

✓ *General Certification Criteria* including components such as audience identification, prerequisites for certification, purposes for certification programs, and forces that promote certification.

✓ *Key Components of Certification* including type of testing, certification requirements, link to licensing, product availability, etc.

✓ *Certification Resources* including type of resources available both internally and externally.

✓ *Benefits of Certification* such as type of benefit and the linkage to organizational goals, objectives, and needs.

✓ *Costs of Certification* including costs for administration, exam development, facilities, etc.

✓ *Rewards, Motivators, and Incentives for Certification,* which includes monetary and nonmonetary incentives such as product credit, discounts, trips, and bonuses.

✓ *Evaluation Practices* including Return on Investment (ROI), satisfaction surveys, performance impact studies, etc.

Under each of these categories are subcategories that are the criteria by which the certification program is assessed.

When using this matrix, simply compare your certification program to the categories included in the matrix and rate each criterion using a scale of 1 to 7 (1 = poor example of the criterion, 7 = a very good example of the criterion). Note this rating in the space provided. It is strongly suggested that comments be made in addition to the numerical rating. This qualitative information will help support the quantitative ratings.

Criteria	Rating	Comments
General Certification Criteria The following sections are used to assess components such as the purpose of the program, content of the exam, and audience identification.		
Purpose of the Certification Program The purpose of the certification program (to increase sales, decrease errors or rework, etc.) is stated clearly.		
General Description of Certification Criteria The content is described in general terms.		
Audience Identification The targeted audience for the certification (including any parameters such as sales quotas, etc.) is identified.		
Length of Program The time it will take to complete the certification is noted.		
Written Policies and Procedures Written policies and procedures are available for how to apply for the exam, where to take the exam, retesting policies, etc.		
Security Procedures Identification is checked at the beginning of testing and a monitor or evaluator is present during the exam, lab, or test. An independent evaluator is used for observation certification.		
Key Components of Certification This category assesses items such as certification requirements, testing, and demonstrations of skills or knowledge.		
Certification Requirements Identification and listing of certification requirements such as apprenticeship, exam, training, etc.		
Job Functional Competencies Identified Performance competencies are identified and are specific to job or function expectations.		

Criteria	Rating	Comments
Linked to Licensing or Product Availability Certification is linked to licensing individuals to perform specific functions or have access to products otherwise unavailable.		
Training Components Relate to Exams Any training offered as a component of the certification program is relevant to performance and the exam.		
Objectives/Goals of Certification Are Outlined The objectives of the certification program are stated and relate to the content of the exam.		
Design Is Psychometrically Sound A multilevel review process was used against the exam to ensure that it is psychometrically sound.		
Design Validated for Performance The exam has been evaluated to ensure those who score high on the exam are also high performers in the workplace.		
Design Is Performance Based The exam is based on job simulations or labs that are specific and contain realistic examples of what may actually occur on the job.		
Certification Is Legally Defensible If certification is used for hiring, promotions, or job-related compensation, the exam is legally defensible.		
Rewards Integrated with Purpose The rewards of certification reinforce the purpose of the program. If the program is to limit rework, rewards and incentives reinforce reduction in rework as part of the certification program.		

Criteria	Rating	Comments
Certification Resources This category is used to specify the types of resources that reinforce and support a quality certification program.		
Administration Support for the exam process is provided which monitors and reinforces the polices and procedures that have been decided upon for the certification program.		
Developers Individuals skilled in psychometrics and instructional design have been hired or contracted with to provide sound design for the exam or any related training materials. The design and quality review process that will be used to develop the exam and any training materials is reviewed against set standards.		
Tracking System A system that tracks scores, registrations, certification mastery, most frequently missed questions, and questions missed least often is in place.		
Subject Matter Experts Industry experts are available and act as consultants in design, review, and targeting maintenance needs.		
Benefits of Certification This section helps assess components such as type of benefits provided, organizational benefits, and benefits to those certified.		
Decrease in Costs The program provides a decrease in costs through decreasing rework, product waste, travel, time, errors, support costs, regulation or compliance penalties, or safety fines.		
Market Share/Sales Certification promotes an increase in sales through increased product availability, targeted prospect lists, sales skills, exclusivity, or promotion through specific avenues such as Web pages.		

Criteria	Rating	Comments
Competitive Advantage The certification is required by customers and provides skills, products, or discounts directly (to which competitors don't have access). The program will allow a reduction in costs that can be passed on to the customer.		
Association Professional Identification The certification is required to practice in this line of business and customers or employers recognize this type of certification as a designation of higher skill levels.		
Performance Improvement Those certified have higher confidence levels or have demonstrated a higher skill or knowledge than those not certified.		
Revenue Is Generated Revenue is generated either through the certification program itself or supporting components to offset the cost of the program.		
Name Identity Certification promotes the product or "name" of the organization, brand, or service, creating customer recognition.		
Accreditation/Regulation/Compliance Certification provides proof of skills so the organization can participate in government or specialized programs.		
Costs of Certification This section identifies the key cost areas for certification.		
Assessment Test/Development The costs can be controlled by outsourcing to expert designers and by using computer automated systems.		
Training and Other Preparation The costs can be controlled through outsourcing the development, but also in contracting with training houses for generic training delivery and relying on subject matter experts for more technical delivery.		

Criteria	Rating	Comments
Administration The costs can be controlled by using an internal source that is multifunctional (such as an internal university system) or by using an external source that allows shared costs across the organizations.		
Legal What has to be reviewed has been identified and attorneys work with specific documents related to these review needs. Legal experts should be involved to a greater extent if the certification results will impact selection or promotion decisions.		
Incentives/compensation Certification incentives or compensation is limited to only a few key items valued by those certified.		
Management Like programs are grouped together and one key manager for these programs has been identified.		
Rewards, Motivators, Incentives This section assesses the components that ensure the success of specific participation motivators.		
Linkage to Program Outcome The incentives or motivators are tied to or promote the results or outcomes desired by those sponsoring the program.		
Ongoing Transfer and Inducement The incentive or motivator creates a desire to continue use or practice of the skill or knowledge that was certified. Those certified are motivated to transfer and continue development of the skill and knowledge that was certified.		
Value of Motivator or Incentive The value of the motivator or incentive has been validated with those certified.		

Criteria	Rating	Comments
Incentive Does Not Detract from the Program The incentive or motivator is complementary to the program and is not given just for the sake of providing an incentive.		
Evaluation Practices This category contains components such as customer satisfaction surveys, reporting, and return on investment.		
Customer Satisfaction Surveys A post-exam survey is distributed that allows participants to rate the administration, exam worthiness, and policies and procedures for the exam.		
Quality Control Standards in place and the exam have been evaluated against psychometric practice standards. The program is reviewed at least once a year and a maintenance schedule is in place. The program has been independently evaluated.		
Reporting Results are tracked and exam statistics for least frequently missed questions, most missed questions, high score, and low score are available.		
Impact of Results Survey The results of the certification exam have been matched to performance results. A follow-up survey is distributed at least to a sample of certification participants to evaluate their satisfaction and the impact of certification on their work performance.		
ROI A return on investment study has been conducted. Costs have been measured against benefits and cost controls have been identified. The importance of measuring the ROI has been determined.		

SCORING THE CERTIFICATION AUDIT MATRIX

In using this audit matrix it is important to preestablish the value of the rating scale. These values are highly dependent on the reason the audit is being conducted and the way in which the results will be used. For example, when using these criteria to assess whether or not a certification program meets best-practice criteria, points are assigned to each criterion and totaled at the end of the assessment. In this case, because a comparison is being made, the higher the number of points the more likely the program is to meet best-practice criteria. In a situation in which the matrix is used to determine the structure and content of a certification program, point values are not given because the matrix is used as a guide rather than an evaluative tool.

22

WHAT QUESTIONS ARE YOU ASKING DURING THE EMPLOYMENT INTERVIEW?

Kent Rondeau

Kent V. Rondeau, Ph.D *is an assistant professor at the University of Alberta in Edmonton, Alberta, Canada. His research interests include the strategic management of human resources in health care organizations. Kent has made numerous presentations and conducted training workshops in Canada.*

Contact information:

Department of Public Health Sciences
Management and Policy Division
University of Alberta
Edmonton, Alberta CANADA T6G 2G3
403-492-8608
kent.rondeau@ualberta.ca

Overview A major goal of human resource managers is to provide equal employment opportunities without regard to an individual's age, sex, race, religion, or ethnic origin. The employment interview provides an important vehicle through which an organization secures the necessary skills, competencies, and aptitudes that compose its diverse workforce. Those conducting hiring interviews must be aware of and sensitive to discriminatory actions that may be deemed inappropriate, or in some cases, constitute illegal actions that may later precipitate a legal challenge.

The purpose of this questionnaire is to assist managers who are responsible for performing the hiring interview. Participants will learn what kinds of interview questions to avoid so as to prevent charges of employment discrimination. Working alone or in groups, participants should be given approximately 15 minutes to respond to the following interview questions, indicating whether they believe each one to be appropriate or inappropriate and why.

EMPLOYEE INTERVIEW QUESTIONNAIRE

QUESTIONS:	APPROPRIATE	INAPPROPRIATE
1. Are you a citizen of this country?	☐	☐
2. Are you married or living common law?	☐	☐
3. Are you willing to work on Sundays and holidays?	☐	☐
4. In what clubs and organizations do you hold membership?	☐	☐
5. Can you provide names and addresses of persons to be notified in case of emergency?	☐	☐
6. Do you have any physical handicaps?	☐	☐
7. What is the first language that you learned to speak?	☐	☐
8. Where do you currently reside?	☐	☐
9. Do you generally go by "Mrs." or "Ms." Smith?	☐	☐
10. Will you supply us with a recent photo of yourself for our records?	☐	☐
11. Do you have plans in the future to have any more children?	☐	☐
12. Do you have any relatives working here?	☐	☐
13. Have you ever been convicted of a criminal offense?	☐	☐
14. Do you have any hobbies or avocations?	☐	☐
15. In the last election, for which political party did you vote?	☐	☐
16. Do you have any disabilities which may affect your job performance?	☐	☐
17. May we have a letter of recommendation from your minister, priest, or rabbi?	☐	☐
18. Where did you go to high school?	☐	☐
19. Is your spouse free to relocate?	☐	☐
20. Do you speak Spanish fluently?	☐	☐

SCORING

What Questions Are You Asking During the Employment Interview?

Score one point for each correct answer.

Question 1: **Inappropriate.** It is an unacceptable practice to ask about national or ethnic origin. Better to ask if the applicant is legally entitled to work in this country.

Question 2: **Inappropriate.** Asking about marital status is a discriminatory employment practice.

Question 3: **Appropriate.** Although it is discriminatory to ask about one's religious affiliations even if they might prevent one from working at certain times, questions about willingness to work a specified work schedule are permitted.

Question 4: **Generally inappropriate.** Asking about organizational memberships is usually discriminatory. However, a request for memberships can be made if membership in a particular organization is a necessary job qualification.

Question 5: **Appropriate.** Asking for the names of persons to be contacted in cases of emergency is a permitted employment practice, but is usually done after employment commences.

Question 6: **Inappropriate.** It is an unacceptable employment practice to ask about physical handicaps, limitations, or health problems. It is better to ask if the applicant wishes to identify any handicaps or health problems that could affect the job applied for, or has other limitations or conditions that can be taken into consideration when determining the job placement.

Question 7: **Inappropriate.** This question attempts to get at a person's national or ethnic origin.

Question 8: **Appropriate.** Asking for an individual's current address in this country is acceptable. Asking about a foreign address (which may indicate national origin) is an inappropriate practice.

Question 9: **Inappropriate.** Asking about marital status is a discriminatory practice.

Question 10: **Inappropriate.** A photo may be used to discriminate on the bases of gender, age, or race. In addition, a photo might also be used to estimate an individual's height and weight. These characteristics may be discriminatory if they act to screen out disproportionate numbers of women, elderly, handicapped, or minority groups.

Question 11: **Inappropriate.** Asking about a person's marital or family status is unacceptable. This question is not job-related.

Question 12: **Appropriate.** The organization may have a stated policy on hiring relatives of current employees.

Question 13: **Generally inappropriate.** Unless the job requires the incumbent to be bonded, it is generally not good practice to ask if an individual has been convicted of a criminal offense.

Question 14: **Appropriate.** However, this question is not job-related. It should not be asked for the purpose of establishing in which clubs or organizations an applicant is a member.

Question 15: **Inappropriate.** Asking questions about political affiliation is a discriminatory employment practice. It is also not considered to be job-related for most employment situations.

Question 16: **Appropriate.** A handicap is relevant to the job only if the handicap prevents the person from adequately performing core job duties or if the handicap, in the exercise of usual job duties, were to be deemed hazardous to the applicant, coworkers, or customers.

Question 17: **Inappropriate.** It is an unacceptable practice to ask questions about religious affiliation. Moreover, it is the duty of the employer to accommodate valid religious observances of an applicant. However, after an individual has been hired, it may be appropriate to inquire about religion to determine when leaves of absence may be required for religious observation.

Question 18: **Inappropriate.** This question may be a convoluted attempt to establish national origin.

Question 19: **Inappropriate.** This question may be used to establish an individual's marital status. It is better to ask if the applicant is free to travel or be transferred to other locales if this requirement is job-related.

Question 20: **Appropriate.** This question is appropriate only if fluency in Spanish can be shown to be a bona fide job requirement. It should not be used to establish someone's national or ethnic origin.

Note: It should be noted that discriminatory employment practices may vary slightly by jurisdiction and may be conditioned by legal precedent.

23

IS VIRTUAL REALITY TRAINING THE RIGHT CHOICE?

Nina Adams and Carol Gunther-Mohr

Nina Adams, *president of Adams Consulting Group, Inc., has discussed using virtual reality as a training tool at more than 50 events and has been featured in over 20 publications. From July 1994 to the present she has worked with Motorola University, Duracell, Biobras Software, S.A., Landis & Staefa, and G.D. Searle implementing a variety of virtual reality-based training programs. In 1997, Adams Consulting was recognized by Motorola University "for ... implementing Virtual Reality Training...."*

Carol Gunther-Mohr, *program manager for Virtual Reality Learning Systems at Research Triangle Institute, has been involved in creating numerous programs that incorporate advanced technologies to improve learning. RTI has worked with military and industrial clients to develop innovative virtual reality-based training programs for the past four years.*

Contact Information:

Nina Adams
Adams Consulting Group, Inc.
3952 Western Ave.
Western Springs, IL 60558
708-246-0766
ninaa@adams-consult.com
www.adams-consult.com

Carol Gunther-Mohr
Advanced Learning Virtual Environments
Research Triangle Institute
P.O. Box 12194
3040 Cornwallis Road
Research Triangle Park, NC 27709-2194
919-541-6062
cgm@rti.org
www.rti.org/vr/

Overview Are you considering technology-assisted methods for delivering training? Have you wondered if virtual reality (VR) is worth exploring? Do you think your organization has the resources and is ready to pursue VR for training?

The Virtual Reality Training Decision Tool can help you answer these questions and evaluate whether virtual reality training programs might increase the effectiveness of your training and improve performance in your organization.

The Decision Tool has two major sections.

✓ The first section helps you decide whether you should consider VR for a specific project.

✓ If your project *is* suitable for VR, Section II helps you decide if you should develop the program in-house or consider outsourcing.

In each section you:

✓ Score (assign values to) a series of project and organizational questions.

✓ Total your scores.

✓ Evaluate your scores using the Decision Tool guidelines.

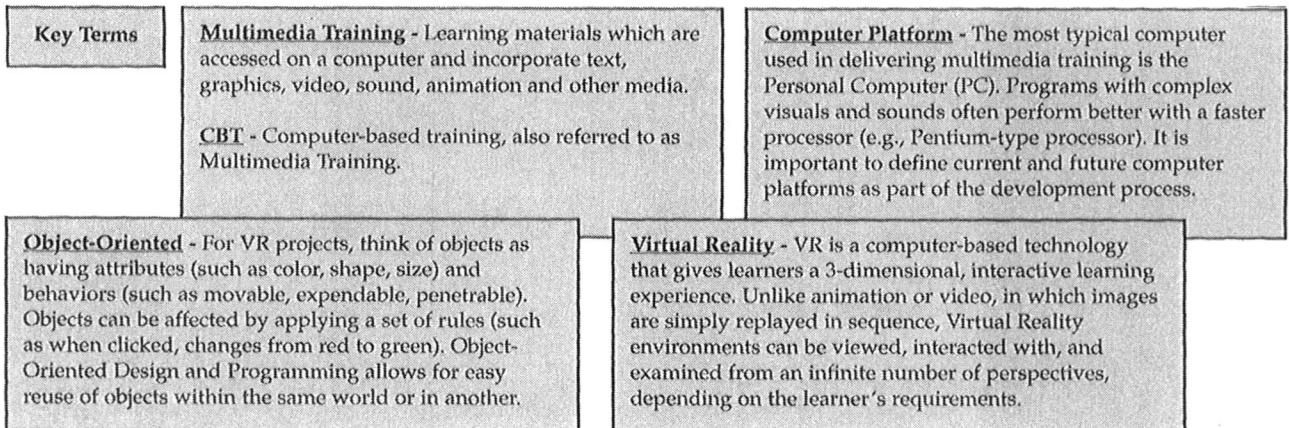

Key Terms	

Multimedia Training - Learning materials which are accessed on a computer and incorporate text, graphics, video, sound, animation and other media.

CBT - Computer-based training, also referred to as Multimedia Training.

Computer Platform - The most typical computer used in delivering multimedia training is the Personal Computer (PC). Programs with complex visuals and sounds often perform better with a faster processor (e.g., Pentium-type processor). It is important to define current and future computer platforms as part of the development process.

Object-Oriented - For VR projects, think of objects as having attributes (such as color, shape, size) and behaviors (such as movable, expendable, penetrable). Objects can be affected by applying a set of rules (such as when clicked, changes from red to green). Object-Oriented Design and Programming allows for easy reuse of objects within the same world or in another.

Virtual Reality - VR is a computer-based technology that gives learners a 3-dimensional, interactive learning experience. Unlike animation or video, in which images are simply replayed in sequence, Virtual Reality environments can be viewed, interacted with, and examined from an infinite number of perspectives, depending on the learner's requirements.

Figure 23-1.

VIRTUAL REALITY TRAINING DECISION TOOL

SECTION I - Should You Consider VR?

Consideration	Instructions	Points	Score
A. Learner Profile			
1. Number of Learners	If: • Fewer than 10 learners • Between 10 & 50 learners • More than 50 learners	0 points 10 points 20 points	
2. Number of training sites	If learners are at: • 1 site • 1 to 5 sites • more than 5 sites	0 points 5 points 10 points	
3. Distance of learners from existing training site	If the average distance learners are from an existing training site: • Does not require overnight stay • Requires overnight stay • Requires many overnight stays	0 points 5 points 10 points	
4. Preferred training schedule	If it is more appropriate to: • Set training schedules • Allow learners to set schedules	5 points 10 points	
5. Risks in the conventional learning environment	If learners in the current learning environment: • Are not exposed to unacceptable risks when they demonstrate critical skills • Are exposed to unacceptable risks when they demonstrate critical skills	0 points 10 points	
6. Preferred learning style	If most learners prefer: • Group learning • Independent learning	0 points 10 points	
7. Current computer proficiency	If learners: • Don't know how to use a computer and don't need a computer for their job • Don't know how to use a computer and do need a computer for their job • Know how to use a computer	0 points 5 points 10 points	
8. Current learner skill level	If learners: • All have the same skill level • Have widely varying skill levels	5 points 10 points	
	Section A - Sub-total		
B. Learning Content			
9. Content already available in interactive format	If interactive training program: • Can be purchased for use without modification • Can be purchased/modified to meet requirements • Must be developed to meet requirements	0 points 5 points 10 points	
10. Type of learning content	If skills are: • Soft (e.g., communications) • Hard (e.g., technical)	5 points 10 points	
11. Interaction with the physical environment related to the learning content	If learning is most effective • Without interaction with the physical environment • With interaction with an environment such as a factory, lab, or other worksite	0 points 10 points	

Consideration	Instructions	Points	Score
12. Interaction with physical objects or equipment	If the most effective learning • Never requires manipulation of physical objects or equipment • Requires manipulation of physical objects or equipment	0 points 10 points	
13. Availability of physical environments or objects	If the actual physical environments or objects are: • Often difficult for learners to access • Not available to learners	5 points 10 points	
14. Availability of content experts	If content questions must be answered and experts: • Cannot be made available • Can be made available	0 points 10 points	
15. Conceptual learning	If content contains concepts which are • Easy to grasp • Difficult to grasp	0 points 10 points	
		Section B - Sub-total	

C. Learning Objectives

Consideration	Instructions	Points	Score
16. Importance of learning by doing	If *performing* skills or tasks rather than just learning about them is: • Not important • Beneficial • Essential	0 points 5 points 10 points	
17. Value of skill practice	If the ability to practice skills and rehearse procedures is: • Not important • Beneficial • Necessary	0 points 5 points 10 points	
18. Importance of consistency	If consistency of content covered is: • Not important • Somewhat important • Very important	0 points 5 points 10 points	
19. Importance of performance tracking	If tracking and evaluation of skills to be performed is: • Not important • Somewhat important • Very important	0 points 5 points 10 points	
20. Need for performance tracking	If performance tracking across multiple courses is: • Not needed • Desirable • Required	0 points 5 points 10 points	
21. Number of times program will be offered	If program will be offered: • 1 time • 1 to 19 times • More than 19 times	0 points 5 points 10 points	
22. Frequency of integrated updates	If integrated updates are needed: • Less than every 3 months • Between 3 and 6 months • More than 6 months	0 points 5 points 10 points	
23. Development time available	If training must be available in: • Less than 3 months • Between 3 and 6 months • More than 6 months	0 points 5 points 10 points	
		Section C - Sub-total	

D. Computing Resources

Consideration	Instructions	Points	Score
24. Availability of computers at learner site	If computer hardware at learner site is: • Not available at all • Available but has to be upgraded • Available	0 points 5 points 10 points	

Consideration	Instructions	Points	Score
25. Consistency of computer platform	If hardware and operating system at learner site is: • Different or not available • Similar • Identical	0 points 5 points 10 points	
26. Configuration of computers	If computers are: • Not available • Stand alone with no network access • On a network (internal or external access)	0 points 5 points 10 points	
27. Availability of troubleshooters	If personnel to keep computers operational: • Cannot be made available • Can be made available	0 points 10 points	
	Section D - Sub-total		
E. Organizational Readiness			
28. Training organization's perception	If training staff view technology-assisted learning as a: • Threat to their job • Possible solution • Great idea whose time has come	0 points 5 points 10 points	
29. Management's past experience with CBT	If past experience with CBT was: • Not favorable • Neutral • Very favorable	0 points 5 points 10 points	
30. General view of technology	If management views technology as: • Awful • A necessary evil • Great	0 points 5 points 10 points	
31. Budgeting scheme	If development costs: • Are separated from costs of delivery • Are included with delivery costs	0 points 10 points	
32. Cash flow available	If cash flow is: • Slow • OK • Good	0 points 5 points 10 points	
33. Management's perception of person making recommendation (optional)	If person making recommendation: • Has a poor track record • Has a great track record	0 points 10 points	
34. Funding sources	Can the project be used for trade shows, other marketing, or community relations, as well as training? • No • Yes	0 points 10 points	
35. Perceptions of others	Is it beneficial for your organization to be perceived as an innovator? • No • Yes	0 points 10 points	
36. Public relations opportunities	If your organization • Would not benefit from articles and other publicity about this project • Would benefit from articles and other publicity about this project	0 points 10 points	
	Section E - Sub-total		
TOTAL	Total of all Categories here:		

Total	Recommended Action
200+ points	VR Multimedia Training can be very beneficial to increase the effectiveness of your organization's training. Consult the Development Options Section.
150 -199 points	VR Multimedia Training should be investigated as an effective solution. Review the sections of this tool for potential barriers and opportunities. Consult the Development Options Section.
0 - 149 points	VR Multimedia Training may not be the best option for your training needs at this time. Use the VR Training Decision Tool in the future to see if conditions change.

SECTION II - Should You Develop In-House or Contract for Services?

Based on your summary score, you are interested in implementing a VR Multimedia Training program. Answer the following questions to help you decide if your organization should undertake the development, or if you should consider outsourcing the project. Consult *Multimedia Training Newsletter,* American Society of Training & Development, International Society for Performance Improvement, or other training organizations for recommendations on experienced VR training developers.

Consideration	Instructions	Points	Score
1. Knowledge of object-oriented design	If staff assigned to the project: • Knows nothing about object-oriented design • Has some knowledge of object-oriented design • Has implemented a project using object-oriented design	0 points 5 points 10 points	
2. Knowledge of 3-dimensional design	If staff assigned to the project • Has never designed a 3-dimensional project • Has designed but not implemented a 3-D project • Has designed and implemented a 3-D project	0 points 5 points 10 points	
3. Knowledge of object-oriented programming	If staff assigned to the project: • Knows nothing about object-oriented programming • Has some knowledge of object-oriented programming • Has used object-oriented programming tools	0 points 5 points 10 points	
4. Availability of production hardware	If computer hardware to produce materials is: • Not available at all • Available but has to be upgraded • Available	0 points 5 points 10 points	
5. Availability and skills of project management staff	If staff has: • Not successfully managed a technology based project • Successfully managed a technology based project	0 points 10 points	
6. Use of existing trainers	If existing trainers: • Will no longer be needed • Can be transferred to new positions • Can be used on VR projects	0 points 5 points 10 points	
7. Time available to undertake initial project	If time available for design and development is: • Equal to or less than 12 months • More than 12 months	0 points 10 points	
TOTAL			

Decision Tool Guidelines II

If your total score for this section is 50 points or greater, your organization appears to be ready to undertake the development of a VR Training program.

If your total score is less than 50 points, you may want to consider selecting a consultant to work with you on your first project.

HELPFUL HANDOUTS

In this section of *The 1998 Training and Performance Sourcebook,* you will find eight "helpful" handouts. These handouts cover topics such as:

✓ Effective writing
✓ Mind mapping
✓ Workplace accessibility
✓ Sexual harassment
✓ Managing time in class
✓ Designing instruction
✓ Managing communication

These handouts can be used as:

✓ Participant materials in training programs
✓ Discussion documents during meetings
✓ Coaching tools or job aids
✓ Information to be read by you or shared with a colleague

All of the handouts are designed as succinct descriptions of an important issue or skill in performance management and development. They are formatted for quick, easily understood reading. (You may want to keep these handouts handy as memory joggers or checklists by posting them in your work area.) Most important of all, they contain nuggets of practical advice!

Preceding each handout is a brief overview of its contents and uses. The handout itself is on a separate page(s) to make reproduction convenient.

It is helpful to read these handouts *actively.* Highlight points that are important to you or push you to do further thinking. Identify content that needs further clarification. Challenge yourself to come up with examples that illustrate the key points. Urge others to be active consumers of these handouts, as well.

24

ARE YOU WRITING MORE BUT ENJOYING IT LESS?

Dianna Booher

Dianna Booher, *a speaker/author/communications expert, is founder and president of Booher Consultants, a communications training company based in the Dallas–Fort Worth metroplex offering courses in writing, grammar, oral presentations, interpersonal skills, customer service, and personal productivity. Booher's clients include NASA, Exxon, IBM, Hewlett-Packard, Conoco, Mobil Oil, PepsiCo, Pennzoil, Texas Instruments, Coopers & Lybrand, Deloitte & Touche, and Frito-Lay. Dianna has authored 35 books. Her most popular titles include* **Get a Life without Sacrificing Your Career** *(McGraw-Hill),* **Communicate with Confidence!** *(McGraw-Hill),* **67 Presentation Secrets to Wow Any Audience** *(Lakewood),* **Clean Up Your Act!** *(Warner),* **Would You Put That in Writing?** *(Facts on File), and* **Ten Smart Moves for Women** *(Trade Life). Booher's work has been excerpted, reviewed, and featured in media as diverse as CNN, Good Morning America, Joan Rivers Show, National Public Radio, the* **Washington Post, USA Today, New Woman, Executive Excellence, Detroit News,** *the* **Minneapolis Star,** *the* **Dallas Morning News,** *the* **Los Angeles Times, Boardroom Reports, Industry Week, McCalls, Success, Entrepreneur,** *and* **Working Woman,** *to name a few.*

Contact Information:

Booher Consultants, Inc.
4001 Gateway Drive
Colleyville, TX 76034-5917
817-868-1200
booher@compuserve.com
www.booherconsultants.com

Overview   In an environment in which time is money, time-pressed executives and associates are reluctant to read verbose communications and often will choose not to, regardless of the communication's potential merit. Writing concisely and still getting your message across takes practice. This handout will show you how to write in a clear and concise style, ensuring your written communications will get read.

ARE YOU WRITING MORE, BUT ENJOYING IT LESS?

A workshop participant recently mentioned the good fortune of her boss: He had just submitted a suggestion that netted him $18,000 from his company's incentive-awards program. Although I can't share the award-winning idea, I will relate what writing rigors he suffered in getting the idea on paper.

He sent a 19-page first draft to his immediate supervisor, who read the paper and suggested cutting it in half. A few days later, he handed the second draft to the same supervisor, who then suggested cutting the proposal to five pages. Being a persevering fellow, he returned with his original idea trimmed to the five-page skeleton. But knowing top-management readers well, the supervisor then suggested one last cut: "Put it on a page."

Upon learning of the $18,000 award, the writer had almost forgotten the painful process of cutting his prose until these words of the vice president who presented the award reminded him: "You were particularly astute to present this complex idea in such few words. A lengthy document on this subject would probably never have been read."

Few writers learn so easily and with so much to gain. Nevertheless, I want to introduce five steps to help you pare your training program proposals, letters, memos, and course brochures accordingly:

1. Consider your audience.
2. Anticipate special problems in your reader's reaction.
3. Outline your message functionally.
4. Develop the first draft.
5. Edit for content, clarity, conciseness, style, and grammar.

Sounds obvious, doesn't it? But you'd be surprised how many blunders marketing divisions of major corporations make by failing to follow just these simple steps.

Step 1—Consider Your Audience

To consider your audience, ask yourself the following questions:

Do I Have a Single Reader or Multiple Readers?

Are you writing to a course participant, her supervisor, or both? How many people are on your distribution list for the evaluation questionnaire? Do you have pass-on readership for the course brochure? Are you writing "through" several people who must approve the proposal or letter before it goes out of the office? If you have mixed audiences, rank readers in order of importance. Then broaden your document to include all levels of readers and their diverse interest in your subject. Most important readers get their information first; lesser-ranking readers must read further into the document to get the details they need.

How Will My Reader Use This Information?

Will the reader have to make a decision based on your details? If so, have you given all the pertinent criteria and facts? Will he merely distribute the information to others who must act? If so, is the information in detachable, complete form? Will the reader have to plead with a boss to attend your seminar? If so, have you given him enough ammunition? What benefits can be expected? Will he have to build on your research? If so, he'll need why's and how's.

What's the Bottom-Line Message to Your Reader?

If you can't summarize your message in a few sentences (often one sentence will suffice), you're not ready to write. How many times do you hear someone say, "Well, I know what I want to say; I just can't say it"? I disagree with that comment. The person doesn't know what she wants to say—that's why she can't get the words on paper. And chances are, even after the words are down in black and white, the reader will still not know what the writer was trying to say.

Examples of bottom-line messages trainers often write:

✓ "We are accepting nominations for second-quarter enrollments in our performance appraisal seminars."

✓ "After investigating communication-skills programs from vendors X, Y, and Z, I suggest we contract with Z Corporation to conduct a pilot program in April for all executive secretaries."

✓ "The standard enrollment procedures were not followed for the October 16 supervisory skills seminar. As a result, the students came with false expectations about the course content. At the conclusion of the course, some participants voiced extremely negative comments and questioned the value of the course in its entirety."

Once you have this narrow bottom-line message in mind, you'll find that most background or introductory remarks, as well as many how and why details, become unnecessary.

How Much Does Your Reader Already Know about the Subject?

What educational background and job experience has he had? How involved in the project has she been?

Not long ago I attended a local ASTD meeting for which the program flyer announced the guest speaker would address "Sequential Training in the Organization." Ten minutes into the presentation about how sales training should be administered to the levels in the organization, from the top executive to the managerial ranks, first-line supervisors, and field reps, the woman beside me leaned over to whisper, "This is not what I expected at all. I thought he was going to talk about sequential training for the individual—from entry-level position to manager."

Even people in the same department or occupational field sometimes speak a different language. As a remedy, sift abbreviations and jargon from your writing when you have multiple readers who may or may not attach your specific meaning to your words.

Step 2—Anticipate Special Problems in Your Reader's Reaction

Will your reader be skeptical about claims or objectives in your course brochure? Are you asking for before-class preparation that a participant won't think necessary? Can you give details about course methods that will overcome reluctance to attend? Do you have a deadline for your reader to meet? Will someone lose face accepting what you say? Will a "yes" to your proposal mean spending more money than was budgeted?

When any of these situations or circumstances are the case, writers must anticipate adverse reactions and plan to overcome them from the start.

If attendees frequently show up to class unprepared, then anticipate excuses of "heavy workload." Insist that preparation is necessary and suggest cancellation if participants cannot prepare. If you must be persuasive about spending unbudgeted money, stack your proposal with whys. If deadlines for cancellations create problems, don't parcel out details about time, location, and travel arrangements in two or three memos; give all the details in the first announcement. If there's skepticism about the credibility of a certain instructor, mention previous class critiques or comments from satisfied managers about on-the-job transfer of skills.

Step 3—Outline Your Message Functionally

Some writers learned the "once-upon-a-time..." organizational format from their first English composition classes and have been using this arrangement happily ever after. Rather than the narrative form, use a functional format. Keeping in mind that length is not as important as the sequence of ideas, a writer achieves both conciseness and clarity by layering the message for multiple readers. About 90 percent of all business communication should answer these four questions in the following order.

What's the Message?

Give the essential, bottom-line message that you decided upon in Step 1: What do you want the reader to consider, believe, or know?

What Action Is Next?

What action do you plan to take now, or what action do you want your reader to take? Do you want her to nominate someone to attend the course? Do you want employee data on the attached form? Will you bill the department for training costs? Do you want approval to hire vendor Smith for a time-management course? Will you schedule a briefing before awarding the contract?

When, Who, Where, Why, or How Details?

The questions that can be answered in a word or short phrase may already be given in your message or action statements. Only if one of these details needs elaboration will you delay it until here. Usually the why and how need elaboration. Why must I bring certain materials to the class? Why have our managers not been satisfied with the program we now offer? How will you use the data you're asking me to collect? How will the topic be presented?

Is There Evidence to Clarify the Message?

Can you attach example forms or questionnaires? Graphs? Training calendar? Breakdown of costs? Copy of previous correspondence or contract?

So what does this four-part functional format have to do with conciseness and clarity? Look at the "Ascending Outline," Figure 24-1.

In this traditional once-upon-a-time format, the writer presents ideas in the order of his research. A reader must trudge all the way up the hill before he gets to stand on the top and understand what the message is really all about; the writer controls the reader's time and forces him to plow through the details before getting to the punchline.

On the other hand, notice that in the "Descending Outline," Figure 24-2, the reader begins on the top of the hill and can see what's coming below. Then, having the basic message and expected action in mind, she can jump off the downhill trail when time or interest dictates and still know she has the essential information.

A vice president may stop after the first paragraph or two: "Employee development has been conducting an in-house supervisory course that focuses primarily on theory and information about management concepts and company policies. We would like to propose additional training for first- and second-line supervisors, focusing on skills only—specific behavioral guidance in supervising and motivating employees to increase productivity.

"The program would be administered with the help of TAG Consulting, Inc., a Phoenix firm. The total cost of $52,000 covers customized behavior models, videotaped introductory and practice sessions, six line managers and/or staff certified by TAG as qualified trainers, two classes (20 participants each) for trained supervisors, and trainer manual and participant workbook for reproduction."

Managers wanting to send staff may read the sections that follow on course objectives, cost breakdown, research on effectiveness and acceptance of program, and perhaps target date for implementation.

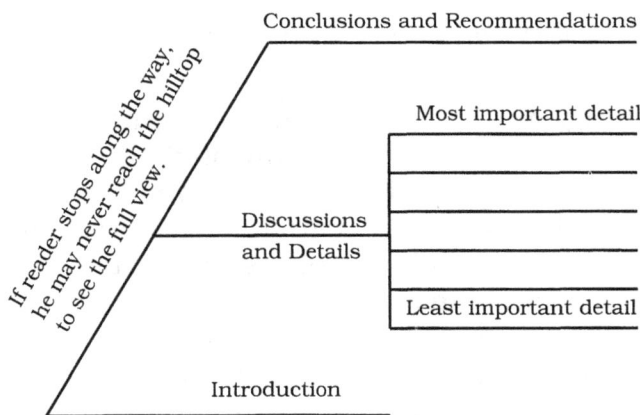

Order of Your Research

Figure 24-1. Ascending outline.

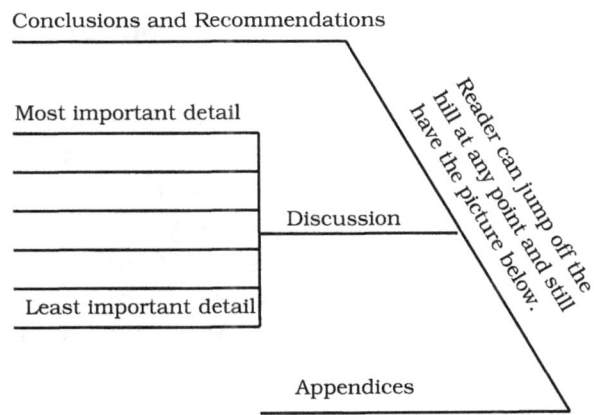

Order of Your Message

Figure 24-2. Descending outline.

The training specialist who may finally administer this program will have to read through all the how and why details to take the action. Another reader in the purchasing department may have to read an attachment to verify that invoices are paid as agreed upon in the contract.

This is the layered effect of details, mentioned earlier. Your audience can read or skim as much or as little as necessary to make a decision or do the required action.

And what does all this have to do with clarity? Plenty. Refer to the memo samples given in Figure 24-3. In the ascending-format memo, notice the reader's reactions added in the margin. The details don't make sense until she gets to the punchline— what's in it for her. However, in the descending-format memo, the reader immediately understands the point of the message and what the writer wants her to do. With this information in mind, she can evaluate the details as she reads through the first time, eliminating the rereading that is all too common in documents written in ascending order.

Step 4—Develop the First Draft

By the time you reach this step, half your work is finished. Developing the first draft should go quickly and smoothly if you have followed the preceding "thinking" steps. All you need do in this step is add flesh to your skeleton: Turn the key words and phrases in your outline into sentences.

Other tips: Dictating the first draft or composing it on a typewriter or at a terminal takes much less time than writing in longhand. In my experience, dictating produces a conversational style, not stilted prose. Third, when dictating or keying into a terminal, you don't fall in love with your words. Words written in longhand quickly become permanent in your mind as well as on paper.

Step 5—Edit for Content, Clarity, Conciseness, Style, and Grammar

Good writing is rewriting. Mark Twain once commented: "The difference between the right word and the almost-right word is the difference between lightning and the lightning bug."

As you've probably found from experience, it's that one missing detail or one awkwardly placed phrase or clause that elicits 14 phone calls or necessitates a follow-up memo.

Always allow a cooling-off period before you edit. Otherwise, you read what you think you wrote. Better yet, have someone who is unfamiliar with your subject proofread the document. When that person comes back to you with questions, don't just verbally explain the unclear parts, answer the questions, or fill him in on the background, and then leave the writing unchanged!

	Ascending Format Memo
	To: All Managers From: Training Director Subject: Employee Performance Appraisal Seminar
So what? I don't work for Mr. Wright!	At Harold Wright's request I have arranged for an Employee Performance Appraisal Seminar to be held for personnel under his supervision. The seminar will consist of five 2-hour sessions during the week of August 1–5, in the mornings. A course outline is attached.
Good. So? *So that's it! Well, I may. What were those details again?*	The instructor, Fred Templeton, is available for an additional seminar to run during the same week in the afternoons, in two-hour sessions. Maximum class size is 14 participants. Mr. Templeton specializes in the sales industry. If you have people you wish to attend, call me so that I may schedule the afternoon seminar.
	Descending Format Memo
	To: All Managers From: Training Director Subject: Interest in Scheduling an Employee Performance Appraisal Seminar
Message here. *OK, I may. I think I'll read ahead for details to make my decision.*	Instructor Fred Templeton is available to conduct an Employee Performance Appraisal Seminar for your staff during the week of August 1–5, in the afternoons. If you have people you wish to attend such a seminar during these dates, please call me so that I may make definite plans to schedule this afternoon seminar.
	Maximum class size is 14 participants, so I will be taking nominations on a first-come, first-served basis. A morning seminar for August 1–5 has already been scheduled for staff under the supervision of Harold Wright; therefore, this is the only date we can consider at this time.
	The instructor specializes in the sales industry. His course outline for the five 2-hour sessions is attached.

Figure 24-3. Ascending format vs. descending format.

✓ Content—Did you create paragraphs by idea and for eye appeal? Are headings informative? Does proportion match emphasis?

✓ Clarity—Delivery of the course textbooks along with the reference library and A/V equipment has been scheduled in late April, pending R&D approval. What is pending R&D approval—the delivery or the scheduling?

✓ Conciseness—Did you write, "The efficiency with which an operation utilizes its available equipment is an influential factor in productivity" (16 words), when you could have written, "Efficiency in using equipment influences productivity" (6 words)?

✓ Style—Do you sound overbearing? Have you included courteous words? Did you motivate the reader by telling her what's in it for her? Do you sound pompous and impersonal? Example: "These assessment instruments should be disseminated to all participants before initiation of the presentation." Instead, try: "Please distribute these questionnaires to all participants before beginning the film."

✓ Grammar—Watch grammatical goofs such as, "Having discussed the problem with all the managers before the first class day, the program has been modified to include the four additional topics." (The program discussed the problem with the managers?)

Effective business writing requires training; success comes from method, not chance. When you must write and when your writing must work, review and practice the five steps detailed here for effective communication. You may not become $18,000 richer, but you can take much of the pain out of the writing process.

25

THE MAGIC OF MEMORY- AND MIND-MAPPING®

Jeanne Baer

Jeanne Baer *is the president of Creative Training Solutions, which has provided performance improvements through training, facilitation, and program design services since 1990. Clients include Chrysler, Campbell's Soup, IDS Financial Services, DuPont Pharmaceutical, Cliff's Notes, and the U.S. Navy. A past president of the Lincoln chapter of ASTD, Jeanne also teaches at Doane College and Southeast Community College in Lincoln. Jeanne's work has been published in three previous* **McGraw-Hill Sourcebooks,** *in two Harvard Business Press training video guidebooks, and in Pfeiffer and Company's* **20 Active Training Programs, vol. 3.**

Contact Information:

Creative Training Solutions
1649 South 21st Street
Lincoln NE 68502-2809
800-410-3178
jbaer@binary.net
www.ncf.carleton.ca/~bk751

Overview   A simple diagramming technique developed by Tony Buzan in the early 1970s is currently used all over the world to boost people's brainpower. His method allows people to explore and retain ideas more successfully.

Buzan called his method "mind-mapping," and applied it not only to brainstorming ideas, but also to learning and reviewing material to be mastered. (Some people refer to this latter technique as "memory-mapping.")

Memory-mapping and mind-mapping are excellent techniques, because they take advantage of the natural way people recall and think. They also give people plenty of "parking space" to record their thoughts.

This handout explains how you can increase your retention through memory-mapping, and how you can effectively explore ideas, alone or with a team, through mind-mapping.

THE MAGIC OF MEMORY- AND MIND-MAPPING®

Imagine that you've got to learn and remember the locations of the states and of the topographical features of the U.S. And further imagine that instead of learning this material by looking at a map, you have to learn it by someone describing the map to you!

While the person details the arrangement of 50 states stretched over the land mass, and the mountains that punctuate and the rivers that flow through the country, you begin to feel a little panic-stricken, trying to grasp and remember it all.

Now imagine someone showing you a map of the U.S. in a giant atlas. Ah—now you can see it all, from sea to shining sea, at a glance! After taking time to study it, you know you understand and can recall what you've seen.

Memory-Mapping: A Picture Is Worth a Thousand Words

A memory map is similar to this map of the United States in that it helps you grasp and recall material more clearly. It's a diagram that features key words and simple pictures to remind you of the concepts you want to learn or remember.

An alternate method of taking notes, it's also a helpful way to review your learning. What makes it even more memorable is that you create it yourself—you don't have to study and try to make sense of someone else's interpretation of important concepts.

If you're like most people, you're probably accustomed to taking notes in a linear or outline form. But your brain doesn't work that way! As you're learning and recalling, your brain creates connections between bits of information organized around a central theme. Memory-mapping is a way of taking notes in this same, natural, interconnected way.

You may have noticed that you're more likely to grasp and remember pictures than actual words. (How many times have we heard that pictures are worth a thousand of them?!) Scientists theorize that's because the right hemisphere of your brain, which stores pictures so accurately, works 1,500 times faster than the left hemisphere, which stores words less accurately.

Memory-mapping takes advantage of both hemispheres. As you draw quick pictures or symbols on your map to accompany your key words, the facts and concepts become firmly anchored in your mind, ready for recall when you need them.

Once you learn how to "map" your learning, you'll find it's fun, creative ... even relaxing! And you won't dread reviewing your notes when they're in the form of imaginative memory maps!

Let Your Right Brain Out to Play: Making a Memory Map

1. Begin by writing the subject of your note-taking in the middle of a sheet of paper. Enclose the subject in a circle, square, or other shape.

2. Add a branch extending out from the center for each key point or main idea you want to remember. The number will vary with the number of ideas or segments presented.

3. Write a key word or phrase on each branch, adding other branches for additional details. Do **not** write whole sentences on your branches; your memory will have difficulty storing and later "seeing" long strings of words.

4. Add symbols, cartoons, or any illustrations for better recall. Don't be afraid to be creative and outrageous. Remember, your brain is more likely to remember ludicrous images than sensible ones!

Mapping Tips to Strengthen Recall

1. Turn your paper horizontally; it gives you more usable space.

2. If you're mapping a chapter of a book or manual, consider giving branches the same titles as the headings or subheads.

3. In addition to key words, jot down abbreviations on your memory map. But use only those you're really familiar with, so you'll recognize them days or weeks later. As you become more skilled at mapping, you'll develop your own shorthand of commonly used abbreviations and symbols.

4. Make important ideas stand out by underlining them, making them larger, or making them especially bold.

5. If you have several colors available, use a different color for each branch. This color-coding will help your brain lock in learning.

6. If possible, play pleasant, refreshing music while you memory map. Experiment to find the music that works for you.

That's Not All: Other Applications

Memory-mapping will not only help you remember what you've already read, it will also help you "get into" what you need to read!

Before you begin an assigned reading, take a few minutes to scan the text. What piques your interest? What questions would you like to find answers to? What questions might you be tested on? Make a map of those questions, with the chapter title or main topic encircled in the center of the page.

Then, read specifically to get your questions answered, and jot down your findings on the memory map. This technique will help you stay focused on the reading and prevent your mind from wandering.

Some skilled memory-mappers make maps instead of taking notes as they listen to a lecture. That way, if a speaker suddenly remembers to make a point about a previous thought, they can easily add it to the appropriate place on the map. Other people prefer to take more traditional notes and then translate them into memory maps afterwards.

As you can imagine, memory-mapping a speech you plan to deliver will boost your recall quite a lot—you'll never write and memorize a speech word for word again! Here's how:

After you've decided what you intend to say, make a memory map of your key points, spicing up the map with colorful pictures that symbolize your points. Consider color-coding entire branches or subtopics of your speech. (Even the process of making the map, you'll find, helps you retain your speech later on!)

Next, as you practice the speech, if you forget a point, simply glance momentarily at your map, with its key words and symbols.

You'll find that when you actually deliver the presentation, you'll easily recall your key words, evocative pictures, and color-coded branches. Many memory-mappers are able to speak entirely without notes; some carry only one page (the map!) to the podium; and a few make a poster-sized memory map and have it tacked at the back of the room, out of audience view, giving them the best of both worlds!

From Memory- to Mind-Mapping

Mind-mapping uses the same diagramming technique as memory-mapping, but for a different purpose. In this case, the map is comprised of random ideas suggested in a brainstorming session. Because participants don't present thoughts in an orderly, vertical direction, and instead bounce and build their thoughts in many lateral directions, mind-mapping offers an interesting and useful way to record ideas and perhaps even increase innovation.

Better Brainstorming for Teams and Individuals

If your team wants to brainstorm via mind-mapping, begin by writing your topic or your problem statement in a circle in the middle of a huge sheet of paper attached to the wall. As ideas are suggested, the recorder jots them down in main or subordinate lines radiating from the center circle.

Once again, an advantage of mind-mapping over listing ideas on a flip chart is that you can add new ideas near similar ones mentioned earlier. This ability certainly makes the eventual sorting of ideas much easier!

Drawing icons isn't nearly as important with mind-mapping as it is with memory-mapping, since your goal is not to remember every phrase on the map. However, because ideas come so fast and furiously during a lively session, a skilled recorder may develop and use a shorthand of certain icons, to keep up with the team's enthusiastic participation.

Does this "great circle route" seem too foreign for you to try? If you use the problem-solving and decision-making tools that are often a part of quality initiatives, you're already using a similar technique—the Ishikawa Diagram. With a mind map, your topic is in the middle instead of at the "head" of the diagram, and the lines coming from it result in more of an octopus shape, versus a fishbone shape.

Explore Your Mental Jungle with a Map!

As you can imagine, mind-mapping is an excellent way to explore your own thoughts on any topic. You can develop plans for projects, training programs, speeches, and more. Some people chart their goals and objectives on a mind map, and some even map what they're thinking and feeling, instead of writing a journal.

To construct your own personal mind map, use 8½ × 11-inch or larger paper. Then simply follow the rules for group brainstorming:

✓ Go for quantity, not quality—let your imagination run wild!

✓ Write as quickly and nonjudgmentally as possible.

✓ Don't worry if it looks or sounds silly—no one else needs to understand or even see your mind map.

✓ Stop when your ideas stop, rest, and perhaps later, you'll want to build on some of the ideas you've already mapped.

Later, you can take a more analytical look at your map. You'll sort, refine, and discard, just as teams do as they begin to make decisions. By this time, thanks to the mind-mapping process, you'll have the makings of a solid, innovative plan! Congratulations, master mapper!

For Further Information

Mapping Inner Space, by Nancy Margulies

Mindmapping, by Joyce Wycoff

Quantum Learning, by Bobbi DePorter

Use Both Sides of Your Brain, by Tony Buzan

26

TWENTY-FIVE TIPS FOR MAKING THE WORKPLACE ACCESSIBLE

Sophie Oberstein

Sophie Oberstein *is the founder of Targeted Training Solutions, an instructional design and training consultancy. She is also an instructor in the training certificate program at Mercer County Community College and teaches courses in Human Resource Management in the MBA program at Drexel University. Sophie has published articles in* **Training and Development Magazine** *on keeping participants enthusiastic and has published an* **Info Line** *on designing creative training efforts. Sophie was a contributor to* **The 1997 McGraw-Hill Team and Organization Development Sourcebook.**

Contact Information:

Targeted Training Solutions
1555 Beechnut Circle
Maple Glen, PA 19002
215-619-7929
SOberstein@aol.com

Overview   Trainers and human resource specialists are already quite familiar with the Americans with Disabilities Act (ADA), passed into law in July of 1992 to eliminate discrimination against qualified individuals with disabilities in the workplace. Provisions of the ADA affect all employment-related activities including recruitment, hiring, training, pay, job assignments, leave, and benefits.

The following handout provides some suggestions to get you started thinking about what you can do as a trainer or human resource specialist to make sure your workplace and your training programs are accessible to everyone. Use the ideas presented here, or call organizations like the Job Accommodation Network to figure out more strategies for accommodating individuals with disabilities. You can reach the network at 1-800-232-9675, or at 1-800-ADA-WORK. Before trying out any of the ideas, remember that determining what accommodation is best for every individual must be done on a case-by-case basis.

TWENTY-FIVE TIPS FOR MAKING THE WORKPLACE ACCESSIBLE

People Supports

1. Pair a person with disabilities with a communication partner. This partner can help out with anything from commonplace issues (e.g., getting things out of the vending machine for a person in a wheelchair) to more involved tasks (e.g., helping a deaf person get called on in a training program when participants don't raise their hands).

2. It is important to help the individual feel at home in the greater work (or training) environment. A walk around the neighborhood or conference center to orient the employee to the location of other services and restaurants is extremely helpful.

3. Some people need directions written out on paper or recorded on audio tape, not just spoken.

4. An interpreter is essential in accommodating a deaf individual, as only a qualified interpreter can assess the best method of communication for each person. ASL (American Sign Language) is a separate language from English and therefore someone fluent in ASL might not be able to understand written or signed English.

5. If someone is totally blind and is uniquely qualified to do a job, such as a lawyer, a reader should be employed.

6. The human service agencies that work with individuals with disabilities in your area are often able to provide people supports free of charge. Agencies in your area that provide services for the hearing impaired, for example, are likely to provide sign language interpreters for free, to loan you phone equipment, or to train your existing staff in deaf awareness issues and/or sign language.

Office (or Training Room) Set-up

7. Some printed materials (e.g., phone extensions, training activities, or company policies) may have to be printed out in a larger font for individuals with some loss of sight.

8. A simple wooden shelf on the desk where employees who are visually impaired can place documents provides a higher surface so they won't have to lean over to read or write.

9. Sometimes all a visually impaired person needs is more light in his or her office or training environment.

10. Building codes must be up to date so that fire alerting systems and smoke detectors are equipped with visual alarms and strobe lights, not just audio alarms.

11. Simple, cheap devices, like locator dots—stick-on labels embossed with dots—can be used to indicate where buttons on the copying machine or other equipment are located.

12. When possible, approach disabled participants prior to any training activity that involves hand–eye coordination or physical activity and ask them how much they want to be involved. Some experiential learning programs and challenge courses are designed to accommodate disabled participants. A directory of these is available from the Association for Experiential Education (AEE). It is called "The Directory of Experiential Therapy and Activity-Based Counseling Programs" and can be obtained by calling AEE at 303-440-8844. You can also call Universal Ropes Course at 803-648-1817.

Equipment

Telephones

13. Deaf individuals should have access to TDD phones that provide a visual display. Key offices within the company should also have TDD to communicate with the deaf employee. For hearing-impaired individuals, a phone with built-in amplification is necessary.

14. A person who can't use his or her hands can use a voice-activated phone with voice dialing or can use a headset so she or he won't have to pick the receiver up.

Computer hardware

15. Smaller keyboards or keyboards with fewer keys are available for individuals who have trouble using their hands.

16. Keyboards can be slanted for easier reach by individuals in wheelchairs.

17. A blind person can have hardware installed that uses synthetic speech or that has a Braille output device. For those with low vision (over 80 percent of those individuals who are legally blind have some usable vision), hardware can be installed to enlarge print or to turn black type on a white background to white print on a black or other colored background.

Computer software

18. Software programs like *Sticky Keys* and *Word Predictors* allow computer users who need to use only one hand to perform two-handed functions (e.g., if you need to hold down both Shift and F8 at one time to activate a function, this program lets you press one, then the other).

Other technology

19. Enlarging machines allow people to place any printed material underneath a glass lens to view it in large print on a computer monitor.

20. A tape recorder is helpful for a visually impaired person who answers calls or writes down messages.

21. Scanning devices can be used to load printed information directly into an enlarging computer terminal.

Job restructuring

22. Modifying work schedules or locations for those employees who have a known relationship with an individual who has a disability may be necessary. There are many alternative staffing options to choose from, including flex-time (working a 40-hour week on your own schedule), job sharing, and telecommuting.

23. The format of examinations and training materials may have to be modified. Exams should not be made easier, but may need to be oral instead of paper based, or vice versa. Training materials may also need to be produced on audio tape instead of on paper. In computer-based training programs, you may need to change the look of your screens, for example using bigger buttons or using keyboard commands instead of the mouse.

24. Some company policies may need to be modified for individuals with disabilities (e.g., leave of absence or absenteeism policies).

25. You may have to vary your standard business card format for a disabled person who wants to be communicated with in one way more than another. For example, you might want to include an E-mail address for a deaf employee rather than a telephone number.

27

SEXUAL HARASSMENT: THE GRAY ZONE

Robert Kaeser

Robert M. Kaeser, Ph.D. *is president of RMK Associates, a training and consulting group. Bob has over 20 years of human resource development, consulting, and training experience in a wide variety of organizational settings. Bob has created and presented workshops for individual clients as well as presenting at local and national conferences. Areas of expertise include: sexual harassment prevention, cultural diversity, change management, and team building.*

Contact Information:

1919 Chestnut St.
Suite 1918
Philadelphia, PA 19103
215-568-1338

Overview Most people today understand that *quid pro quo* sexual harassment is against the law. However, the concept of a hostile work environment is much more complex and difficult to interpret. The "gray zone" refers to that area of behavior where it is often unclear whether sexual harassment is occurring or not. This concept is best developed with a group through discussion and the use of examples. However, the overriding determinant of harassment is whether or not the behavior is "unwelcomed."

This leads to the issue of appropriate versus inappropriate workplace behavior. The point to be made is that while a behavior may not constitute hostile work environment sexual harassment, it still may not be appropriate workplace behavior. The following handout can be a helpful tool in illustrating this point.

Additionally, the handout can be used to clarify some important differences between *quid pro quo* and hostile work environment harassment. Often in *quid pro quo* situations, the harasser has organizational power over the individual being harassed, the nature of the incident is very serious, and frequency is less. On the other hand, hostile work environment harassment may involve a harasser who has little authority over the harassed person, the nature of the incident tends to be less serious, and the frequency of occurrence is greater.

Application During the course of a sexual harassment prevention workshop, participants frequently are very interested in knowing what constitutes a hostile workplace environment. The areas of casual touching, telling jokes, and the use of what is, to some, offensive language will come up naturally in discussion. This is an excellent opportunity for the facilitator to make some important points.

It is not the **intent** of behavior that determines whether it constitutes hostile work environment harassment, but the **effect** it has on others.

While some behaviors are not technically illegal, they are of questionable appropriateness in the workplace. So even if no one objects to the behavior, it may be best to discontinue it.

Some people who are offended by certain behaviors may be reluctant to say so. Just because people are not complaining doesn't mean that they find the behavior acceptable.

If we would be uncomfortable saying or doing something in front of loved ones or family members, it is probably inappropriate in the workplace.

SEXUAL HARASSMENT OVERVIEW

I L L E G A L

QUID PRO QUO

Harasser has **POWER** over harassed.

The behavior is of a **SERIOUS** nature.

The behavior may be one-time or very **INFREQUENT.**

HOSTILE WORK ENVIRONMENT

Harasser may have little or **NO POWER** over harassed.

The behavior may be of a **LESS SERIOUS** nature.

The behavior may be **REPEATED FREQUENTLY.**

_____ THE GRAY ZONE _____

L E G A L

INAPPROPRIATE/UNPROFESSIONAL

Behaviors that may be legal, but are unacceptable in the workplace

---

APPROPRIATE/PROFESSIONAL

Behaviors that are both legal and professional in the workplace

28

FOUR WRITING CHALLENGES AND WHAT TO DO ABOUT THEM

Brooke Broadbent and Lise Froidevaux

Brooke Broadbent *specializes in training needs analysis, instructional design, and technical writing. He has written numerous courses, books, and articles about computer-related training, training methods, and workplace safety. He is a senior associate with Friesen, Kaye and Associates and consults globally. Friesen, Kaye and Associates is a 30-year-old, internationally renowned training and consulting group offering a complete curriculum of train-the-trainer workshops, needs assessment and custom consulting services, and outstanding instructional design software.*

Lise Froidevaux *was born and educated in French-speaking Switzerland. Now residing in Ottawa, Canada, she does translation, editing, and general management as a partner in Broadbent Associates.*

Contact Information:

Friesen, Kaye and Associates
3448 Richmond Road
Ottawa, Ontario, Canada
K2H 8H7
1-800-FKA-5585
info@fka.com
www.fka.com
www.magi.com/broadb/ba.

Overview Writer's block, lack of editing services, lack of resource information, problems preparing a final version. Have you encountered these four writing challenges? This helpful handout provides up-to-date suggestions for responding to these challenges.

FOUR WRITING CHALLENGES AND WHAT TO DO ABOUT THEM

Today's Challenges

Writing, never easy, has become a feat of self-reliance in recent years. Company editors who once helped tweak documents have been right-sized. Funds to hire editors on contract have evaporated. Hawk-eyed supervisors and colleagues who commented on our draft documents have become endangered species—casualties of reengineering. Likewise, there are fewer resource centers and librarians to locate the perfect background information for our projects. For "Lone Ranger" mobile workers, or teleworkers, or consultants, there is no "Tonto"—nobody to save our skins. Clients, internal and external, expect first-class work. They engage us to produce top-quality documents and are not sympathetic to circumlocution, typos, and dumb errors. To make matters even more challenging, everybody expects a spiffy document—a hurdle for human resource practitioners who have not had an opportunity to learn the finer points of desktop publishing!

Help Is Available

Three resources help to cope with the writing challenges identified above. Powerful word processing software contains features that take some of the guesswork out of writing. The Internet is chock-full of information to help you write. Finally, if you are lucky, a third resource, family-based "editors," can also help.

WRITING CHALLENGES AND SOLUTIONS

CHALLENGES	SOLUTIONS
1. writer's block *symptoms:* angst, sweaty palms, procrastination, general anxiety	✐ Turn on your PC and write—anything. ✐ Anticipate your readers' questions and craft answers. ✐ Address the five W's: who, what, when, where, and why. ✐ When you have a clear vision of your piece, use the outline feature in your software to structure a plan. ✐ Let your plan sit a few days, review, sleep on it. ✐ With a clear plan and a fresh mind—go for it. ✐ Still stymied? You can access a cornucopia of writing tidbits at *Purdue University's Writing Resources* (http://owl.english.purdue.edu/writing.html). ✐ Need to go further in your cybernetic quest for writing resources? Try *Indispensable Writing Resources* at http://www.stetson.edu/~hansen/refmat.html. ✐ Web sites have a way of disappearing; if you have trouble accessing the foregoing sites, use a search engine, look up the title of the site, and find the latest URL.
2. lack of editing services *symptoms:* You dread delivering documents to clients because you fear they will find typos on the first page, 10 seconds after you hand over your masterpiece.	✓ Your "editor-partner," your "editor-friends," and your children may have the capacity to become skillful reviewers. ✓ When you have a few paragraphs of your piece, show them to these editors and ask an open question like, "What do you think?" ✓ Encourage your entourage to provide quick, clear, constructive comments. ✓ Grammar-checking software always helps me eliminate a few errors that my spell checker missed, like a dropped 's' or a missing period.
3. lack of resource information *symptoms:* In your bibliography, you cite only articles you have published, or worse yet, draft articles you hope to publish one day.	⚖ *Online Resources for Writers* list links to libraries, research and facts, and other information. Check out these resources at http://www.nwu.org/nwu/links/linkhome.htm. ⚖ Search for hard-to-find articles in back issues of *Training* magazine at http://www.trainingsupersite.com/rsrchset.htm. ⚖ Access *ERIC Internet Resources*, about training and education, by pointing your Web browser to the ERIC home page at www.aspensys.com/eric/. ⚖ Internet search engines like Lycos (www.lycos.com/) and Alta Vista (www.altavista.com/) will find you information on just about anything from their extensive WWW catalogs. ⚖ To get the best results from a search engine, take a few minutes to learn to target your search strategy; check this out near the top of individual search engine Web sites under terms like *advanced features, customize your search,* or *search tips.*
4. problems preparing a final version *symptoms:* There is no final version, just a few unformatted electronic files and a PowerPoint presentation that you call your final report; but deep down you know this is not going to satisfy your client.	📖 Styles, templates, and automated formatting features of your word processing software will help you produce professional-looking documents. 📖 For example, under File, New, current versions of WordPerfect and Word have templates that will step you through hassle-free writing of memos, reports, faxes, and other documents you need to write. 📖 If styles, templates, and automated formatting are mumble-jumble to you, use the on-line help feature of your word processor to learn more about them, at Help on your main menu.

29

SIXTEEN GUIDELINES FOR MANAGING TIME IN CLASS

Scott Parry

Scott B. Parry, Ph.D. *is chairman and cofounder of Training House, Inc. Since 1971, Scott has published over 600 hours of materials for the training field including books, assessments, training programs, games and simulations, surveys, and self-inventories and workshops for trainers. He is active in ASTD and ISA and conducts workshops around the world.*

Contact Information:

Training House, Inc.
P.O. Box 3090
Princeton, NJ 08543
609-452-1790
TrngHouse@aol.com

Overview   Trainers are managers. We manage people (trainees, other presenters, AV support, etc.). We manage resources (facilities, equipment, food service, etc.). And we manage time (start, finish, eat, and stay on schedule).

Course developers put time estimates on each activity and exercise. But these are merely guidelines. Different classes will require different amounts of time to reach the objectives of a given learning exercise. Yet the length of the course is fixed and can't be expanded to accommodate a group that is slower, or highly verbal, or fascinated by the subject.

To what degree is the enrollment in a course controlled? Is it limited to those who have the **need** and the **prerequisites** (experience, knowledge, etc.)? A homogeneous group is much easier to manage and keep on schedule than a heterogeneous group.

Each time we teach a course, our repertoire of anecdotes, examples, and experiences gleaned from participants gets larger. Each offering of a training program should be richer than its predecessors.

Add to this the tendency of the sponsors or clients to think of new subjects that should be included in the training—new content to be "worked in" next time you run the course.

In short, we've just identified four factors that make the management of classroom time extremely difficult. They are:

✓ the differences in learning time from group to group and from individual to individual;

✓ the degree to which your participants constitute a homogeneous or a heterogeneous group;

✓ the expanding repertoire of the instructor that becomes richer each time a course is taught;

✓ the tendency to add new topics to a course without deleting or shortening existing topics.

Consider this situation. You are midway through a course you've taught several times. Yet this group is less experienced than past ones, and you are two hours behind where you should be. What should you do?

1. Tell participants that "We'll have to step up the pace, cut down on the questions and discussion, and eliminate some of the hands-on exercises so as to cover everything and still get out on time."

2. Study the remaining schedule during a break and decide which of your presentations can be eliminated or shortened without losing the practice sessions (hands-on applications) and without extending the length of the course.

Before reading further, decide which option you should pursue. The trade-off here is one of content vs. process. Option 1 prefers **content:** It's important to cover **everything,** even at the expense of comprehension and retention. Option 2 prefers **process:** It's important that participants achieve **mastery** of what we do cover, even if this means jettisoning some of the content.

Which is better? That depends. (A diplomatic and safe answer, albeit less than satisfying!)

If you're teaching personnel policy, EEO, OSHA compliance, or some other topic that is heavy in information, documented in handouts or manuals, and your main objective (sometimes legalistic) is to make sure that participants were **exposed** to the policy and rules, then Option A might make more sense.

If you're teaching skills (supervisory, selling, data entry, assembly, troubleshooting) and your main objective is to develop new habit patterns and improve one's performance, then Option B might make more sense. It's essential that your participants achieve **mastery** of the key skills and techniques, even at the expense of less important ones.

Here we arrive at the crux of the time-management dilemma: How you manage your time in class, as in life, depends on your objectives and priorities. Your decision to retain or to jettison a given activity or exercise should be based primarily on the degree to which it moves your participants toward the attainment of the key learning objectives. Whether it's fun ... whether they love it ... whether it's one of your favorites ... all these are secondary considerations.

There's a tendency among inexperienced instructors to worry about having enough to say and enough material to fill the allotted time. Seasoned trainers know that participative instruction often takes more time than indicated on the schedule or lesson plan. Their concern is with getting participants out on time. The guidelines that follow should help you in fulfilling your responsibility for managing time in class.

SIXTEEN GUIDELINES FOR MANAGING TIME IN CLASS

1. The time estimates for each exercise are expressed in minutes and not in clock time (since we don't know when you plan to start each day). We suggest that you enter the expected clock times in the margin beside each exercise so that you can see at a glance throughout the day whether you're running ahead of or behind schedule.

2. You may also want to record your actual time spent on each exercise (or your actual clock time at various checkpoints). This might be helpful the next time you administer the program—you'll know where to modify the pace.

3. Don't worry if the group takes less time than you anticipated to read a handout, make a report, discuss a point, etc. Rather than filling the allotted time (which may slow the pace and cause the day to drag), you should move on to the next exercise. You may be grateful for the extra time later in the day when you need it for another learning activity. (And no instructor ever got bad reviews for letting a class out early!)

4. You're expected to make trade-offs from one exercise to another—to rob Peter to pay Paul. When the course was developed, the flow of instruction (learning sequences) came from a "master plan" in the mind of the course designer. There was a logic to it. But participants are not privy to this logic.... They ask questions and introduce information out of sequence. Thus, effective time management involves knowing the content and purpose of each exercise. If these are covered in an earlier exercise, then on a subsequent exercise you may find that you need less time than the course designer estimated. Conversely, if the content and purpose aren't being met in an exercise, you might conclude that "the group isn't ready yet" and bring them out in a later exercise. Make note of this in the margins of your instructor guidelines.

5. When participants raise issues that you'll be getting to later in the course and that cannot be answered in a minute or two, you may want to start a follow-up list. Tape a sheet of flip chart paper to the wall and label it "Follow-Up." Then, each time a participant raises a question or topic that can be better addressed later, make note of it. Add the participant's name (and add a note on your lesson plan, indicating when you'll bring it up). Incidentally, this sheet is also a great place to put questions you don't know answers to, or topics that are political "hot potatoes" that you want to clear with someone before addressing. The list buys you time to do your homework.

6. Sometimes participants have their own agendas and will raise issues that don't relate to the purpose of your class. (Their psychological needs don't always mesh with your logical or chronological needs!) What can you do? Here are several ways of dealing with the participant who raises an irrelevant issue:

    ✓ If it can be addressed and dismissed in a minute or two, handle it. This is easier than making a scene!

    ✓ Ask the participant how the issue relates to the objectives of the exercise or class (which you have made known in advance).

    ✓ Explain that the issue is one you'd like to address, but that you can't take the time to do it justice during class. Ask the person to see you during the break (at lunch, etc.), along with anyone else who might be interested.

    ✓ If the same person continues to bring up irrelevant or personal issues, talk to him or her during a break or after class.

7. If you're running behind schedule, you can use subgroups to pick up the pace. A subgroup of 2 to 4 persons will usually reach a conclusion much more quickly than the full class will.

8. Similarly, by using subgroups for a division of labor, you can speed up an exercise. For example, suppose the class has just read a four-page folder followed by six questions you were going to discuss in full session. But they took longer to read the folder than other classes have taken. Break them into three subgroups and give two different questions to each, to discuss for 2 minutes and report on for a minute. Total time: 5 minutes, compared with 10 to 15 minutes in full session.

9. If the flip chart is being used to record ideas and responses from participants, you may save time by pre-lettering the headings on each sheet prior to class and by appointing a recorder to write the entries during class. You can't lead discussion and write simultaneously, and much time is lost with everyone waiting while you record a point before going on to the next point. A recorder can be writing the point just made while you're eliciting and interpreting a new point. And the recorder will have more time than you to print or write neatly and spell correctly.

10. Similarly, use participants to distribute handouts, collect assignments, go off to make copies, turn on the projector in the rear, turn off lights, and so on. You can thus be instructing the group while these administrative chores are being handled.

11. The example you set for punctuality will determine the group's behavior in starting on time and returning from breaks and lunch at the designated time. Similarly, class should end at the scheduled time. If you do have to run over (an exception rather than the rule), you should negotiate this with the group and not assume that they are your captive audience.

12. Participants will work faster, the pace will move better, and breaks will be shorter if you can have your own coffee and refreshment service in or near the classroom. The same holds true of the proximity of phones, toilets, eating facilities, and so on. (We recognize that you may have little, if any, control over facilities.)

13. When you need to break into subgroups, instead of sending participants off to break-out rooms and losing 5 minutes each way, have the subgroups work in different locations in the main room. Or select a seating arrangement in which participants can sit in subgroups that are focused on the front of the room.

14. When you break the class into subgroups, give them a time limit and have each team appoint a timekeeper to make sure the group stays on target and is ready to reconvene on time.

15. Use a wristwatch or alarm clock that has a soft buzzer. At the start of each exercise, set it to go off 5 to 10 minutes before the end of the exercise. This is your reminder to begin the wrap-up.

16. Have the participants elect a class president. Equip this person with two handheld signs (about the size of Ping-Pong paddles). One is the octagonal red STOP sign, which the president can hold up 2 to 3 minutes before the indicated end time of each topic or session (especially if you haven't begun your wind-up). The other sign is the triangular YIELD sign, which is used to call your attention to someone who has a hand up and needs to be recognized. (It helps to seat the president where the entire class is in view.) These signs are a graphic way of letting the group know that time management is a shared responsibility.

30

SIX PRINCIPLES FOR DESIGNING INSTRUCTION

Anne Marrelli

Anne F. Marrelli, Ph.D. *is a Senior Human Resources Consultant for Hughes Electronics. She designs and develops programs, processes, and tools to assist the Hughes companies in developing highly competent and motivated employees. Anne has over 16 years of experience in learning and development and performance improvement. She has published many articles in* **Performance Improvement, Technical and Skills Training,** *and other publications and has received several local and national awards for her work in instructional design. Anne was a contributor to* **The 1996 McGraw-Hill Training and Performance Sourcebook.**

Contact Information:

Hughes Electronics
Loc. CO, Bldg C01, M/S C136
P.O. Box 80028
Los Angeles, CA 90080
310-568-6737
afmarrelli@ccgate.hac.com

Overview How can you help adults learn? Six fundamental principles of adult instruction and how to apply them are explained in this handout. By focusing on these principles as you design and develop instruction, you can create effective learning experiences and facilitate the transfer of that learning to the job.

The six principles are:

✓ Connect new knowledge to prior learning.

✓ Design instruction for different learning styles.

✓ Provide active practice and feedback.

✓ Relate learning to job performance.

✓ Establish that learners are responsible for their own learning.

✓ Create a climate of mutual respect and collaboration.

SIX PRINCIPLES FOR DESIGNING INSTRUCTION

Principle 1: Connect New Knowledge to Prior Learning

The single most important factor in effective learning is prior knowledge. The knowledge that learners already possess strongly influences what information they attend to, how that information is perceived, what they judge to be important or relevant, and what they understand and remember.

People learn by assigning meaning to new material. Meaning is generated by activating existing knowledge structures in the brain and relating the new material to existing knowledge. The existing knowledge base is then restructured to incorporate the new information. The restructured knowledge is encoded into memory.

Your learners have a rich store of knowledge and experience. It is essential to build explicit connections between this store of knowledge and the new knowledge and skills presented in the instruction.

Applying Principle 1

✓ Describe how learners' prior knowledge can be used to understand or apply the new knowledge or skill.

Example 1: For a statistics course, explain that the math necessary to apply statistical methods is the arithmetic and basic algebra they already know.

Example 2: Give examples of how measures of central tendency are used in our everyday lives such as the average miles our cars get per gallon of gas (mean), the median salary in our profession, or the most popular food in the family pantry (mode).

✓ Briefly review the prior knowledge needed to understand the course content.

Example: Provide review exercises and feedback on the mathematical operations needed to compute a mean.

✓ Explain the relationship of the new information to be presented to previous learning. If possible, show a chart, graph, or model depicting the relationship between prior and new knowledge or skills.

Example: If you are beginning a module on calculating standard deviations, demonstrate that to calculate a standard deviation, you first have to compute the previously learned mean.

Principle 2: Design Instruction for Different Learning Styles

People learn in different ways. The three basic learning styles are: visual (learning by seeing), auditory (learning by hearing), and kinesthetic (learning through body movements). Facilitate learning for all participants by using a variety of instructional methods.

Applying Principle 2

✓ Plan how you can efficiently present the same new information in a variety of ways. Spend a few moments talking with your learners about learning styles and explain that you will use a variety of learning activities to match their preferred learning modes.

Example 1: A lecture (auditory learning) can accommodate the needs of all learners if you prepare slides or charts with the key points (visual learning) and distribute partial handouts (kinesthetic learning). To create partial handouts, prepare a list of the important points you will cover but leave blanks where key words or phrases should be. As you talk, learners are to follow along and write in the missing words.

Example 2: Distribute a written case study with questions to answer (visual learning), divide the class into groups to discuss the case and formulate answers (auditory), and ask them to write the answers to the questions, act them out in a role play (kinesthetic), or share them orally with the class (auditory).

✓ Vary the instructional methods in each course module so that all learners have the opportunity to receive information in their preferred modes.

Principle 3: Provide Active Practice and Feedback

Effective learning and transfer of that learning to the job require active practice in realistic situations. To efficiently process and remember information, learners must work with it in some way. Practice enhances understanding and retention by increasing the number of connections between the new information presented and existing knowledge. Learners also need feedback on their practice to know if they are processing information correctly.

Applying Principle 3

✓ Plan enough time in each module of the course for practice and checking learners' progress. Some practice activities can be assigned as homework.

✓ Consider carefully what you want your learners to learn and plan practice activities that will build this kind of learning. Do you want them to remember or recognize facts? Perform procedures? Understand and apply concepts? Interpret and apply principles?

✓ Ask learners to perform the practice activities individually or in pairs. Practice is only effective if each individual actively participates. Some learners may not fully participate in group activities.

✓ Offer practice activities suitable for each learning style and encourage participants to select the activity that will be most effective for them. You can ask learners to complete the same type of task in their preferred mode.

Example: Ask learners to explain the benefits and importance of a procedure or the key points of a concept or principle. They can choose to do this by creating a radio commercial, rhyme, or song (auditory), preparing and reading a mock press release (visual), or preparing a demonstration (kinesthetic).

✓ Explain to your learners the rationale for each practice activity.

✓ Provide explicit directions. Offer both oral instructions and instructions printed on a flip chart, viewgraph, or handout.

✓ Browse through several of the excellent books on active learning and training games for ideas for creative and effective practice activities.

Principle 4: Relate Learning to Job Performance

Adults approach learning with a problem-centered orientation. They need to know the practical value of what they are learning, i.e., how it applies to their work and how it can improve their performance.

Applying Principle 4

✓ Present several examples of how adding the new knowledge or skill to prior learning can enhance job performance or marketability.

✓ Tell a story about your past experiences with the content, demonstrating how having the knowledge or skill helped you solve a problem or achieve a goal.

✓ Ask several learners to briefly share a relevant experience and explain how the knowledge or skill helped them or could have helped them.

✓ Base instruction and practice activities on the types of problems and situations that learners will actually face in their jobs. If possible, have learners work on an actual project or problem for their organization.

✓ If possible, tailor the instruction to the job interests and needs of the specific learners.

✓ Ask your learners about their information needs and prepare lists of resources for them including books, journals, trade magazines, professional or trade associations, conferences, and Internet sites.

Principle 5: Establish That Learners Are Responsible for Their Own Learning

Adults need to accept responsibility for their own learning as they accept responsibility for the other facets of their lives. When they enter a classroom, adults sometimes revert to the childhood dependence of "Teach me." You must quickly establish that each learner is in charge of his or her own learning.

Applying Principle 5

✓ Begin the course with an exercise in which each learner explains what she or he wants to learn. As these topics are covered in the course, refer to the learners who mentioned that a topic was of special interest.

✓ Explain at the beginning of the course that each person is responsible for his or her own learning and that it is up to each to participate in the class activities or not.

✓ Encourage learners to select the practice activities they think will most enhance their learning.

✓ At the end of each module, spend a few minutes asking learners to share how they will apply the knowledge or skill just learned to their work.

✓ Try using a learning contract in which each learner specifies what he or she wants to learn and the activities he or she will pursue to achieve that learning.

Principle 6: Create a Climate of Mutual Respect and Collaboration

Adults in a relaxed and positive frame of mind learn most effectively. A climate of mutual respect and collaboration is important for learning. Learners need to see themselves, each other, and the instructor as mutual collaborators in an interesting learning experience.

Applying Principle 6

✓ Decorate the classroom with fresh flowers or plants and colorful posters. Make the learners feel like special guests.

✓ Create a welcome poster with each participant's name.

✓ Think carefully before selecting an icebreaker to begin the class. Many popular icebreakers can embarrass less gregarious adult learners. Beware of activities that require people to remember names or facts and those that require people to reveal personal information.

✓ Make a special effort to call learners by name. Use name tents until you learn each person's name.

✓ Use warm, positive communication. Phrase your comments and suggestions to learners respectfully.

✓ Ask learners for examples from their work experiences relevant to each course topic.

✓ Encourage questions and class discussions.

✓ Explain at the beginning of the course that you expect to learn from each person in the class because each person has a unique wealth of experience. Reinforce this idea by asking learners to comment on their areas of special interest or expertise when you discuss these topics.

✓ Provide alternative learning experiences for those who prefer not to participate in some of the group activities.

✓ Share anecdotes of your own learning and on-the-job experiences and encourage learners to share their experiences.

✓ Speak privately with uncooperative or disruptive learners. Try getting them involved by giving them a special role to play or task to complete.

31

MANAGING YOUR COMMUNICATIONS WEB

Jacqueline Hall

Jacqueline Hall *is an independent consultant, specializing in process improvement, team performance and change management. Ms. Hall has eight years of organizational development consulting and training experience, plus five years in line management. Her clients include firms in engineering, finance, education and professional services. Jacqueline coauthored the article "Walking the Talk: Here's a Real Example," and is an examiner for the Louisiana Quality Award Foundation. She is a member of the Association for Quality and Participation and the American Society for Training and Development.*

Contact Information:

Pathways Consulting
29529 Parker Branch Road
Albany, LA 70711
504-567-5543
jkhall@exit1.i-55.com

Overview Managing your communication process is important to the overall effectiveness of an organization. Miscommunications can result in low morale, wasted time, errors, and poor customer relations, all of which impact the organization's bottom line. Use the following questions and worksheet to analyze the effectiveness of your communications.

MANAGING YOUR COMMUNICATIONS WEB

Much like a web, our communications move upward, downward, and horizontally through individuals and groups. Our ability to communicate clearly significantly impacts our effectiveness with others. Communication is a process, and as a process it can be managed and improved. As you complete the worksheet, ask yourself the following questions:

Communication Type. What am I communicating? Examples include project status, organizational goals, performance feedback, appreciation/recognition, organizational changes, new positions, to name a few.

Purpose. Why am I communicating?

Desired Outcome. What actions do I want to occur as a result of my communication? What level of understanding is needed?

Decision Type. Is this information based on a command (one-way communication of a decision which is final), consult (requesting input for consideration prior to the communicator making a decision), or consensus (the communicator asks those receiving the message to arrive at a decision all can live with) decision?

Audience. Who will be receiving the message? What communication style might they be comfortable with?

Channel. What channel or channels will be most effective to achieve my purpose and desired outcome (e.g., voice mail, memo, group meeting)?

Timing/Frequency. When do I want people to have this information? Is this communication time-sensitive? That is, must its receipt coincide with a specific action or specific calendar? Should it be communicated more than once?

Setting. What location and atmosphere would be most appropriate?

Who Communicates. Am I the right person to communicate this message? If not, who is? Should more than one person communicate this message?

COMMUNICATION PROCESS PLANNING WORKSHEET

Type of Communication	Purpose of Communication	Desired Outcome of Communication	Decision Type	Audience	Channel	Timing/ Frequency	Setting	Who Communicates

287

PRACTICAL GUIDES

In this section of *The 1998 Training and Performance Sourcebook,* you will find nine practical guides. These "how to" guides are short articles containing useful ideas and guidelines for implementing training and performance support initiatives.

You will find advice about such topics as:

✓ the internet and intranets
✓ on-line instruction
✓ training strategy
✓ self-directed learning
✓ workshop design
✓ problem-based learning
✓ single- and double-loop learning
✓ college internships
✓ meetingware

Each guide contains step-by-step advice. Several have examples, illustrations, charts, and tables to enhance your understanding of the content. You will find that these guides are clearly organized and easy to read.

Four suggested uses for the practical guides are:

1. Guidelines for your own consulting, facilitating, and training interventions.
2. Implementation advice to be shared with peers and people who report to you.
3. Recommendations to senior management.
4. Reading assignments in team building, organizational consultations, and training programs.

32

HOW TO USE THE INTERNET AND INTRANETS AS LEARNING AND PERFORMANCE TOOLS

Diane Gayeski

Diane M. Gayeski, Ph.D. *is internationally recognized as a pioneer in interactive media, and as a researcher, consultant, and speaker on organizational communication and learning systems. As a partner in OmniCom Associates, she's led over 200 client projects involving the assessment and adoption of new technologies and policies for training and performance improvement. Her research and publications have won awards from the International Society for Performance Improvement, the Association for Educational Communications and Technology, and the International Society for Business Communicators. The author of seven books, she maintains an academic affiliation as associate professor of corporate communication at Ithaca College.*

Contact Information:

OmniCom Associates
407 Coddington Road
Ithaca, NY 14850
607- 272-7700
gayeski@omnicomassociates.com
www.omnicomassociates.com

On-line learning and performance support tools have never been more powerful, cost-effective, and easy to produce. Organizations can leverage publicly-available information and can collect, organize, and disseminate internal information very efficiently using standard computer hardware and software.

Creating a Dynamic Information Environment

The Internet and its related standards and technologies—E-mail, newsgroups, and World Wide Web sites—have created a whole new paradigm for dissemination of information within and among organizations. Because today so many employees already have computers with an Internet connection (either at home or work or both), there suddenly is a built-in communication network, essentially free to trainers and performance consultants.

Many of the problems of conventional training and job aid approaches, such as difficulty of updating, cost of distribution and duplication, challenges in scheduling training and finding necessary content, and barriers to providing just-in-time information, are now much easier to overcome. Along with the rapid rise in adoption of this technology has come a set of new ideas about how to manage organizations and how to ensure that employees have the skills and concepts they need to perform well. The learning organization, self-directed work teams, and communities of practice all share a common thread of ideas that emphasize collaboration and continuous learning rather than top-down and controlled instruction. This guide will outline the various terminology and options available using on-line systems, and will explain how you can quickly and cheaply implement performance improvement projects using the Internet or an internal Web site (***intranet***).

Types of On-line Systems

Although E-mail and Web sites are the most common uses of the Internet and intranets, there are other related standards and applications that are useful for training and performance support (see the table below). The applications can be organized on two axes: the bandwidth, or what kind of data representation the application supports, and time, either synchronous or asynchronous. All Internet and intranet applications support at least text, and many also allow you to display graphics and play audio and video clips and animation sequences. These latter media require a lot of data, so the file sizes are large and in many cases the time to download these images and clips is unacceptably long. A newer data type is called ***virtual reality,*** or VR. These are "artificial worlds" which you can explore on the screen by moving your mouse around to "travel" through a space, or type in commands to interact with objects or beings. The time dimension is divided into synchronous applications in which parties must be on-line at the same time together, and asynchronous applications in which parties can communicate sequentially with each other over time by sending messages, having them stored on a central server, retrieving them, and responding.

Each of these applications holds many opportunities for training and performance improvement specialists. I'll give a few examples:

Bandwidth	synchronous	asynchronous
Text	On-line conferences, such as CompuServe or AOL "live" guest speakers, MUDs, and MOOs	E-mail, newsgroups and mail list groups, groupware such as Lotus Notes
Graphics	On-line whiteboard collaboration	Web sites, group scheduling and project management programs, personal news gathering services
Audio and video	Internet phone, desktop video conferencing such as CUSeeMe	Web sites, FTP (file transfer protocol)
Synthetic worlds	On-line chat systems with avatars	Virtual reality-enabled Web sites (VRML)

Text/Synchronous

It's possible to have on-line conferences in which participants sign onto a system at the same time and type messages back and forth to each other. CompuServe and AOL have "chat rooms" that are organized by areas of interest, and users can electronically meet there and chat in real time. These services also have famous authors and speakers as guests each night, and members can sign on and have a dialogue with them. Another interesting set of applications is called **MUDs** or **MOOs**—multiuser dungeons, or multiuser object-oriented programs. Although their most popular application today is on-line games, like versions of Dungeons and Dragons, this technology holds a lot of promise for instructional and informational applications. When you sign onto a MUD, you're presented with text or graphics that describe the space; you then navigate through it by typing in commands to move or to interact with other people who are signed on, and other artificial life forms. So, for example, you could have a MUD that's a representation of your company's headquarters; users could type in commands to walk through the lobby, ask the receptionist where the training department is located, take the elevator to the third floor, and visit your new safety lab.

Text/Asynchronous

There are literally thousands of special-interest groups on the Internet that are organized into list serves, forums, or newsgroups. For example, on CompuServe, there's a trainers and training forum and an intranet forum; these are special areas that allow members to post comments and questions to other forum members. A similar application is a **list serve.** To join one of these, you send a message to the group's "owner" saying you'd like to join (almost all of these are free). Then, each day you're sent (via E-mail) a set of messages that other users have sent into the list. Three popular list serves are TRDEV-L, Webtraining List, and LO-L, groups in training and development, Internet- and intranet-based training, and the learning organizations, respectively. Members of these lists send in questions, solicit recommendations from colleagues, advertise products, job vacancies, and services, and engage in lively discussions about theory and practice in these areas. There are list serves and electronic news groups on almost any topic you can think of, from rock bands to raising goats to programming languages. They are a terrific source of straightforward and quick answers from colleagues and for finding resources, such as videotapes or books on a topic.

Of course, we shouldn't overlook simple E-mail; this can be used to contact trainees before or after a class to answer questions or better introduce or consolidate information. Sending a document attached to an E-mail message can allow you to electronically distribute a survey or manual without having to incur duplication and shipping charges. This is especially useful when you need to work with subject matter experts or trainees who travel a lot—typically their E-mail follows them wherever they go.

One way to send, organize, and store messages from a group involves applying a type of software called *groupware*; perhaps the best-known product in this category is Lotus Notes, but there are also now many programs that can be embedded in Internet or intranet Web sites. This type of software allows users to display sets of icons or titles of topics under which are listed "threads" of back-and-forth messages. It's very much like E-mail except that everyone's responses are saved and available to be read at any time by members who have access to the site. This is an excellent way to capture and organize ideas and questions from a group. For example, instead of developing a whole course on conflict management, you might start an on-line discussion group among members of your organization with expertise in this subject, and members who need the examples and hints these experts can provide. The novices can post questions and real-life examples, and the subject matter experts can respond directly. All of these questions and answers are saved and can be searched and browsed. Although this does take the time of SMEs, in many cases it involves less time than developing or teaching typical courses and it can directly and rapidly address real organizational issues at a very low cost.

Graphics/Audio/Video Synchronous

Thanks to the rapid deployment of more powerful computers and standards for graphics and media, more applications now support a wider variety of modalities. One interesting set of products allows you to conduct conferences over a local area network or the Internet, either with two people or with a whole group. All of these conferencing products allow users to at least type information back and forth, but most do a lot more: for example, you can use an ***electronic whiteboard*** to sketch out graphics on your screen. All other conference participants can see this whiteboard and can also write on it and edit and move objects—so you could, for example, collaborate on the design for a new product or develop a list of priorities for a strategic plan. Many applications also let users see each others' computer screens and hear live audio; in this way, an instructor could teach a course on spreadsheets by actually displaying her screen and mouse movements to logged-on users, who can also hear her voice and respond in real time.

Desktop videoconferencing systems are becoming popular and very inexpensive. By purchasing a golf-ball-sized video camera for under $200 that plugs into the parallel port of the computer and sits atop your screen, and by licensing software that costs under $100, you can exchange voice and pictures with another person or with a whole group. In fact, Cornell University developed software called CUSeeMe that supports desktop videoconferencing on Macintosh and Windows-based computers and is free to download from their Web site. Again, because people are typically logging onto the Internet from a local information provider, there are no long-distance charges involved as there would be in a typical phone conference. A potential downside of this type of conferencing, however, is the speed of your connection to the Internet, and the general traffic pattern on the Internet when you're using it. Typically, the audio and video are delayed and not as smooth and clear as we expect from a phone or television set, and sometimes the resolution and delays are downright unacceptable. However, improvements in these technologies are taking place quickly and soon these should be not only extremely cost-effective, but also commonplace in corporate training. Using this technology, I have, for example, "brought in" guest speakers or involved clients in meetings when they were not able to take the time away from work to fly to another city. You could, for example, connect a camera and laptop computer to an available phone line on a factory floor and send audio and images of a broken machine to an SME who is across the world.

Graphics/Audio/Video Asynchronous

Web sites, either posted on the Internet for public access or posted on an organization's intranet for internal use only, are now the most popular way to share graphics, audio, and video on-line. The best reasons for using this standard in training and performance support are:

1. Web documents are very easy to create. New editors that generate code in **hypertext mark-up language** (html), the standard for Web pages, are as easy to use as a full-featured word processor or desktop publishing package. In fact, most of the current versions of word processing and desktop publishing software, like Word for Windows, Word Perfect, Pagemaker, and even electronic slideshow programs like PowerPoint and Astound, allow you to save your work in html format. Check to see if your software already does this.

2. Web sites are relatively inexpensive to build and maintain. True, some organizations have spent millions on their sites by installing high-powered computers anticipating millions of "hits" or "visitors" per day and by hiring expensive graphic artists to design the pages. But for many information applications, a relatively standard personal computer can act as the "server" or storage place for the documents. In most organizations, the information systems department has or can inexpensively purchase a server. If you don't want to maintain your own server and you have access to the Internet from a local Internet service provider or **ISP**, you can generally store a few megabytes worth of Web pages (generally 100 or so pages and graphics) for free as part of your monthly account payment. Once the overall design for the site is complete—how the information will be laid out in various documents and what the graphic "look and feel" will be—it's relatively simple for anybody with basic word processing skills to update it. The cost of an intranet can often be paid for by just eliminating the updating and reprinting of long documents, like policy manuals, that have a wide distribution.

3. You can update information on Web sites easily and frequently. As easily as editing a document and saving it, you can "publish" a new version of a document on your site. This means that your audiences always have current information, like new phone numbers, new dates for courses, etc. Many organizations now publish only electronic versions of internal phone directories, manuals, newsletters, or training schedules.

4. Using Web features, users can actually access databases and do a lot of the updating or registration procedures that were formerly done by memos and clerks. For example, users can browse a training department's set of Web pages, read course descriptions, and register themselves into a course. Their input automatically updates a database that is accessed by the training department. Many organizations also do their benefits open enrollment and allow employees to update their personnel records on-line.

5. The medium is two-way. It is very simple to build in a place for users to fill in surveys or forms, post a question or helpful response, or send E-mail to the "owner" of the Web site. So you can collect data from the visitors to your site. For example, in a training site, you could include a page that asks the person to suggest courses that they'd like to see offered. Or, before enrolling someone in a course, you could require them to take a pretest online which would be immediately and automatically scored, determining whether their registration would be accepted.

6. Information is easy to "navigate." Because of the hypertext linking that is easy to set up in Web documents and because of its ability to support graphics, animation, audio, and video, many different kinds of information can be stored. Many organizations are offering entire courses on the Web—this new medium is called *web-based training.* Learners can select topics, click on hotwords to get more information or definitions, and actually see video clips or animation, or hear audio related to the topic. There's no need to have slide projectors, VCRs, manuals, and audiotape players; all of the functions of these are combined in the computer and Web browser. Many organizations actually use Web sites as a place for instructors to store all their course presentation materials in one place instead of carrying around reams of papers and other media. They can dial into the intranet or Internet from a computer and display the Web pages using an LCD panel on an overhead projector or a computer projector.

7. It's easy to link to sites outside your own to refer your users to up-to-the-minute news, information on competitors or customers, or sources of research. Although there's a lot of "junk" on the Web, there are also very sound research papers, news stories and press releases, and amazing pictures and statistics. So you could create a course in business literacy on your intranet that included material you developed as well as links to outside sources that would be continuously updated.

Don't overlook other standards for graphic, audio, and video information retrieval other than the Web. The most popular application is FTP or *file transfer protocol.* Using this protocol and a simple Internet connection, it's possible to download digital files containing text, computer programs, graphics, audio, animation, or video onto your computer's hard drive. Most software companies now post updates or "bug fixes" to their programs on their Internet sites, and using FTP, their customers can download these new programs directly and without cost.

Many other popular office productivity software packages can be run on an internal network, allowing users to collaborate on documents or manage projects. One application is a meeting scheduler;

each person maintains his or her appointment calendar on the computer and this information is available to all others in a defined group. When you wish to schedule a meeting, you can check out a person's calendar and book yourself in, or can type in a whole list of parties you wish to be present and ask the computer to find a mutually available time.

Finally, one of the rapidly emerging Internet/intranet software applications is personal data gathering programs. These programs ask individuals to define a set of topics and/or set of sources they wish to follow, and then whenever the user signs onto the Internet or clicks on an "update" button, the program pulls from its database of up-to-the-minute stories a personalized electronic newspaper. Currently, the most popular of these is PointCast. You can download PointCast free from their Internet site and specify which industries, stock prices, companies, cities, newspapers, and even state lotteries you want to follow. All of this is presented in attractive screens which allow you to browse through headlines, select weather reports for cities all over the world, and so on. PointCast can also be set to act as your screen saver, in which case it displays animated headlines and reports to keep you updated throughout the day. All of this is supported by advertising, which is seen in small portions of the screen and is also tailored to your profile of age, location, and interests. Tools like these are good ways to inexpensively and constantly keep people updated on world and business events that may be very important to their job performance.

Virtual Reality Applications

Currently, most virtual reality (VR) programs on the Internet are oriented to games and to virtual "chat rooms" in which users can choose a virtual "being" called an *avatar* to represent themselves on the screen. VR programs can be entirely fictitious places developed in 3-D software, or they can represent actual rooms and spaces. To create a 3-D version of a room, the developer actually shoots multiple digital pictures of a room, spinning around to get individual pie-shaped shots of all 360-degrees. Then those images are electronically stitched together, and people can look around the 360 degree images by moving a mouse around in the space. This technology holds a lot of promise for allowing people to virtually experience and explore an environment—like taking a virtual orientation tour of a company or allowing them to work in an environment by operating equipment and manipulating objects. One current application of VR in training is a meeting room reservation system that's currently posted on the intranet of a large facility. This allows people who want to reserve a training or meeting room to look around the kinds of rooms that this company actually has available, seeing what each entire room looks like, what the view from the third row of seats or from the podium looks like, and what types of media and controls are available to the presenter.

SOURCES OF ON-LINE INFORMATION

If you have access to the World Wide Web, you can check out these sites for information and examples, and to actually download applications that are discussed in this article. Please note: Web addresses *do* change; these were correct at the time of publication.

Name of company or service	What to look for	The address or URL
PointCast	download Pointcast network, a free personalized electronic newspaper	http://www.pointcast.com
Asymetrix	examples of how their CBT authoring tool, ToolBook, can create Web-based training	http://www.asymetrix.com
Macromedia	examples of how their CBT authoring tools, Director and Authorware, can create Web-based training using their Shockwave software plug-in	http://www.macromedia.com
White Pine	free demo of enhanced CUSeeMe desktop video teleconferencing program	http://www.cu-seeme.com
TRDEV-L site	Web site for the training and development on-line list serve operated out of Penn State University; has links to many training-related sites and summaries of discussion topics	http://train.ed.psu.edu/trdev-l/
Learning organization list serve	discussion on the theory and practice of the "learning organization"	http://world.std.com/~lo
Multimedia Training on-line newsletter and discussion group	discussions about using the Internet and intranets in training	http://www.multimedia training.com
OmniCom Associates Web site	on-line articles, research reports, and analysis tools related to new technologies and practices in training and performance	http://www.omnicom associates.com

33

HOW TO BE AN ON-LINE INSTRUCTOR

Zane Berge

Zane L. Berge, Ph.D. *is the director of the Training Systems Graduate Program at the University of Maryland. Dr. Berge's experience in the instructional design and educational technology fields include teaching and consulting in higher education and business, as well as an extensive list of publications and presentations. He has coedited seven books on computer-mediated communication: a three-volume set,* **Computer-Mediated Communication and the Online Classroom: Higher and Distance Education** *(Hampton Press, 1995) and a four-volume set,* **Wired Together: Computer-Mediated Communication in the K-12 Classroom** *(Hampton Press, 1997).*

Contact Information:

UMBC
Department of Education
1000 Hilltop Circle
Baltimore, MD 21250
410-455-2306
berge@umbc2.umbc.edu
http://star.ucc.nau.edu/~mauri/zane.html

So, you want to teach on-line? Is that different from face-to-face instruction? Are the students going to react the same as if they were together in a classroom? What do you have to do differently to motivate students, manage the environment, and model appropriate behaviors in the on-line classroom? Following is a synthesis of on-line practice that will help you design and instruct on-line.

Introduction

A prerequisite to the use of computer-mediated communication (CMC) when facilitating on-line instruction is access to a high level of computing power and a reliable telecommunication infrastructure. That said, it should be emphasized in the strongest way that when developing and delivering *instruction*, whether on-line or not, the use of technology is secondary to well-designed learning goals and objectives. What distinguishes on-line instruction from entertainment or recreation is the purposefulness of the designers and developers in provoking certain intelligent responses to the learning materials, context, and environment.

This guide will list the roles and functions of the on-line instructor in computer conferencing (CC). Simply stated, computer conferencing is "direct human–human communication, with the computer acting simply as a transaction router, or providing simple storage and retrieval functions" (Santoro, 1995, p. 14). Regardless of the level of technology used for CC—such as E-mail, mailing lists, MOOs (short for Multiuser, Object-Oriented), MUDs (short for Multiuser Dungeon or Multiuser Dimension), BBSs (bulletin board system), computer conferencing systems, or the Web—certain instructional tasks must be performed for successful learning. It may not create the best learning environment to rely solely on CC. But used alone or in conjunction with other media, such as audio conferencing, classroom delivery, or printed materials, CC can be used to provide an effective instructional system.

Types of Interaction in Learning

In essence, learning involves two types of interaction: interaction with content and interpersonal interaction (i.e., interaction with other people). Both are critical in many types of learning. As an educator designs a course that is to promote higher order learning—such as analysis, synthesis, and evaluation—rather than rote memorization, it becomes important to provide an environment in which both kinds of interaction can occur. Technology available today, like CC, allows interaction with and about the content. In the past, while this interpersonal interaction has occurred almost solely between instructor and student in distance education, it is increasingly possible for students to interact with one another, even when geographically separated. Again, different channels of communication can hinder or facilitate interpersonal interaction and interaction with content. It is a combination of technologies and media that provide an environment rich in various opportunities for interaction that the designer can use, provided the strengths and limitations of each are taken into consideration.

Interpersonal interaction doesn't necessarily require real-time (synchronous) communication. Therefore, interaction among instructor and students can be independent of time and place. Designers of on-line instruction need to be aware that the higher the content density of the materials to be learned, the more self-pacing is the responsibility of the learner. High-density content may be better delivered via recorded media such as printed text, videotape, or on a Web site—all of which can be revisited by the learner at his or her convenience and individual pace.

The Role of the Instructor When Teaching
in the CC Environment

Clearly the most important role of the on-line instructor is to model effective teaching and accept "the responsibility of keeping discussions on track, contributing special knowledge and insights, weaving together various discussion threads and course components, and maintaining group harmony" (Rohfeld & Hiemstra, 1995, p. 91).

There are many necessary conditions for successful on-line tutoring, which have been categorized into the following four areas (Berge, 1995): pedagogical, social, managerial, and technical. Not all of these roles need to be carried out in their entirety by the same person. In fact, it may be rare that they are. A brief description of those roles follows.

Pedagogical (intellectual; task)—Certainly, some of the most important roles of on-line discussion moderators/tutors revolve around their duties as educational facilitators. The moderator uses questions and probes for student responses that focus discussions on critical concepts, principles, and skills.

Social—Creating a friendly, social environment in which learning is promoted is also essential for successful moderating. This suggests that "promoting human relationships, developing group cohesiveness, maintaining the group as a unit, and in other ways helping members to work together in a mutual cause" are all critical to the success of any conferencing activities.

Managerial (organizational; procedural; administrative)—This role involves setting the agenda for the conference: the objectives of the discussion, the timetable, procedural rules, and decision-making norms. Managing the interactions with strong leadership and direction is considered a sine qua non of successful conferencing.

Technical—The facilitator must make participants comfortable with the system and the software that the conference is using. The ultimate technical goal for the instructor is to make the technology transparent. When this is done, the learner may concentrate on the academic task at hand.

Notes to the Tasks of the On-line Teacher

The overall categories are arbitrarily made by the author. Some tasks are contradictory. There is considerable overlap with some tasks among categories. This is probably because there are issues that cut across two or more categories that make them particularly challenging! For example, if it is said that the mechanics for giving feedback on-line regarding a student essay assignment need to be devised (as oppose to writing on the margins in hard copy, for instance), should this be under pedagogical, technical, administrative, or social issues? A case could be made for each being the appropriate category. The following recommendations come from many sources and much experience. A complete listing of sources can be found in the References and For Further Reading sections of *"The Role of the Online Instructor/Facilitator"* (Berge, 1996a).

Pedagogical Recommendations

Have clear objectives. Participants must believe their on-line interaction is time well spent.

Maintain as much flexibility as you can. Because of the individuality of the learners, courses need to remain flexible and the instructor needs to support this. Rather than presenting an elaborate seminar agenda at the outset and a complex process for students to fulfill, follow the flow of the conversation, while guiding it toward the subject.

Encourage participation. The use of various learning options can stimulate learner participation and interaction—small group discussion, debates, polling activities, dyadic learning partnership exchanges, and one-on-one message exchanges recognizing students' messages are some of the activities to use when encouraging participation.

Maintain a nonauthoritarian style. It is usually better to avoid the "authority figure" role when teaching on-line, especially with adults.

Be objective. Before generalizing to the conference about a contribution, consider such things as the tone and content of the posting, the author and his or her skills, knowledge, and attitudes that you may know about from prior conference postings, and time of the posting in relation to the conference thread.

Don't expect too much. On-line instructors need to be content if two or three well-articulated, major points are communicated in a particular thread of discussion.

Don't rely on off-line materials. Summarize the assigned readings on-line so that the discussion in the CC remains mostly self-contained.

Promote private conversations as well as those in the CC. Design opportunities for private conversations between two or more people who you suspect have similar interests in the content.

Find unifying threads. Instructors can weave several strands of conversation into a summarization that may prompt people to pursue the topic further.

Use simple assignments. Group assignments are appropriate to this media, but an overcomplicated design in them is not.

Make the material relevant. Develop questions and activities for learners that relate to the students' experiences.

Require contributions. In credit courses especially, students can be required to sign on and contribute substantively a certain number of times. With some computer conferencing systems, it is possible and may be appropriate to require a participant to respond to the topic or question under discussion before he or she can access the answers posted by other participants.

Present conflicting opinions. Instructors can draw attention to opposing perspectives, different directions, or conflicting opinions that could lead to debates and peer critiques.

Invite visiting experts. Guest experts may join the conference with students to respond to posted contributions, or so students can ask questions of the visitor.

Don't lecture. Experience strongly suggests that a long, elaborate, logically coherent sequence of comments yields silence. Instead, use open-ended remarks, examples, and weaving to elicit comment and other views.

Request responses. The instructor may ask particular learners for comments on a topic or question, then give them time to respond, for instance, "by tomorrow."

Social Recommendations

Be accepting of lurkers. Recognize that there will be "lurkers" in the conference and they may never participate with comments. Some people learn by listening to others so do not assume learning is not taking place. Both lurkers and any latecomers to the class must be acknowledged and welcomed.

Guard against fear in your conference. Fear of public ridicule often stifles participation in CC. Be gently accepting of students' comments and deal with exceptions off the list.

Watch the use of humor or sarcasm. It may be wise not to use humor or sarcasm due to different cultural and ethnic backgrounds that may be represented on the CC. Using text-based communications, it is especially difficult to construe intent and tone from on-screen text, unless you know the students very well.

Use introductions. The facilitator should encourage the participants to introduce themselves, to help build the sense of community.

Facilitate interactivity. A sense of interactive participation is often promoted by using special introductory techniques, dyadic partnering, and some assignments that facilitate informal discussion among learners.

Praise and model the discussant behavior you seek. Reinforcing and modeling good discussant behaviors, such as by saying, "Thank you" to students who respond effectively on-line, can be helpful to encourage courtesy and interaction.

Do not ignore bad discussant behavior. Request change (privately) in poor discussant behaviors and have a written "netiquette" statement to refer to.

Expect that flames may occur. Participants may breach etiquette and respond with harsh or vulgar language. If this problem should occur, the tutor needs to react and remind people (privately) about computer etiquette.

Managerial Recommendations

Informality. Depending upon the instructional objectives of the course, the instructor may decide that informality should be encouraged. One way to stress the informality of this communication medium is to let people know that perfect grammar and typing are much less important than making their meaning clear. It's simple to edit items that will become part of the group's report later.

Distribute a list of participants. Distribute, or make available to all subscribers to the conference, a list of participants so that private messages can be addressed to individuals and not to the list.

Be responsive. Respond quickly to each contribution. One way of doing this is by posting a personal message to the contributor or by referring to the author's comments in a post to the conference. In some conferences, it is not advisable to respond to each individual contribution, but better to respond to several at once by weaving them together. Experience with the content and students will need to guide the instructor; test different ways to see what works most effectively.

Be patient. Messages sometimes are not acknowledged or responded to for days or weeks by conference participants. Contrast the last recommendation concerning responsiveness with this one: Be prepared to wait several days for comments and responses, and don't rush in to fill every silence with moderator contributions.

Provide for administrative responsibilities. Coordinating and providing information about activities for such things as registration, admissions, student counseling, normal bookstore activities, and many other administrative functions are issues that are often unanticipated by the novice on-line instructor.

Request comments on metacommunications. Request metacommunications by inviting participants to tell how they feel about the course within the conference.

Synchronize and resynchronize. As much as possible, ensure that all students begin in unison and in an organized fashion. Also, periodically design ways that students can "restart" together.

Be mindful of the proportion of instructor contribution to the conference. As a rule, instructors or moderators should contribute from 25 to 50 percent of the on-line material.

Model procedural leadership. The on-line tutor should initiate procedures and stifle frustrating procedural discussions. Change what isn't working, but don't allow the conference to be taken over by discussion of failed procedure rather than content or more useful discussion.

Use private E-mail for prompting as is appropriate for discussion. Using private messages, the facilitator can urge participants to join in the discussion, to initiate debates, and to solicit suggestions.

Be clear. Succinctly and clearly state the conference topic and the expectations for students within the conference. Clarify the topic and expectations throughout the conference proceedings.

Don't overload. The instructor should pace the conference so that the equivalent of about one long post per day is made. If the participants have a lot to contribute, the moderator should contribute less so that the slower students can keep up.

Change misplaced subject headings. Immediately change the subject line on a contribution posted under a wrong discussion heading to the more appropriate one.

Handle tangents appropriately. Return inappropriate digressions to the author or guide the participants back to the original topic.

Vary participants' amount of contribution. If there is a participant who appears overly outspoken, ask that person (privately) to wait a few responses before contributing. Similarly, ask less outspoken individuals to participate more actively.

Student leaders. It is perfectly reasonable to design elements of most on-line instruction so that students could take turns as assistant moderators and lead the discussion. This needs to be determined by the content of the class and the skill, knowledge, and attitude of the students. Again, one instructor does not necessarily need to execute *all* these roles and tasks solely.

Plan preparation time. Instructors find that planning, developing, and distributing course materials requires a substantially greater lead time for preparation than may be anticipated at first.

End the sessions. Decisively end each discussion thread and the conference. Conclude discussions so that they don't drag on after they have served their purpose.

Have experienced instructors. Avoid having a first-time instructor also teach on-line the first time.

Technical Recommendations

Use technical support. Using face-to-face tutorial sessions for novice computer conference participants is recommended, but not always possible. If it is possible, it may be useful to have technical support people available at these sessions, and available to answer E-mailed or telephoned inquiries. Before the conference begins, the instructor should know who is available for technical support that might be needed beyond his or her skills level.

Provide feedback. Provide swift feedback, especially to technical problems.

Develop a study guide. A common reader, study guide, or workbook that addresses both the content and any common technical concerns is important. These could serve as the basis for discussion and provide introductory information, description of course activities, resource materials, and other information about the course components or procedures.

Provide time to learn. Learners need support as they learn and use new software features. Provide adequate time for novice users to be comfortable with the technology before they must participate.

Use new methods of indicating feedback. One needs to develop standards for on-line feedback to students' work, such as how corrections or notes to the author can be accomplished working on-line versus with hard copy.

Promote peer learning. Encourage novice E-mail or E-conference users to work with more experienced peers.

Avoid lecturing. Single contributions should be limited to no more than two screens. Longer postings are hard to read on-screen, become tedious, and impede discussion. If lecture is in order, it is better to send the lecture separately as a reading, either electronically to be downloaded, or by mail.

Limit direction. It is important to not give too much direction. Learners will often rebel if the structural design of the conference is excessive.

Summary

Each computer conference, regardless of the technology that carries it, has a different "feel" about it. What may work in one setting with one group of people may not work in another. Both the teacher and each student are challenged by new roles, functions, and tasks they need to perform (Berge, 1996b). While instructors are asked to more clearly articulate their goals and methods to others in the development team, students are also asked to take more responsibility for their learning. It takes time for student and instructor to develop effective use of technologically mediated instruction, and it takes time for students to learn in this environment.

For instructional situations to be successful, there often needs to be more discussion among the students than the one-way transmission of facts and information from teacher to student generally allows. On-line instructors need to be aware that this can make some students and faculty profoundly uncomfortable. Take positive steps to build both confidence and communicative competence in on-line instruction.

Computer conferencing usually should not be the only medium one uses to create the elements in a learning environment. If your instructional goals and objectives lend themselves to the instructor focusing on the right questions to ask, rather than the right answer to give, then computer conferencing should be given serious consideration as an effective medium for communication within the instructional system being designed.

REFERENCES

Berge, Z. L. 1996a. "The Role of the Online Instructor/Facilitator." [Online.] http://star.ucc.nau.edu/~mauri/moderate/teach_online.html

Berge, Z. L. 1996b. "Changing roles in higher education: Reflecting on technology." *Collaborative Communications Review.* McLean, VA: International Teleconferencing Association. pp. 43–53.

Berge, Z. L. 1995. "Facilitating computer conferencing: Recommendations from the field." *Educational Technology.* 15(1) pp. 22–30.

Feenberg, A. 1986. "Network design: An operating manual for computer conferencing." *IEEE Transactions on Professional Communications,* PC29(1) pp. 2–7, March.

Gulley, H. E. 1968. *Discussion, Conference, and Group Process* (2nd). New York: Holt, Rinehart and Winston, Inc.

Kerr, E. B. 1986. "Electronic leadership: A guide to moderating online conferences." *IEEE Transactions on Professional Communications,* PC29(1) pp. 12–18, March.

McCreary, E. 1990. "Three Behavioral Models for Computer Mediated Communications." In Linda Harasim, ed. *Online Education–Perspectives on a New Environment.* New York: Praeger Publishing.

McMann, G. W. 1994. "The Changing Role of Moderation in Computer Mediated Conferencing." In the *Proceedings of the Distance Learning Research Conference.* San Antonio, TX April 27–29, pp. 159–166.

Paulsen, M. F. 1995. "Moderating Educational Computer Conferences." In Z. L. Berge and M. P. Collins, eds. *Computer-Mediated Communication and the Online Classroom. Volume 3: Distance Learning.* (pp. 81–90) Cresskill, NJ: Hampton Press.

Rohfeld, R. W. and R. Hiemstra. 1995. "Moderating Discussions in the Electronic Classroom." In Z. L. Berge and M. P. Collins, eds. *Computer-Mediated Communication and the Online Classroom. Volume 3: Distance Learning.* (pp. 91–104) Cresskill, NJ: Hampton Press.

Santoro, G. M. 1995. "What Is Computer-Mediated Communication?" In Z. L. Berge and M. P. Collins, eds. *Computer-Mediated Communication and the Online Classroom. Volume 1: Overview and Perspectives.* (pp. 11–28) Cresskill, NJ: Hampton Press.

34

HOW TO DEVELOP
A TRAINING STRATEGY

Susan Barksdale and Teri Lund

Susan Barksdale *is the founder of Front Line Evaluators, a training consulting firm specializing in evaluating training effectiveness. Susan conducts organizational assessments for strategy design, return-on-investment evaluations for performance improvement initiatives, and instructional material audits. She was a contributor to* **The 1997 McGraw-Hill Training and Performance Sourcebook.**

Teri Lund *is a partner in the firm Baldwin & Lund Services, which provides consultation in performance improvement methodologies and develops strategies for training and development within organizations and entities. Teri conducts return-on-investment evaluations and develops evaluation strategies. She also contributed to* **The 1997 McGraw-Hill Training and Performance Sourcebook.** *Susan and Teri have recently formed Strategic Assessment and Evaluation Associates, LLC, a business entity through which they offer licensing agreements for their various methods and tools.*

Contact Information
Susan Barksdale
25 NW 23rd Place, #6 - 412
Portland, OR 97210
503- 223-7721
sbbfle@msn.com

Teri Lund
4534 SW Tarlow Court
Portland, OR 97221
503-245-9020
tlund_bls@msn.com

What strategies should you deploy to ensure that you are aligned with business objectives and provide performance value for your organization? How do you gain management's approval for the programs and services you need to provide? This guide provides a process and tools for developing a training and development strategy for your organization.

Managers who are accountable for providing performance improvement and training development strategies for their organizations are faced with change as never before. Organizations are faced with responding to market demands quickly and efficiently while integrating new technology at an ever-increasing pace. The pervasiveness of technology is forcing everyone who supports or supplies performance improvement opportunities to rethink what is needed, how it should be delivered, the resources needed to support the delivery, and how to identify results.

In today's environment organizations operate on a new set of assumptions, which include:

Employees will support cross-functions. Employees will be trained in a variety of skills that promote integrated business processes, which cut across an organization's functions. This cross-functional approach will ensure quick responses to changing market demands and enable the organization to maintain its competitive advantage.

Delivery methods integrate. The channels, suppliers, and partners through whom organizations deliver products and services are driving the need to integrate parallel processes. Customers drive the value chain and the integration of these processes ensures lower costs, higher satisfaction, and higher quality to the customer. Now training must ensure not only that an employee is fluent in his or her own organization's processes, products, and procedures, but in other companies' as well.

Customized product lines are key to success. No longer can an organization offer one product and compete successfully. Customers demand customization to meet diverse needs without paying a surcharge or penalty. This forces employees to continually identify new methods to deliver a product or service in a multitude of "flavors."

Change is constant. Competitive demand and technology are forcing products to change at an ever-increasing speed. New techniques, technology, and procedures are being discovered daily. In this environment continuous improvement is a requirement and not a "best practice." Employees need methods to continually improve and enhance their current skills and knowledge as well as avail themselves of new technology, processes, products, and services quickly and efficiently.

A worldwide view is critical. Today's work environments and processes are no longer limited to single sites or divisions or global boundaries and, in order to maintain competitive positions and meet business drivers, organizations are constantly looking for ways to improve work practices. Organizations find themselves competing with the best companies in the world. Employees have diverse training needs that reflect differences in culture, language, and sensitivity to local customs.

The Need

The need to provide employees with analytical skills to refine and create new products, services, and processes has become paramount, as has the need to manage day-to-day operations and employees who are expected to produce the products, services, and processes and respond appropriately to the customer. A single strategy or technique for providing training and performance improvement within organizations is no longer workable.

Instead, the training manager must define a set of strategies that outline the performance improvement products, services, methods, and evaluation tools that will provide information delivered just-in-time to a diverse set of employees. Information and learning must be collaborative and up to date. Learners must take the initiative and be provided with the resources to direct their own learning. Instruction must be provided in a manner that allows for learners to access the level of detail and simulations that meet their learning needs. Organizations must have systems to identify when learning has been successful and when additional learning or remedial opportunities are needed.

The Process

To create these performance-driven strategies the following process is recommended:

Step 1: Analyze the business environment. Identify and affirm the business drivers and corresponding performance needs facing the organization.

Step 2: Prioritize the performance needs. Determine which needs to respond to first in order to ensure impact to the organization's business objectives and promote ongoing value.

Step 3: Determine strategies. Outline the products, services, processes, and methods that will need to be in place to meet the performance needs. This includes what will be delivered, how it will be delivered, and the resources needed to ensure delivery on time and within budget.

Step 4: Prioritize resources. Define the resources that will be critical to the delivery of the strategies and when these resources will be needed.

Step 5: Formulate the plan for delivery. Identify the tasks, milestones, time frames, and delivery for implementation of the plan to meet the strategies and resource requirements identified in Steps 3 and 4.

Step 1: Analyze the Business Environment

Identifying the business drivers (such as loss of market share or competition) and/or affirming if they still exist and can be affected by the performance intervention or training solution (if the business drivers are known) is the first step in the process. There are external business drivers and internal business drivers.

External business drivers are forces outside of the organization that trigger change. They include:

✓ *Economic drivers.* Upturns or downturns in the economy. Embargoes or trade restrictions and other "economically driven" situations.

✓ *Human resource drivers.* Shortages of resources or of certain skills. Union demands or contracts. The need for employees to balance family and work relationships.

✓ *Government drivers.* Regulation or deregulation that forces change in competition or the environment as a whole.

✓ *Public perception drivers.* The public's viewpoint of the organization. This may be influenced by press coverage of an event or situation that arose outside of the organization's control.

Internal business drivers are forces within the organization that trigger change. Sometimes internal business drivers are responses to external business drivers. Typically there is a stakeholder for the driver within the organization that increases the importance of creating a performance improvement strategy. These drivers may include:

✓ *Market/customer drivers.* Changes in customer demographics, definition, and needs that place demands on products or change product design. Increased competition or other changes in how the organization views the marketplace in which it competes.

✓ *Technology drivers.* New innovations and technology that create opportunities or needs for change in information keeping and processing.

✓ *Change in system, process, or key policy drivers.* Changes in work processes, systems, or key policies that change employee skill or behavior requirements.

✓ *Shareholder or financial drivers.* Responses to Wall Street or bank demands for higher profits or lower costs reflected on the balance sheet.

An organization initiates business objectives and strategies to respond to the business drivers. For example, if the business driver is Increased Competition, a response may be the need to cut costs in other parts of the organization in order to reduce prices for the customer and undercut the competition.

The performance need defines what individuals need to achieve in order to support the business drivers and corresponding business response. For example, if increasing market share was an identified business driver, the business response is to sell more products within the product family to a customer. The performance need identified is increased product knowledge and recognition of which products within the product family complement each other and are potential prospects for the customer base.

Performance needs usually drive a training program or performance intervention. These same performance needs also define the value to the organization and why the organization should invest in the intervention. It must be kept in mind that not all causes of performance problems are indicative of the need for training or can be solved by training. In our rapidly changing world the problem often is multifaceted and so, then, is the solution. It is important to determine the actual role training has in contributing to the performance results, especially before investing funds for design and development.

To define the performance need it is critical to recognize current skill, knowledge, and behavior levels. If an impact is to be made and measured, there must be a "baseline."

To identify the business drivers and clearly define the performance need, an analysis of the organization's business environment should be conducted. Tool 1 is provided to assist in the design of this analysis. It identifies key business environment questions, the answers to which could be provided by:

✓ Senior Management
✓ Managers or Supervisors
✓ Participants/Employees/Users

These questions can be asked in various formats including interviews, focus groups, and forums.

The information gathered through the analysis will be the basis for the remaining steps of this process.

Step 2: Prioritize the Performance Needs

In Step 2, the needs that must be responded to in order to ensure impact to the organization's business objectives and promote ongoing value must be determined. The information gathered in Step 1 is helpful in prioritizing the performance needs. Key information to prioritize includes:

✓ Definition of Business Drivers
✓ Key Business Strategies
✓ Key Challenges

TOOL 1   KEY BUSINESS ENVIRONMENT QUESTIONS

Business Environment Questions	Organizational Findings
What key challenges face our organization in the future?	
What factors in the business environment are forcing change for our organization?	
What major business strategies will require employee support?	
What skills and knowledge will be required to support those strategies?	
What do you see as our organizational strengths and weaknesses?	
What skills and knowledge does our workforce need to develop to combat these weaknesses? (How critical is it to develop the skill or knowledge in our workforce?)	
What do you see as training's role in meeting current and future knowledge and skill development needs? Who else is accountable?	
How would you measure the success of training in the future?	
By which methods or means should training be delivered to employees? To users? To yourself?	
What constraints do you see impacting training?	
What current skill gaps do you see in our workforce population? What is the evidence?	
In visioning the future of our organization what "future required" skills, knowledge, or behaviors are currently absent or need development in our workplace?	

✓ Audience
✓ Performance Need by Audience
✓ Organizational Strengths
✓ Organizational Weakness

Tool 2 demonstrates how this information can be displayed as a matrix to facilitate the analysis and prioritization of the performance needs.

Using this matrix, six questions are asked to determine the priority of the performance need. These questions each represent one point and are asked for each performance need. For example, the Competition performance need was given a priority 1 assignment as it received a "6," meaning that each question was answered with a yes response.

1. Does the audience represent a sizable population in the organization? (The greater the audience the greater the potential to impact the overall organization's performance.)

2. Does the performance need cut across the organization? (For example, three cross-functional groups have been identified for Cost Management. The opportunity to assist in closing communication gaps and creating consistent processes is greater in this situation.)

3. Do current training products or services exist that could resolve the need? (This is a quick-fix and an easy win.)

4. By correcting the need will multiple business drivers or business strategies be met? (A need that supports multiple business drivers and strategies will be more critical to an organization's long-term survival than other needs.)

5. Is the organization's weakness a key factor in implementing future business visions and strategies? (This is a pay-now or pay-later question. By impacting the weakness, future plans may be implemented earlier which provide long-term opportunities for organizational success.)

6. Will a current organization strength be improved through correcting the performance need? (Best-practice companies continually look for the means to improve their strengths and maintain a competitive edge.)

Once the performance needs have been prioritized, the three or four key performance needs become the foundation for determining the department's strategies.

TOOL 2   ANALYSIS MATRIX

BUSINESS DRIVERS	BUSINESS STRATEGIES	KEY CHALLENGES	AUDIENCE	NEED BY AUDIENCE	STRENGTHS	WEAKNESSES
Competition	Launch new laser product in first quarter	Sales force understanding key benefits	Sales	Benefit identification New strategies to influence customer base	Strong marketing skills Deep customer relationships	Deployment of products Understanding of competition
Cost Management	Reduce product packaging costs so funds can be allocated to R&D	Identify methods to reduce costs	Manufacturing Customer Service Managers/Sups	Innovation Understanding of problem and issue	Considered to be lean and mean	Difficult to cut back further without compromising product lines

Step 3: Determine Strategies

There are four primary goals involved in completing this step:

1. Identifying or clarifying the mission and accountabilities of the organization's training/performance improvement group in the next 1 to 3 years.

2. Outlining the products, services, processes, and methods that will be provided to meet the performance needs.

3. Identifying the resources and methods that will be developed and executed to ensure delivery on time and within budget.

4. Identifying the changes and tactics the group will deploy to ensure training/performance improvement processes and practices will meet current and long-term organization needs.

Tool 3 is provided to assist in determining the strategies that best meet the organization's need.

Once the key strategies are defined, the next task is to document the strategies. The final document will be a marketing tool as well as a road map for the implementation of the overall training/performance improvement strategy. Tool 4 is a sample Table of Contents for you to use in structuring your plan.

Step 4: Prioritize Resources

Once the plan has been accepted by management, the next step in the process is to prioritize the resources that were identified within the plan. Resource prioritization takes into consideration the various strategy components and the relationship between the components and three key relationships:

1. The Business Environment
   - ✓ Business Strategies
   - ✓ Business Goals and Objectives
   - ✓ Business Measurement Criteria (Result Indicators)
2. Performance Need
   - ✓ Skill and Knowledge Requirements
   - ✓ Constraints
   - ✓ Long-term Impact
3. Training/Performance Improvement Customers
   - ✓ Demographics
   - ✓ Performance Requirements
   - ✓ Tools, Locations, Resources, Delivery Methods

TOOL 3   DEFINING THE STRATEGIES

Component	Current Environment	Future Need
What is the department's role for: ✓ Training ✓ Education ✓ Employee Development ✓ Organizational Development ✓ Career Development ✓ Performance Improvement ✓ Other:		
What deliverables are you providing or should you provide to the organization for: ✓ Training ✓ Education ✓ Employee Development ✓ Organizational Development ✓ Career Development ✓ Performance Improvement ✓ Other:		
Which parties are accountable for training and performance improvement?		
What are the accountable parties, roles in training and performance improvement?		
Where does/can training and performance improvement make the biggest business impact on the organization, and how?		
Which products/services are most important to your clients? Why?		
What products/services need to be developed and why?		
What delivery methods support or will support the products and services?		
What delivery methods will or should you support? ✓ Classroom ✓ EPSS ✓ Laboratory ✓ CBT ✓ Internet/Intranet ✓ Multimedia ✓ Satellite/Company TV ✓ University Concept ✓ Library ✓ Self-study (Paper-based)		

Component	Current Environment	Future Need
What are your customers' delivery needs?		
What can or should be outsourced? Why?		
How do your products/service contribute to the business strategies?		
What processes and procedures support the department's deliverables?		
Which of the processes need to change, and how?		
What improvements are needed for processes or procedures within the department, and why?		
Which business strategies have the greatest impact on the department, and why?		
What is the department's greatest strength?		
What is the department's biggest weakness?		
What resources are required for the following components within the department? ✓ Delivery ✓ Instructional Design ✓ Technology ✓ Evaluation ✓ Assessment ✓ Organizational Development ✓ Consultation ✓ Management		
What are the key measures of success for the department?		

TOOL 4 STRATEGIC PLAN TABLE OF CONTENTS

Training and Performance Improvement Strategic Plan
Table of Contents

Executive Summary
✓ Key Business Drivers
✓ Key Business Strategies
✓ Challenges for the Future
✓ Summary of Current Environment
✓ Strategic Assumptions for the Future
✓ Strategic Actions and Response to Performance Needs
✓ Performance Indicators for the Future

Training and Performance Improvement Charter
✓ Mission Statement
✓ Guiding Principles
✓ Action Plans

Current Environment
✓ Current Strategies
✓ Current Resources
✓ Current Strengths
✓ Current Improvement Areas
✓ Key Customers and Identified Needs
✓ Results Compared to Performance Indicators

Quantitative Plan
✓ Identified Performance Needs
✓ Linkage of Performance Needs to Business Drivers and Strategies
✓ Delivery Strategies
✓ Product and Service Strategies
✓ Technology Strategies
✓ Resource Needs to Support the Strategies

Key Performance Indicators
✓ Evaluation Techniques
✓ Expected Results
✓ Metrics and Measures to Indicate Business Value of Strategies
✓ Key Performance Measures
✓ Financial Accountabilities
✓ Planning, Priorities, and Accountability Process

Resource Requirements
✓ Staffing
✓ Equipment/Technology
✓ Capital Budget
✓ Expense Budget

It is important to identify where these relationships and components overlap and prioritize resources accordingly.

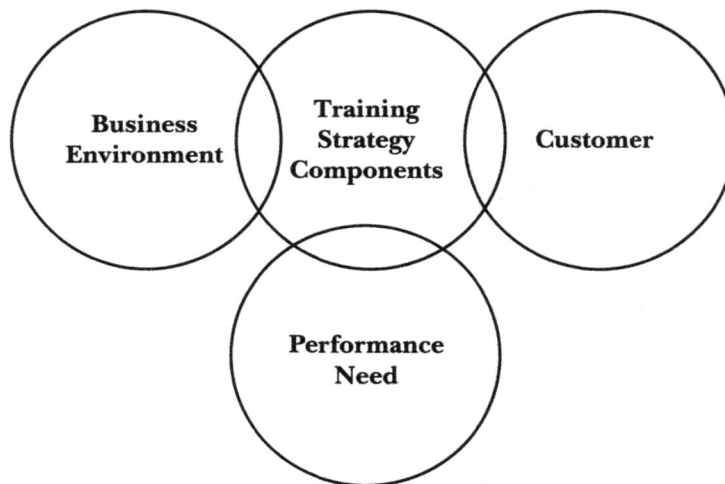

Figure 34-1. Resource Prioritization by Relationship Overlap

The availability and commitment of the resources that have common relationships are of the highest priority because they can ensure the plan is implemented successfully and on time. Identifying these resources prior to implementation of the plan will ensure that the strategy will be implemented on time and meet the key performance indicators. These resources are critical to the achievement of desired results that create business value.

Step 5: Formulate the Plan for Delivery

The final step defines the tasks, milestones, time frames, and delivery for implementation of the plan to meet the strategies and resource requirements identified in Steps 3 and 4. The final tool presented in this guide outlines the key issues to consider prior to finalizing the implementation plan.

Conclusion

Identification and publication of a training strategy will help everyone in your organization understand the role of training and performance improvement and respond to individual accountabilities. Aligning your strategy with the key business strategies and performance needs helps gain commitment and management recognition of the value your department provides to the organization in the short and long term.

TOOL 5   KEY CONSIDERATIONS

1. Have the prioritized resources been identified and has commitment been solidified?

2. Are the training or performance improvement stakeholders in the communication cycle?

3. With which organizational processes does the implementation plan need to align? (For example budget, outsourcing, procurement, etc.)

4. Who will need to be involved in identifying milestones and sign-offs?

5. What tactics need to be deployed (tasks) and who will do it (accountability)?

6. In what order do the strategies need to be implemented?

7. What dependencies have been identified?

8. What additional information needs to be gathered?

9. What are the next steps that need to take place?

REFERENCES

Brinkerhoff, R. 1987. *Achieving Results from Training*. San Francisco: Jossey-Bass.

Hagel, J. and A. Armstrong. 1997. *Net Gain*. Boston: Harvard Business Press.

Hills, M. 1996. *Intranet Business Strategies*. New York: Wiley & Sons.

Kaplan, R. and D. Norton. 1996. *The Balanced Scorecard*. Boston: Harvard Business Press.

Mintzberg, H. 1994. *The Rise and Fall of Strategic Planning*. Boston: Harvard Business Press.

Montgomery, C. and M. Porter. 1991. *Strategy*. Boston: Harvard Business Press.

Robinson, D. and J. Robinson. 1989. *Training for Impact*. San Francisco: Jossey-Bass.

Svenson, R. and M. Rinderer. 1992. *The Training and Development Strategic Plan Workbook*. Englewood Cliffs, NJ: Prentice-Hall.

Willis, B. 1994. *Distance Education Strategies and Tools*. Englewood Cliffs, NJ: Educational Technology Publications.

35

HOW TO DEVELOP SELF-DIRECTED LEARNING MODULES

Sophie Oberstein

Sophie Oberstein *is the founder of Targeted Training Solutions, an instructional design and training consultancy. She is also an instructor in the training certificate program at Mercer County Community College and teaches courses in Human Resources Management in the MBA program at Drexel University. Sophie has published articles in* **Training and Development Magazine** *on keeping participants enthusiastic and has published an* **Info Line** *on designing creative training efforts. Sophie was a contributor to* **The 1997 McGraw-Hill Team and Organization Development Sourcebook.**

Contact Information:

Targeted Training Solutions
1555 Beechnut Circle
Maple Glen, PA 19002
215-619-7929
SOberstein@aol.com

Companies have been exploring alternatives to traditional classroom training for the past several years. While several new options for self-directed learning have been cropping up recently involving new technologies like the Internet or an intranet, one way of conducting self-paced, non-classroom instruction has remained popular. It is the self-directed learning module, or workbook, and its use is still quite common and effective. This guide examines the steps involved in developing such a module.

Why is the self-directed learning module being utilized? It provides a necessary alternative to classroom training, but is not as costly initially as some other options. It allows an individualized approach to learning, but does not require computer literacy or comfort with technology. It can be completed by employees on-the-job, at home, or on an airplane. It can be completed by hundreds of employees at one time. The downside? It is hard to update and maintain.

Several factors contribute to successful self-directed learning modules.

What Goes on the Cover Page

Generally, a cover page should include the following components:

✓ **Introduction**—A few sentences describing what the module is about.

✓ **Objectives**—What will participants who complete the module be able to do or what will they know that they don't know now?

✓ **Recommended completion time**—This should be listed as a range (e.g., 2–4 hours) to promote the self-paced concept. You might wish to mention the time needed to read and complete the module as well as the time needed to try out module concepts on the job or in discussions with the supervisor (e.g., "2–4 hours, plus additional time to research your client company").

✓ **Required materials**—What resources will the participant need to have on hand in order to complete the module (e.g., client contract, pricing schedule, company newsletter)?

✓ **Table of contents.**

Icons

Icons used throughout the module keep it visually appealing and informative. Some common icons to include are:

✓ Hand pointing icon: Read on to find out more about this concept.

✓ Calendar page with *meet with supervisor* written in icon: Before moving on, share your responses or have a discussion with your supervisor.

✓ Book icon: Refer to another module (or another resource) for more information.

✓ Key icon: Sample responses can be found in the module's answer key.

✓ Lightbulb icon: Used to indicate a tip to make answering a question or learning a new concept easier.

✓ Finger with string tied around icon: Used to indicate a key point.

Whatever icons you use, they should be consistent within a module and across all modules in a series.

In addition, when you have any of the following pages in your module, you may wish to create an icon to use on that page: Summary, Test Your Knowledge, Next Steps, Glossary, Resources, or Appendix.

Other Conventions

Let participants know up front any additional conventions that you will be using in the module. For example:

✓ "For the purposes of simplicity, all employees will be referred to as female and all customers will be referred to as male. The matching gender-specific pronouns will be used."

✓ "Acronyms will be used once they have been defined. Acronyms will be printed in bold font and can be looked up in the back of the module."

You may want to create a separate "Getting Started" module to let participants know what icons and conventions will be used throughout a series of modules.

Graphics

A self-directed learning module on paper should be no less visually appealing than a training program on CD-ROM. Wherever possible, include relevant graphics—pictures, copies of forms, decorative borders, etc. Most word processing programs include standard pictures that you can insert. Disks containing additional icons are available at bookstores. For a charge, artists can draw pictures to create visual appeal or to accompany an exercise (e.g., "Which of these two employees is making a good impression based on her appearance?" or "Which of the employees in the picture are providing excellent customer service?")

Content

There is no reason a self-directed learning module can't be as interactive and as fun as classroom training or any other methodology. Too often, workbooks are simply textbooks that do not offer participants any opportunity to practice new skills or to apply their knowledge on the job. When activities are included, they are usually pen and pencil tests with true/false, match-up, and multiple choice items. This does not have to be the case. To keep your module interesting, you might want to include:

✓ **Observations**—Have participants look for the things they've learned in the module on the job. Provide them with a format for note taking.

✓ **Self-assessments**—If observing others doesn't seem feasible, have participants assess their own skills and knowledge.

✓ **Interviews**—Provide interview guides and let participants seek out answers from experienced colleagues.

✓ **Scavenger hunt**—Have participants seek out annual reports, newsletters, organization charts, or mission statements to answer some generic questions.

✓ **Case studies, examples**—Illustrate learning and show participants what's in it for them to master the module's content by providing relevant and realistic case studies and work examples. You might want to include questions on the cases.

✓ **Interactive activities**—Instead of telling participants, for example, that information should be communicated in a logical order, show them what it's like when information isn't presented in a logical order. Have them rearrange it so that it makes sense. Instead of telling participants that industry knowledge is sometimes valued over sales skills, provide them with the "resumes" of two job applicants and let them choose the one they would hire. Instead of listing what questions they should ask a client in a given situation, let participants think about what they want to know and create their own questions. Have them try out their questions on a supervisor or peer.

✓ **Role plays**—Even role plays are possible in a self-directed learning program. You might provide worksheets that ask the participant what they would do in a given situation. The module might then direct them to try out their solutions with a supervisor or colleague.

✓ **Video- or audiotapes**—Depending on the topic of your module and your budget, you can also use the self-directed workbook in conjunction with a video- or audiotape.

Testing

Self-directed programs usually include tests to determine if the participant has successfully mastered the module's content or to allow participants to "place out" of a module. A few things to remember about these tests include:

✓ If the participant does not "pass" the test the first time, there should be a second posttest available. If some time has passed between taking the first and the second test, you can use the same test questions in a different order.

✓ The test should not be the only way to determine whether the participant is familiar with the module contents. A discussion with the supervisor of key points from the module should be part of the evaluation process. This discussion can be formal or informal but the supervisor should have a list of suggested topics and questions for this assessment meeting.

✓ Participants should also be asked to evaluate the self-directed learning program upon completion. It is especially useful to ask whether they found the module to be on the right level for their knowledge and experience and to find out how long the module took to complete.

Answer Keys

Answers to activities should be included in the module so the participant can check his or her answers and move on or repeat a section of the module. Putting answers on the same page or on the following page can enhance the temptation to cheat. Creating an answer key in the back of the module is another way to provide answers. Overall, however, the responsibility for learning in a self-directed program is the participant's, so you don't have to try too hard to conceal answers.

Consistency

In a series of multiple modules, several developers may contribute different modules. It is crucial that someone read all of the modules with an eye toward ensuring consistency and eliminating duplication. Terminology, processes, philosophies, writing style, and variety of activities should all be looked at. Information that occurs in more than one module can be eliminated by using icons that refer readers of one module to the module where the new concept was first introduced.

Supervisor Guides

The term "self-directed learning program" implies that participants can complete training on their own. Your modules should stand alone so that participants can complete them without any interaction, because sometimes supervisors are too busy to support the learning and sometimes there is no supervisor.

However, in an ideal world, self-directed learning is supported by a manager or supervisor. The supervisor should receive copies of the modules the participant is to complete but also a guide that allows him or her to understand what the modules contain without having to read an entire module.

The supervisor's guide should contain:

✓ A cover page identical to the participant's.

✓ A description of the supervisor's role in the self-directed learning process (a sample appears at the end of this article).

✓ A short list of the activities and explanations provided in the module.

✓ A detailed description of each page of the module including the learning point. This detailed summary should include suggestions of when and where the supervisor should check in on the employee or schedule a progress meeting or a discussion of key points.

✓ Module discussion topics and questions.

✓ An answer key.

✓ Answers to the mastery test.

Format

It is easiest for participants to complete self-directed learning modules if they are bound separately. This allows participants to take one module with them wherever they are going. You may want the bound modules to be 3-hole punched so that they can be stored in a binder when completed.

When you have a series of modules, it is usually easiest to send them out all at once, regardless of whether the participant will be completing all modules in the series. This is because it is easier for your training coordinators or administrators to keep track and also because if some modules refer to other modules, the participant will need to be able to refer to them.

When you have a series of modules, it is important to consider what unifying elements they will have and how you will tell them apart. For example, every module might contain the same graphic on the cover but each module might have a stripe of a different color down the side. The supervisor's guide for the module might be printed on a different color paper to distinguish it from the participant materials but to keep it in the same family.

A Final Note

Make sure you put copyright information inside the module's front cover. This will prevent your program from being duplicated by other companies. It may also be necessary, especially when the module's content is sensitive or contains trade secrets, to include the phrase, "for internal use only" on the bottom of each page.

THE SUPERVISOR'S ROLE (SAMPLE PAGE)

The success of this self-directed learning program is up to you. You can ensure that your staff learns through this program and that the learning is relevant and applicable on the job.

To help your team members succeed with this program, you can:

✓ *Provide time for the employee to complete the selected modules.* It is advised that you allow your employee undisturbed time to complete the module. Recommended completion time for the module is listed on the cover of this guide. Times are listed as ranges as the modules are to be completed as quickly or as slowly as the employee needs and desires.

✓ *Provide the employee with the materials necessary to complete the module.* The materials the team member will need for the activities and exercises included in the module are also listed on the cover of this guide.

✓ *Determine with the employee what client account she or he will use to complete the module.* Most of the activities in this self-directed learning program involve applying ideas in the modules at an actual client company. Make sure that the employee has an appropriate client account in mind as she or he goes through the module.

✓ *Guide the employee through the exercises, activities, and learning contained in the module.* Throughout the section of this guide entitled "The module in detail," there are tips to help you know when to meet with the employee and what to discuss or review.

✓ *Ensure the employee has mastered the module's key points.* This includes reviewing the employee's answers to the "Test your knowledge" section at the end of the module as well as using the discussion topics and questions in this supervisor's guide to assess his or her knowledge of the module's content.

More experienced employees may wish to complete the "Test your knowledge" section before reading the entire module. Even if she or he passes the test the first time, it is important for you to use the discussion topics and questions from the module with this employee. She or he may be missing out on something from the module when placing out of it.

✓ *Complete the module assessment form with the employee.* Your employee cannot be certified in the self-directed learning program without completing and sending in to Training & Development a completed assessment form for each module in the program. The forms ask you and the employee to assess the employee's mastery of the module's objectives after completing the module. The assessment form also asks questions to help Training & Development improve the modules for future program participants.

36

HOW TO DESIGN A WORKSHOP

Niela Miller

Niela Miller *founded People * Systems Potential to help individuals and organizations fulfill their potential as well-functioning systems with the capacity for learning, growth, and change. She provides a variety of consulting and training services aimed at the "people skills" side of life and offers both public and on-site workshops and seminars in personal and professional development, as well as experiential and expressive coaching for individuals and groups.*

Contact Information:

P.O. Box 132
Nagog Woods, MA 01718
508-264-4565
NielaM@aol.com

Designing a learning experience for adults requires a specific set of skills that are separate from the subject matter being taught. This guide will help you design your workshop so that the adult learner will get the most out of his or her learning experience.

The general principles in the design process are:

1. In adult education, learners are the ones primarily responsible for their learning and the facilitator is a guide in acquiring the skills needed.
2. Good learning design is based on experience, is flexible, is balanced between structure and flow, is interactive, and pays attention to the whole person (physical, emotional, intellectual, and spiritual).
3. Satisfying adult learning experiences generally take place in a supportive, relaxed, informal atmosphere.

Step 1. Find Out What Attendees Need and Expect

In order to match your design with the learning needs of your attendees, you must have some basic information that will help you to gear your exercises, input, and sequencing to your learners. You should get this information prior to the workshop. If you aren't able to do that, here are some things you can do.

Large Group Activity

Choose some categories to respond to with a show of hands. Find out whether there are exceptions. In this way, visible data is available to all and attendees with common interests can identify each other.

Example: "How many of you are currently running meetings? How many of you would like to?" "How many of you are from corporate settings? Non-profit organizations?" "Who else is here and not covered by these categories?" "Call out some typical problem areas for us to look at."

Small Group Activity

Ask attendees to introduce themselves and make a brief statement about what they want out of the workshop. You might ask them to mention what specific areas of interest they have in the workshop topic.

Step 2. Convey Your Goals and Plans for the Workshop

You cannot successfully design a workshop unless you have goals that are clear and realistically based on the needs of attendees, the requirements of the situation, and the time permitted. By sharing your intentions, you give attendees a chance to adjust their expectations or to influence your plan, so that the experience is mutually satisfying.

Activity

Share your goals for the workshop. Let attendees know what they can expect from you and what you expect from them. If certain plans are inflexible, let them know. Also tell them how Step 1 has influenced your design.

Step 3. Present Group Building and Support Exercises

To establish an atmosphere of cooperation, trust, respect, and ease, it is often necessary to help attendees become acquainted and share some feelings and data about themselves and their experience with the subject matter. More learning can take place when people recognize each other as potential resources and are relaxed. You might want to use one of the following.

Large Group Activity

Ask attendees to form small groups of four to six. These can be random or based on common interest. If it doesn't matter to you, give them the choice. These can be "home groups" to which they return periodically to share tasks, feelings, ideas, etc.

Small Group Activity

Provide the opportunity for sharing first impressions, questions, feelings, and introductions.

Step 4. Present the Initial Experience

The initial experience helps in several ways:

- ✓ It involves the attendee on a personal level, which creates interest in what is to follow.
- ✓ You begin to establish some norms for working toward the goals of the workshop.
- ✓ The participants begin to discover their inner resources and to take responsibility for their learning.
- ✓ Some ideas may begin to form that are applicable for later learning.

Activity

Give the attendees something to do that taps into their personal experience, is related to the subject matter in some way, and is shareable with others.

Step 5. Share the Experience with the Total Group

Here you begin to establish yourself in your role of educator, as well as facilitator of a process. You stress what is relevant in light of your goals. You also establish the opportunity for attendees to begin to learn from each others' experiences and to see the value of personal experience for learning. You help attendees focus on the important elements of the workshop.

Activity

Bring the whole group together. Ask them to share what was important to them or what they learned from this initial experience.

Step 6. Proceed with the Main Body of the Workshop

You are now ready to fulfill your learning goals with an appropriate activity, while attending to the stated needs of attendees to which you have agreed to respond. In other words, you are carrying out your contract.

Principles

- ✓ Good workshops allow for flexibility and change.
- ✓ Both the facilitator's and the attendees' needs must be taken into account.

✓ Learning takes place best in a supportive, relaxed, open atmosphere suited to the age and experience of the attendees.

✓ Learners can take a lot of responsibility for their learning if they are helped with the skills for learning.

✓ Learners usually learn more from doing than from listening or watching. Include all three if possible.

✓ Good learning is interactive, not just between facilitator and attendees, but among attendees.

✓ Learners need time to reflect and assimilate.

✓ A balance should be provided between stillness and activity, structure and flow, providing information (teaching) and bringing forth material from attendees (educating), thinking and feeling.

✓ Evaluation and feedback are essential parts of the learning experience.

Activity

The activity should be based on what came out of the initial experience. The facilitator might demonstrate the skill and then ask the attendees to practice in pairs and give feedback to each other. Next have them repeat the exercise with someone else, then share their learning with the large group and evaluate.

Step 7. Give and Receive Feedback and Evaluation

It is important now to tie together the experiences of the workshop and to draw out the learning that has taken place. It is also necessary to know how the process has worked for attendees, what remains unclear, what helped or hindered learning, so that you can respond appropriately with either more information, more practice, more sharing time, etc. to fulfill the goals of the workshop.

Activity

Find out what attendees have learned about the subject that they either did not know or were not clear about before, and what value it has for them. Encourage them to evaluate the workshop and your performance in light of the stated goals. Attendees might also want feedback from you and each other.

Step 8. Option: Build on Prior Learning

If time permits, it's a good idea to strengthen and solidify what has been learned thus far in the workshop. It also provides an opportunity for attendees to take more responsibility to further their own learning experience and to use each other as resources.

Activity

Send attendees back to "home groups" to try out ideas they have for further practice and experience in the areas of learning they need to strengthen. Each person in the group can receive feedback and ideas from the others as well.

Step 9. Complete Unfinished Business

When you leave, both you and the attendees should feel that you can say goodbye to this experience satisfied that you've done what you could to achieve the stated goals and to express reactions to the experience. This is also the time to summarize what has been learned and its value to all, in addition to whatever possibilities exist for next steps or additional learning in this subject matter or related areas.

Activity

1. Fulfillment of learning objectives

   Ask attendees to summarize what they've learned in short phrases or words. Write these on flip charts. Relate them to stated goals and whether the goals have been fulfilled or not.

2. Applications

   Ask how attendees will make use of what they have learned both professionally and personally.

3. Problems

   Find out what is still unclear or needs more work. You won't have time to do anything about it now, but at least participants have time to make explicit statements or ask questions, which will help them figure out how to fill in the gaps later.

4. Responses to workshop design and facilitator

   In Step 7, the emphasis in the feedback was on the particular learning that was taking place, plus an interim check-in about how the workshop was going. Now you want to get more substantial feedback about attendees' thoughts and feelings on any aspect of the workshop. This helps them to leave the experience feeling more finished and it helps you improve your design next time.

37

HOW TO MAKE A C.A.S.E. FOR PROBLEM-BASED LEARNING

Rick Rogers

Rick H. Rogers *is manager of compliance training for Astra USA, Inc., a manufacturer of ethical pharmaceuticals, as well as an adjunct professor of management at Bentley College. Rick has over 23 years of experience in writing and presenting technical and management programs. He is a past president of the Bio-Pharmaceutical Education and Training Association (B.E.T.A.) in New England, chairs the PDA's international interest group on training, was a contributor to* **The 1996 McGraw-Hill Training and Performance Sourcebook,** *and is a past winner of the PDA's Eddy Award.*

Contact Information:

Astra USA Inc.
50 Otis Street
Westborough, MA 01581-4500
508-366-1100 X2811
rhrccarc@tiac.net
www.tiac.net/users/rhrccarc

This guide lays out models for both the design and delivery of cases used in a problem-based application of learning.

Have you ever bemoaned the situation when your students go back to their work sites and cannot successfully perform what you have just spent megabucks trying to teach them to do? Remember that a trainer *does not* get paid to deliver training. A trainer gets paid for what the participants are able to do back on the job after they *finish* with training. Among the tools trainers have to assist the participant in this learning transfer is one that is far too often overlooked: the case. This is also referred to as problem-based learning.

The power of the case as an instructional design tool is really quite simple. It is a form of role play. With a case, the instructor puts learners in a situation in which they simulate the cognitive and verbal tools they will be required to use in the "real world." When this is done publicly, as in a classroom setting, the dissonance created by the role play creates powerful reinforcers for the participants' new behavior.

Problem-based learning can be as simple as one sentence, or as complicated as a long case. Its power lies in its ability to simulate situations students will actually encounter and give them the practice to skillfully face the real situations later. The present guide presents two models. The first lays out how to design a case, and the second suggests how to skillfully facilitate a case.

C.A.S.E. Design

The purpose of the case is to simulate a situation the learners will actually face, to give them the opportunity to apply the tools presented in class, and to present the learners with a problem to solve or a decision to make. The keys to designing a successful case are straightforward. (See Figure 37-1.)

1. *Contextual Learning.* Adults learn best when they feel they control their own learning, when they can apply the content of the training session to a problem or situation of their own design and current needs. Many otherwise competent training sessions fail to allow the participant to experiment with the content of the training session in the context of a situation relevant to the material. An example of this problem is in the academic environment, where students complain that tests "are too hard." The tests are not really too hard. The students just have trouble remembering in the test-taking environment material that was learned in the classroom environment. The context is different. The students have trouble applying what they have learned to questions on the exam. In the training situation, this is devastating.

   The first step, then, is to design the case in the context of the participants' own job setting. Make it a real problem, one that they are likely to encounter in their everyday schedule. Make it a case that fits their needs *today,* and that looks and feels just like the situation you want them to apply the content in tomorrow.

   Example: *A technical training session for computer repair technicians could present a case in the form of a simulated "customer service request" wherein a repair request was received from a customer. The request could*

How to <u>Design</u> Your C.A.S.E.

C.   **CONTEXTUAL** learning

A.   **ACTIVATION** of prior knowledge

S.   **SPECIFICITY** in encoding

E.   **ELABORATION**

Figure 37-1

set out the customer's description of the symptoms, efforts to correct the situation, and list of error messages.

From these data the student technicians would have to apply the problem-solving skills presented in the workshop in order to work toward identifying the cause of the problem and a likely solution. The "assignment" for the case could be a series of questions the technician would ask the customer in order to uncover the most likely cause of the problem, and what the technician's possible response would be to each question.

2. *Activation of Prior Knowledge.* One of the biggest differences between adult and child learners is the level of experience they bring to the learning situation. The child's experience is understandably limited, while the adult brings a rich texture of prior knowledge. The case design should take advantage of four aspects of the adult learner's prior knowledge.

First: Make sure the case is framed in the context of the concepts that need to be grasped. Make the students *use* the skill points developed in the course.

Example: *Radiation safety training: A case could place the participant in the situation of a supervisor at a nuclear reactor faced with assigning workers to move and store radioactive materials just received at the plant.*

Second: The case should set out some kind of problem-solving situation. The goal is not just analysis, but to make a decision, to take action using the tools from the session.

Example: *A class of bank branch managers have a loan application on the desk. Approval of the application is not clear-cut. The managers must use the approval decision matrix just taught them to recommend approval or rejection.*

Third: Make the case as concrete as possible. Pie-in-the-sky situations are great for brainstorming sessions, but do little for giving participants the opportunity to apply their newfound skills.

Example: *Medical students facing their surgical residency can be given real case histories and asked to diagnose the patients and recommend a course of surgery, under an experienced surgeon's guidance.*

Fourth: The complexity of the case should match both the skills being taught and the skill level of the students.

Example: *In the surgical resident situation above, residents are learning very delicate and complicated skills. They are also in the fifth or sixth year of medical training, and have already received quite a bit of education. Case assignments don't have to be long, but will likely be complex and require considerable skill. In contrast, a case used to illustrate equipment start-up procedures for new forklift operators will likely be uncomplicated and straightforward.*

3. *Specificity in Encoding.* Case designs must have a close resemblance to problems and situations the participants will actually face as they apply their new skills. The case can be fictional, but must

represent real decisions. Four steps can help in achieving the correct specificity. Pick situations:

✓ that the students will face most frequently;

✓ with the most potentially serious outcomes;

✓ at the extremes, the most urgent problems or most life-threatening situations;

✓ that are frequently handled poorly by practitioners.

Example: *Flight scenarios for pilot training should obviously include the most threatening situations, such as loss of power or loss of controls on the aircraft. Force your business students to deal with the situation in which their company is on the brink of financial disaster. Drill psychologists with the extremes of human behavior.*

4. *Elaboration.* Remember that cases work because they are a form of role play. As with any role play, the more active the individual's participation, the more dissonance they will experience, and the more behavior change one should expect. The better case designs will find more than one way to make the students elaborate on their participation, such as:

✓ answering questions (on paper and in class);

✓ taking notes, completing diagrams;

✓ discussing subject matter in class (and outside of class);

✓ teaching others;

✓ writing summaries of the case;

✓ presenting and defending recommendations.

Example: *My favorite elaboration has long been the unexpected presentation, a kind of simulation. This can be done formally by assigning roles to defend during the following class. It is also a powerful tool used informally, and unexpectedly. Lead the class up to an important issue, then point to one student and say something like, "Okay, John, let's assume* **you** *are the manager (physician, pilot, bank teller, etc.) in this case. Turn to Mary next to you and tell her what you would say to Mr. Smith when…."*

C.A.S.E. Delivery

Experience recommends that the discussion of cases, particularly longer ones, is best facilitated using a "funnel" questioning sequence (see Figure 37-2).

Start the discussion with a series of open-ended questions to generate discussion and provide a platform for the application of class materials. As the discussion develops, the facilitator gradually guides the students toward the crux of the case. The crux of the case can be whatever decision or action the facilitator wants to illustrate.

Four Keys to Delivery

This method of case delivery has proven very effective if the facilitator keeps four key suggestions in mind. (See Figure 37-3.)

Case Facilitation Sequence

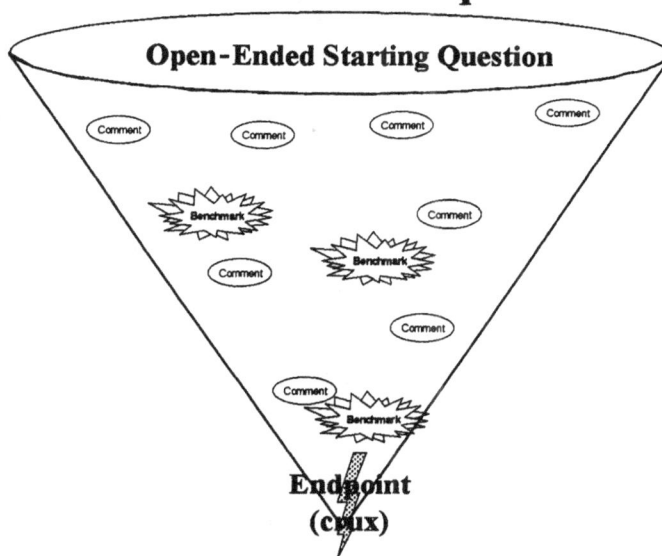

Figure 37-2

1. *Capture Benchmarks.* Important points will be offered up by the class during the case discussion. Comments that are central or critical to the endpoint (crux) sought can be thought of as benchmarks. When these benchmark comments are presented:

   ✓ Reinforce the participant offering them up.

   ✓ Refer back to them and their authors as reinforcers during the discussion.

   ✓ Mention them and their authors in the summary.

   Example: *"Good point, John. (Then to the class.) Do all of you see how John's comment (relates to the theory being taught in the case)?"*

2. *Anxiety: <u>Don't</u>.* One of the advantages of the case method is that the participants have done a great deal of work in coming to their solution to the problem. Keep in mind that in better cases there is frequently no one, absolutely correct response. The purpose of

---

How to <u>Deliver</u> Your C.A.S.E.

C.   CAPTURE benchmarks

A.   ANXIETY: Don't

S.   SKILL PRACTICE mentally

E.   ENDPOINT

Figure 37-3

the case is to apply the tools from the session to a real situation, not necessarily to get to a particular answer.

Realize that the instructor really doesn't know exactly what is going to happen during the discussion. All the instructor knows for sure is where the discussion will end up (see Endpoint, below), not where the discussion is going to go. All that are really needed are:

✓ facilitation skills, principally the skills of positive reinforcement and questioning to keep the discussion going, and

✓ benchmarking (from above) to tie the discussion together.

Example: *A few years ago I was asked to substitute in a Business Policy class for a professor who was ill. I was told that the case scheduled for this session was the "Head Ski" case.*

By way of background, Business Policy is a capstone business course typically taken by business majors during their final semester before graduating. The students must put in considerable preparation before coming to class to discuss a new case each week. Further, the "Head Ski" case is a classic, and has been used, probably, by every Business Policy teacher in the last 20 years. I have taught it myself literally hundreds of times.

On the appointed day I met the class, briefly set out the reason for their professor's absence, and began discussion of "Head Ski." My first (open-ended) question was something like, "Okay, who wants to lay out the basic problem presented in the Head Ski case?" A student in the first row quickly raised his hand.

To my horror the student said, "We did Head Ski last week. This week we were assigned Ajax Widgets!"

I had been given the wrong case assignment! Not only had I not prepared for "Ajax Widgets," I had never even heard of the case.

One could consider this a perfect example of an opportunity for the instructor to experience what might be described as "some level of anxiety."

Without hesitating I replied, "Oh, yes! Ajax Widgets. Great case. Okay," pointing to the young man who had so unknowingly wrecked my morning, "why don't you summarize for the class the strategic points you think the author was trying to lay out for you in this case." This is a classic opener for the funnel questioning sequence described above. In fact, it might have been the question I would have asked had I actually prepared for the case.

I reinforced the young man's contribution, and the class moved the discussion forward in nice fashion. I benchmarked a number of significant points as they came up, and 90 minutes later I led the class into an improved understanding of a key strategic skill they had identified during their discussions. Whether this is the skill point the case author had in mind, I haven't a clue. I've never used the case again.

The crux of this example is of course that the students were well prepared. What's important is the role play dissonance created in the students, not the instructor's anxiety.

The role of a facilitator in a problem-based learning situation is that of a coach, a guide, a resource to help the students apply their skills and learn for themselves. The facilitator may need to guide the discussion if the group gets off track or begins to spend too much time on one point. However, in a well-prepared class the facilitator's job will largely be to get the group going, and then stay out of the way! One can often facilitate a case discussion quite nicely while sitting in the back row, not saying a word.

3. *Skill Practice Mentally.* As pointed out above, most case discussions will start without an exact picture of what is going to happen during the discussion. The facilitator will, however, have a general idea of the key points that are likely to come up, and of the crux, the "ah-ha," that is the goal of the case. This is enough to allow mental role play in preparation for facilitation.

Some instructors will go so far as to stand in front of a mirror and practice their gestures and body language for a case discussion. For others it is enough to run through the key benchmarks in their minds, playing out possible responses to questions and how they might handle the closing. For a brand new case the facilitator can do this while preparing class notes. Once prepared, the facilitator can rehearse in the car on the way to class.

What parts of the discussion should the facilitator role play mentally? Not the whole session. Remember that the actual discussion is unpredictable anyhow. At a minimum it is recommended to role play the very beginning of the discussion (the opener), the very end (the "ah-ha"), and most of the key benchmarks expected during the discussion.

Example #1: *What is the <u>first question</u> you ask? It should:*

✓ *be open-ended enough to allow a wide range of remarks;*

✓ *be easy enough to answer so that the discussion will start quickly;*

✓ *somehow tie in to the "ah-ha" you hope to achieve with the case;*

✓ *relate to each of the participants personally.*

ASK: *"How many of you in class have experienced the kind of problem Mr. Jones had in the case? How did that make you feel? Describe the situation for the class."*

Facilitate this question until you have enough discussion points for your purposes, then pick the one point with which you want to continue and ask a follow-up question of its author.

NOTE: Keep a backup opener question ready, just in case the original does not generate the discussion desired.

Example #2: *What is the <u>closing</u> question? This is a question, or sequence of questions, that leads the participants into an understanding of the crux of the case as the instructor wishes to use it. In contrast with the opening question, the closing sequence should:*

✓ *be closed-ended and force the audience into the understanding sought;*

✓ *somehow tie together the several benchmark comments of the discussion;*

✓ *actually be a possible solution to the problem set out by the case;*

✓ *relate to each of the participants personally.*

In order to role play this mentally, start with the last question and work forward about two questions. Such a sequence might look like this:

ASK: *"Will you personally be facing a situation similar to Mr. Jones in the case? Is this a realistic situation? If you actually go back to your job and do (the skill point set out by the case), will you be more effective in your role as a (whatever)? Will this have benefit to you personally with (more money, improved status, saved lives, more effective work group, etc.)?"*

4. *Endpoint.* The most important aspect of delivering a case is to have a clear mental image of the final sequence of the discussion, of where the students should end up, what the central crux of the problem is (at least as the instructor plans to use it). This endpoint should:

✓ be related to the material covered in the class;

✓ relate to the participant personally;

✓ be directly related to something they are doing in their jobs right now.

ASK: *"Let's see a show of hands; how many of you feel more comfortable now in doing (whatever skill it is you have been teaching them)? How many of you <u>will</u> go back and try to do (whatever)? If you <u>do</u> go back to your workplace and do (whatever), are you likely to be (more successful, safer, better prepared, etc.) in your job? Is this likely to result in (some benefit) to you personally?"*

Get to Work!

When the objectives of training include skill building or the application of concepts to real-world situations, the case is a valuable addition to the instructor's design skills. Participants who can relate training to their own situations and practice new skills through the case design will be better able to perform when they get back to their job settings. Isn't *their* performance back on the job what *you* get paid for? If these participants do perform better on the job as the result of your efforts, isn't this likely to be a positive reflection on your skills as a trainer?

Make a **C.A.S.E.** for your problem-based training. It reflects on you!

38

HOW TO TEACH THE CONCEPT OF SINGLE- AND DOUBLE-LOOP LEARNING

Diane Stoy and Jennifer Wild

Diane B. Stoy, Ed.D. *is an assistant professor in the Organization Learning and Development Program at the University of St. Thomas School of Education, St. Paul, Minnesota. Dr. Stoy is an organization development consultant with special interest in teaching action science, performance consulting, and building transnational organizations. The chair of the Southern Minnesota ASTD International Special Interest Group, Diane is an active member of the Organization Development Network, the American Society for Training and Development, the OD Institute, and the Society for International Training, Education, and Research.*

Jennifer L. Wild, Ed.D. *is an adjunct professor at Marymount University in Arlington, Virginia and at George Washington University, Washington, D.C. Dr. Wild is President and CEO of Wild Consulting, a firm focusing on expanding learning organization concepts and skills. Dr. Wild is an experienced behavior scientist and OD practitioner with over 20 years of scholarship in organizational assessment, action science, group dynamics, and consulting in business and education. Jennifer and Diane are coauthoring a new book on teaching and learning action science.*

Contact Information:

Diane Stoy
University of St. Thomas
School of Education
2115 Summit Ave.
CHC #131
St. Paul, MN 55105
612-962-5384
DBSTOY@STTHOMAS.EDU

Jennifer Wild
Wild Consulting
8301 Armetale Lane
Fairfax Station, VA 22039
703-643-1353
104757.1626@compuserve.com

The concept of single- and double-loop learning has been in the literature since 1974 (Argyris and Schon, 1974). Although **The Fifth Discipline** *(Senge, 1990) has stimulated a resurgence of interest, many HRD and OD practitioners struggle with training others to understand and apply these concepts. Successful integration of double-loop learning into an organization's repertoire of skills increases the organization's ability to sustain continual learning. This "how-to" guide, developed from the authors' consulting practices with national and international organizations, provides a step-by-step process for helping others learn and apply these concepts in the workplace.*

Background

Practitioners in HRD and OD often struggle with how to apply important and meaningful *theoretical* concepts within their organizational settings. One concept that has captured the interest of numerous professionals and still remains elusive to many is how to help organizations become "learning organizations," i.e., those organizations that recognize the critical importance of learning to business success and build learning into daily business operations. An important subset of organizational learning is the concept of single- and double-loop learning. Single-loop learning is learning that occurs when one makes an error and corrects it by examining and altering actions, rules, or strategies involved in producing certain consequences. Double-loop learning involves not only an examination of the strategies but also of the values and belief systems that informed those strategies (Argyris, 1993). Single-loop learning can lead to fire fighting and "more of the same" methods that cause organizations to expend resources on solutions that do not work and problems that reoccur. Double-loop learning can lead to *sustained* learning and change.

Key Words and Concepts

✓ *Learning organizations:* organizations that are able to reproduce positive results purposefully, detect and correct error when it surfaces, and continually reflect and evaluate the assumptions upon which organizational actions are based.

✓ *Single-loop learning:* learning that occurs when one makes an error and corrects it by examining and altering actions, rules, or strategies involved in producing certain consequences.

✓ *Double-loop learning:* learning that occurs when one makes an error and corrects it by examining and altering not only actions, rules, or strategies involved in producing certain consequences but also the values and belief systems that informed those strategies.

✓ *Governing value:* the principles, standards, beliefs, or accepted and valued qualities that govern action.

✓ *Action strategy:* the acts, processes, or theories that are used by an individual, in a group, or in an organization.

✓ *Consequences:* the results of action strategies for an individual, group, organization, or system.

Goals

✓ To increase awareness of the concept of single- and double-loop learning.

✓ To recognize the value of incorporating double-loop learning into an organization's culture.

✓ To be able to apply this training in an organizational context.

Preparation and Materials

✓ Write "Why Errors Resurface" on the top of a flip chart page and leave it blank.

✓ Write the 3 flip chart pages for "Sam's Loop Before," as described in the lesson.

✓ Write the 2 flip chart pages for "Sam's Loop After," as described in the lesson.

✓ Write "Consequences After" on the top of a flip chart page and leave it blank.

✓ Provide 1 blank flip chart page and 1 marker for each group of 5 to 6 participants, as described in the lesson.

✓ Provide single- and double-loop *Before* and *After* overheads and handouts (one copy for each participant), as described in the lesson.

1. Prior Knowledge and Experience (15 minutes)

Ask participants to think of a time when they have seen the same error being played out over and over again in a fire fighting or "more of the same" fashion. Have them share the experience with one other person in the group. After a few minutes of sharing, ask the group what they think caused the error to resurface. Write their answers on the "Why Errors Resurface" flip chart.

2. New Knowledge and Information (20 minutes)

(10 minutes)

Divide the large group into smaller discussion groups of 5 to 6. Ask participants to think of a time when they thought that an error was detected and corrected in a lasting way at the individual or organizational level. Ask them to jot down on a sheet of paper their initial thoughts about the differences between an error that is corrected and an error that resurfaces. Ask for the groups to write their responses on the blank flip chart pages. After the small group has had a chance for discussion, ask for volunteers to share their information with the larger group. As each group reports, hang its flip chart up in the room. Look for patterns and themes that emerge from the large group discussion and point out similar responses.

(10 minutes)

Explain the concept of single- and double-loop learning. (See resource list for original works on the process.) Tell the group that we all create action strategies. Action strategies have consequences that are either pleasing or disturbing. When we are unhappy with the consequences of actions we create, we typically rely on single-loop learning to provide us with an alternative action that we hope will provide a different consequence. However, there are governing values that exist, "master programs" or theories that are informing the actions that we create. If we do not examine the master programs, the actions that we create may look dissimilar on the surface; however, since they are ruled by the same governing value, they may create similar consequences, i.e., more of the same, more of the fire fighting approaches that are not effective. In other words, by using single-loop learning processes, we may be creating and recreating the very consequences we hoped to avoid.

3. Modeling and Practice (40 minutes)

(5 minutes)

Tell the group about Sam. Sam is a mid-level manger who has been having difficulty in his job and has called you because he seems to be playing out the same errors over and over and doesn't understand why. Explain to the group that you asked Sam to describe his action strategies to you and this is what Sam said. Provide the following prewritten flip chart for the group:

Action Strategies (Before)

✓ Little direct feedback on performance problems.

✓ Change subject when people disagree.

✓ Highlight and emphasize when things go well.

✓ Blame system or time (not people) when error occurs.

SINGLE-LOOP AND DOUBLE-LOOP LEARNING

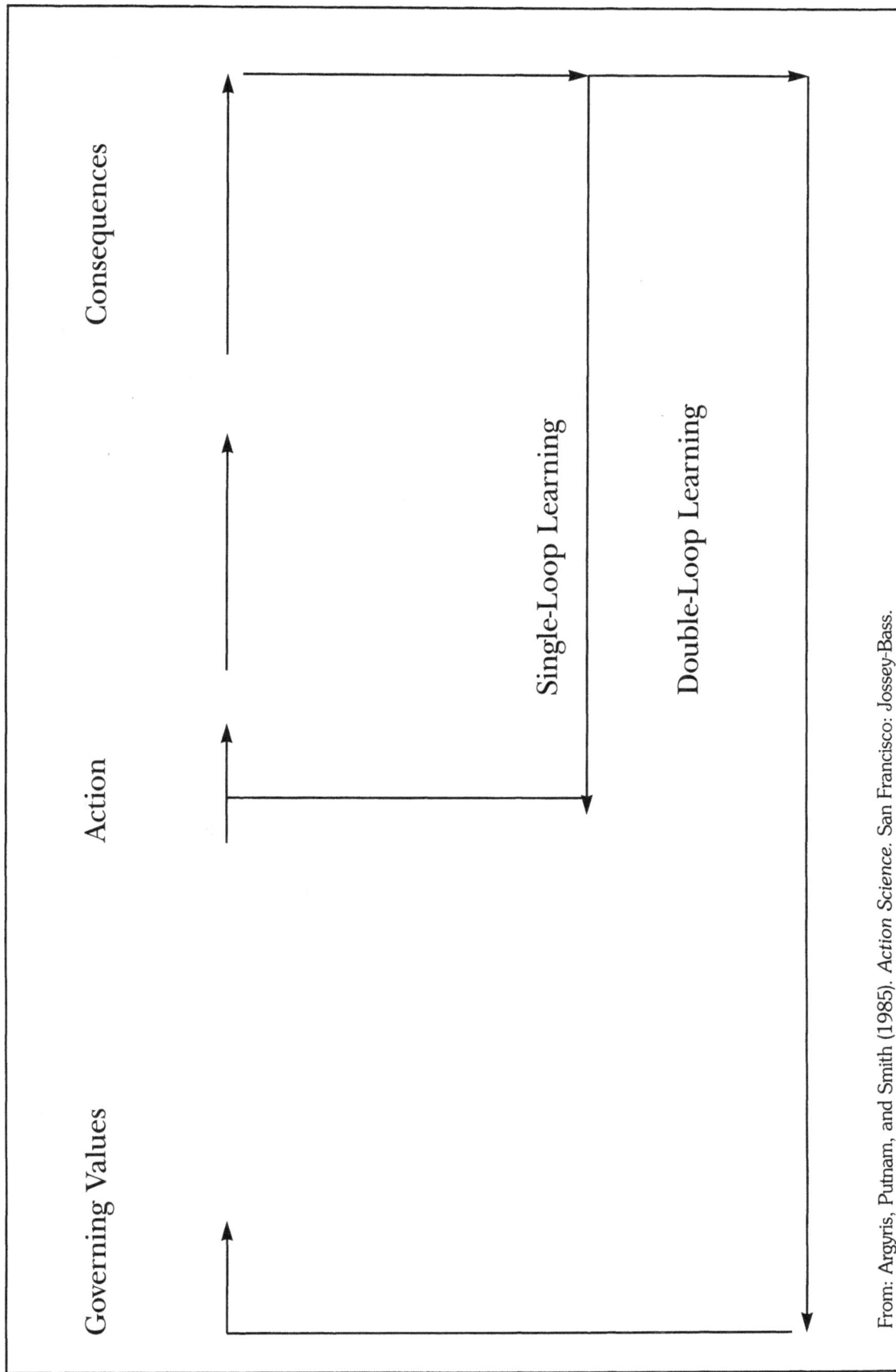

Governing Values   Action   Consequences

Single-Loop Learning

Double-Loop Learning

From: Argyris, Putnam, and Smith (1985). *Action Science.* San Francisco: Jossey-Bass.

(5 minutes)

Explain that you then asked Sam to provide you with the consequences he thought those actions were creating for him. Provide the following prewritten flip chart for the group to see and place this flip chart to the right of the previous one so that the actions lead (left to right) to the consequences:

Consequences (Before)

✓ No change in employee performance.

✓ Frustration that people do not improve.

✓ Status quo of unit performance on all levels.

✓ Mediocre performance rating (self) as a manager.

Explain that even though Sam had attempted to change his actions, the consequences he created did not achieve the desired change. Sam needed to reflect on the governing values that were informing his actions and change those before meaningful sustained change could occur. Have the group meet in their small groups and try to come up with what Sam's governing values might be. When the groups reassemble, have them report some examples.

(5 minutes)

Clarify for the group that Sam had to think carefully and reflect on his governing values because they were so embedded in his very nature. Tell the group that you then asked Sam to provide you with the governing values he thought might be informing his actions. Provide the following prewritten flip chart for the group to see and place it to the right of the action strategy flip chart:

Governing Values (Before)

✓ People are fragile—they hurt easily.

✓ People like those who are nice—I want to be liked.

✓ If you can't say something nice, don't say it at all.

✓ People have difficulty changing.

SAM'S LOOP-BEFORE

Governing Values	Action	Consequences
People are fragile—they hurt easily	Little direct feedback on performance problems	No change in employee performance
People like those who are nice—I want to be liked	Change subject when people disagree	Frustration that people don't improve
If you can't say something nice, don't say it at all	Highlight and emphasize when things go well	Status quo of unit performance on all levels
People have difficulty changing	Blame system or time (not people) when error occurs	Mediocre performance rating (self) as manager

(10 minutes)

Explain to the group that you then worked with Sam to develop different action strategies based on new governing variables. Sam first revised his governing values and came up with new ones that were more congruent with what he actually believed about employees' work and himself. Tell the group that you then asked Sam to provide you with the governing values he created—the ones he would like to see informing his actions. Provide the following prewritten flip chart for the group to see:

Governing Values (After)

✓ People are resilient; they need direct feedback to grow.

✓ Being nice and being direct can occur simultaneously.

✓ It is unfair to withhold information that can help others.

✓ Change is a matter of choice.

(5 minutes)

Explain that these new governing values led to new action strategies. Inform the group that you asked Sam to provide you with the new action strategies he would like to see implemented. Provide the following prewritten flip chart for the group to see:

Action Strategies (After)

✓ Learn the principles of effective feedback and give it regularly—both good and bad.

✓ Be open, but stand your ground—do not change subject when differences occur.

✓ Give people choices (alternatives) and provide them with skills when necessary.

✓ Hold individuals accountable for mistakes and successes.

(10 minutes)

Give the group the following handout and ask them to meet with their small groups and discuss what they believe the new consequences for Sam's behavior might be.

SAM'S LOOP-AFTER

Governing Values	Action	Consequences
People are resilient—they need direct feedback to grow	Give regular feedback (good & bad)	?
Being nice and being direct can occur simultaneously	Stand ground—do not change subject	
It is unfair to withhold information that can help others	Give people choices (alternatives)	
Change is a matter of choice	Hold people accountable for mistakes/success	

After each group has a chance to reflect, ask for groups to report and chart their responses on the prewritten "Consequences" flip chart.

4. Application (20 minutes)

Ask participants to think of the organizational issue they mentioned at the beginning of the session—one that keeps occurring over and over again. In the same paired groups that met at the beginning of the session, ask participants to talk through what might be the governing values influencing the action strategies that recreate unwarranted consequences. Spend 10 minutes for each individual in the pair. Ask for a volunteer pair to share one of their examples.

5. Reflection (20 minutes)

Introduce questions that encourage reflection and application. Have participants meet in their small groups and discuss the following questions. Ask the groups to report back to the large group so all can benefit from each others' thinking.

1. How would an organization benefit from double-loop learning?
2. Who would you engage in this training activity?
3. How would you introduce the need for this training in your organization?
4. How would you advocate for the time needed to conduct this type of training?
5. What next steps would you engage that would improve transfer of learning?
6. What barriers to learning this concept can you identify?
7. How would you overcome them?

RESOURCES

Argyris, C., R. Putnam, and D. Smith. 1985. *Action Science*. San Francisco: Jossey-Bass.

Argyris, C. and D. A. Schon. 1974. *Theory and Practice*. San Francisco: Jossey-Bass.

Argyris, C. 1993. *Knowledge for Action*. San Francisco: Jossey-Bass.

Senge, P. 1990. *The Fifth Discipline*. New York: Doubleday/Currency.

39

HOW TO DEVELOP COLLEGE INTERNSHIPS

Boni Sivi

Bonita Sivi *is a managing partner at Thomas Baker Associates, a full-service training and consulting firm founded in 1986. She worked in high technology organizations in training and organization development for 15 years, starting in engineering training. Earlier, she taught mathematics and computer science at the University of Pittsburgh. She specializes in management and team development and executive coaching. She helps technical people acquire stronger communications and interpersonal skills. She is the 1998 Immediate Past President of the 500-member Central Florida Chapter of the American Society for Training and Development and a contributor to* **The 1997 McGraw-Hill Training and Performance Sourcebook.**

Contact Information:

Thomas Baker Associates
31640 Wekiva River Road # 100
Sorrento, FL 32776
800-300-6738
352-735-1030
tbaker@digital.net

College internships: You're missing out if you don't have them. There's no doubt that well-managed college internship programs can greatly benefit both the organization and the individual students involved in them. In today's fast-paced workplace where the urgent can drive out the important, interns can concentrate with good management on important projects that may be driven out currently by urgent daily crises. You can create a successful internship program by following the ideas in this guide.

Yes, it's true. Just when you have them trained, they leave! College interns, when you first think about it, can be more of a challenge than you might want to take on. But, performance improvement and training and development are what you are all about. Practice will make you good at it.

Six Steps to Developing Internship Programs

To develop an internship program, follow these steps:

1. Sell the idea to your manager.
2. Call universities to begin developing relationships with internship decision makers.
3. Hone your people-development skills.
4. Plan your internship program.
5. Interview possible interns.
6. Follow up carefully with internship requirements.

Step 1: Sell the Idea to Your Manager

Sell the idea of internships to your manager. Be sure the organization you work for will support the concept.

The first objection will probably be, "But what will we pay them with?" It is not necessary to have a paid internship if you choose people from majors in which it is difficult to get a job without experience.

Another objection might be, "But we have no place to put them." In a very crowded organization that was growing fast, two interns did much of their work and research at home and in the university library. When they came to the work site, they used a conference room. This was all explained ahead and the experience worked out very well.

One manager did not believe that interns could accomplish anything and would be in the way. He lost all doubt when he saw the new employee orientation program he wanted seem to appear overnight while regular employees worked on even more important projects.

Plan to select students who may have some difficulty getting into the field they are majoring in. Human Resources and Human Resource Development have been ideal for meeting this requirement. Entry-level students have a difficult time getting a position because employers want at least some experience. Recent job market realities have allowed employers to find employees with experience, thereby excluding recent graduates without experience.

Step 2: Call Universities and Develop Relationships

Contact schools in your area that offer majors in the area in which you work or in closely related majors. Interns can be majoring in disciplines at both the undergraduate and graduate levels in human resources, human resource development, industrial/organizational psychology, business, organizational communication, etc. Talk to professors in the departments. Offer to speak to their classes on subjects in which you have experience that would be of interest when relating the theory of the class to the experiences the students will be having on jobs.

Step 3: Hone Your People-Development Skills

If you work for a larger, well-known organization, you may receive an offer to have an internship immediately. If you work at a smaller organization, you may need to build your credibility as an intern sponsor by speaking to classes over a period of time. It also helps to have educational credentials yourself.

The internship advisor from the school will probably interview you and visit you at your work site. Be as credible as possible. Explain where the interns will be working and sell the resources they will have. Will your manager, who may have more credentials than you, be able to spend some time with them? Do you have an area where they can work? Will they have access to a computer?

Your goal, even at this point, is to establish your organization with you as intern advisor as a desirable place to do an internship. Internships are as good as you make them. Use your skills in managing people. Find out what their needs are and match those needs to the needs of your organization. Establish your internships as a place of learning and creativity, not of drudgery and clerk work.

After you have been approved as an intern site, the university will tell possible interns about you. Interns generally interview with several organizations before making a decision. Always dress professionally and treat them with the respect any job candidate appreciates. Explain what you expect from interns. You can sell the experience that you are offering them.

Once interns accept positions with the organization, meet with them to determine what hours they will be working and what they will be doing.

Step 4: Plan Your Internship Program

When designing an experience for an intern, always consider the following:

a. Allow the intern to select his or her hours within your normal working hours. Especially if you are located more than 20 miles from the school, they may not want to drive at peak traffic times or when they have other classes they may be taking. They may even do some of their work off-site.

b. Allow them flexibility with their schedules so they can take final exams, complete important assignments, and observe school breaks. You may want to allow them to change their schedules so they can attend special employee functions. Always invite interns to organization parties and events as part of their intern time.

c. Emphasize learning about the business end of the organization. Point out how projects are linked to the organization's strategic objectives and intent, financial information, products and markets, and the nature of the business. For their own future it is important that all employees and interns understand as much as they can about the organizations' products and services, the markets, market issues, and other organizational issues that will allow them to see the connection between your strategic goals and what the organization is trying to achieve.

Be sure to address the learning styles of your individual interns. Refer to Kimberly Ishoy's article, "How to Adapt Your Training to Different Learning Styles" in *The 1997 McGraw-Hill Training and Performance Sourcebook*.

d. Have interns pay attention to the financial condition of the company. Help them to learn basic financial information and how to interpret it.

e. Start them with a small project that they can complete from start to finish. Just as with any employee, explain the project thoroughly, and check their understanding. Often a beginning project might be a word processing software application tutorial to get them up to speed on your software. Do not assign clerical work to interns unless you want your organization to be avoided like the plague when interns are deciding where to do their internships. Many interns will choose a non-paid internship over paid internships that have a reputation of giving them meaningless clerk work. Insist, however, that interns are responsible for the clerk work generated by their assigned projects. Refer to Chip Bell's article, "How to Give Great Advice and Feedback" in *The 1997 McGraw-Hill Training and Performance Sourcebook*.

f. Arrange for interns to meet and if possible to work with others who have similar interests—perhaps someone who is a little ahead of them, like an employee who did an internship last year and is now doing an entry level job.

When dealing with interns:

✓ Give them the whole project and expect excellence.

✓ Let them work away from the organizational environment.

✓ Give them the opportunity to attend enjoyable organizational events on internship time.

✓ Be flexible about their hours.

✓ Don't make them do clerk work.

✓ Be sure they meet other interns and employees.

Step 5: Interview Possible Interns

When interns are given your site as a possible internship, it is important to be as encouraging and professional as possible when that first phone call is answered. If it comes in as a voice mail message, be sure to return the call promptly. Consider all the advantages and disadvantages your internship has. Emphasize the advantages: "You'll have your own office area." Deemphasize the disadvantages: "Yes, we are a longer drive from your room at the university, but we work with interns to have them drive at low traffic times."

Continue to emphasize the positive qualities once they are interviewing. Show them around the areas of your company. You may be used to your fitness center, but interns may see it as a great incentive: "Yes, interns can use the fitness center."

Follow up with interns a few days later to find out if they have questions or concerns about doing their internship in your organization.

Step 6: Follow Up with Internship Requirements

Be sure you know the requirements of each school's internship program. Some students are required to keep daily journals. Some must write a paper on their experience. Others must submit projects. Be sure you know the requirements, and then help the student assemble the needed information. Include visuals when possible. They can be a great influence for a better grade, or they can sell your internship program to future attendees who often have access to what was turned in by previous students.

Intern Experiences

What are some of the things you can accomplish using interns?

✓ An intern did a culture survey of the organization.

✓ An intern learned a course by first being a participant in it, then observing it and being debriefed by the instructor, then teaching small parts of it, increasing the percentage taught each time until she could teach the whole thing.

✓ Two interns working together developed a new employee orientation program.

Sometimes certain internships become so popular that the school's intern advisors may call you to say they have more interns than you think you can manage. One semester the university sent four interns: one graduate student and three undergraduates. At first it can be unsettling, but you may remember, for example, the Level Three study you had been wanting to do on your basic supervision course. First, clear it with your manager, who may agree along with you to take the risk and allow interns to evaluate one of your programs. In our case, the graduate student and several university professors designed the study. Under their direction, the three undergraduates performed all of the interviews. A control group was matched with the study group by age, gender, length of time with the organization, length of time in supervision, and other variables. The managers of the participants were also included. The result was an extensive study designed by a team of experts—knowledge and time that was not available in our organization at that time.

Interns can be great to hire as employees. You are very familiar with their skills, work habits, and how they fit into your culture. Many interns go on to become excellent employees of the sponsoring organizations. Others become great resources in professional organizations you volunteer in.

Lynne, while interning, took a job in the organization's supplemental job pool doing all types of fairly unskilled jobs around the fast-growing organization. She learned the business by working in the lowest levels of many departments while she was a student. She was able to obtain a clerical position through which she learned about the engineering of the products. When an opening occurred in Human Resources, she was hired immediately. The company downsized, and she was laid off and took a job for a short time with another company. When an HR professional in the original company quit, she knew the job and was hired immediately at a higher level. The company continued to downsize, but she was the last person to be let go in the Human Resources department, where she had learned everyone's job and gotten extensive experience in all facets of Human Resources. This experience made it easier for Lynne to get another job.

Rick, another intern, was employed by the local community college's grant program located at the company. When the grant ended he was hired as a full-time regular employee at the company.

Another intern was graduating in May, doing her internship in the marketing department her last semester. The marketing department wanted to hire her and had an opening in February. At the risk of losing the requisition, they waited for the intern to graduate in May. Yet three of her marketing major roommates did not have jobs a year later.

One organization's president "volunteered" to employ Marc, an international customer's son, for a summer of "working in the United States." Speaking very little English, Marc was placed in the marketing department. Marketing asked the intern advisor, because of her experience with interns, to see what she could do. She enrolled Marc in an English as a Second Language program at the local community college as close to full time as possible. Then two interns taught him a desktop publishing software application program. Among the three of them they published, on their own, the longest and best employee newsletter the company ever put out. Needless to say, it wasn't long before the marketing department wanted Marc back!

The Downside Is Small

There are some downsides to internships, but with good management, problems can be minimized.

Internships can cause jealously in departments. Naturally the intern advisor gets much of the credit for the work being done. Other professionals might feel threatened by such credit, knowing that you did not really "do" all that work. The solution: Get interns for them, but be sure to train your colleagues extremely well, or you could lose all the credibility you have built up with the school and with the students (who do talk to each other). Unfortunately, some professionals perceive interns as gophers (go for this, go for that) and treat them as such, making interns very frustrated—especially after they heard what a great experience they would have.

Some internships are required by the university program, and you may acquire interns who aren't motivated to get much work done. This is rare, but it can happen.

Since students can be naive and not used to the work environment, it can be important to watch for sexual harassment. In one case the intern advisor found out late in the internship that a young male employee was harassing two female interns. Fortunately it did not result in a lawsuit for the organization, and the employee was disciplined. The interns were reluctant to discuss their problem because they wanted to do well on their internship.

Becky, a conscientious intern, decided at the end of her internship that she was changing her major back to education because she never saw anyone work as hard as her intern advisor did. She thought teaching would be easier. Little did she know that her intern advisor's job teaching in the public schools for years prior to this incident was the hardest job she ever had!

Sometimes interns do not dress appropriately. Speaking frankly at the interview about dress can avoid this problem.

In Summary

Even those of you who work in small consulting firms may be able to have interns. Get started today by calling university departments.

40

HOW TO USE MEETINGWARE AND FACILITATORS FOR EFFECTIVE MEETINGS

Jana Markowitz

Jana Markowitz *is the founder of The Collective Mind, a consulting firm specializing in meeting facilitation, groupware consulting, and management seminars to improve business productivity through collaborative work. Jana lectures in the Executive Masters program at Christian Brothers University Business School and is a contributing author to* **Groupware: Collaborative Strategies for Corporate LANs and Intranets.** *She is a member of the American Society for Training and Development (ASTD), the International Association of Facilitators (IAF), the Organization Development Network (ODN), and the Human Factors and Ergonomics Society (HFES).*

Contact Information:

The Collective Mind
5305 N. Clover Dr.
Memphis, TN 38120
901-682-0830
jmarkowi@odin.cbu.edu

Is your business day a series of long, unproductive meetings? There is technology available to help you have shorter, more effective meetings—meetingware. Read this guide to find out the types of meetings that can benefit from the use of technology. Also, be prepared to prevent the negative effects technology-assisted meetings can produce if not handled correctly.

Meetingware

"Groupware" is any computer software used to support collaborative work. A specific type of groupware known as "meetingware" is used to support team meetings where participants generate ideas, make decisions, or perform other group functions.

Meetingware (also known as an electronic meeting system—EMS, or group decision support system—GDSS) consists of personal computers networked together with one computer for each participant. The meetingware software on the network server and on each participant's PC enables individuals to list ideas, vote, and comment. A facilitator guides the meeting process by posing questions to the group through the software. Participants respond by keying answers on their PCs. Responses scroll across the participants' screens so each person can respond or add comments to others' responses anonymously and simultaneously. The system displays voting results seconds after they are gathered and maintains a complete record of the meeting which is available (via printing or on computer disk) as soon as the meeting ends. Products in this category include Ventana's GroupSystems, McCall, Szerdy and Associates' CA Facilitator, and Eden Systems' Meeting Room.

People who see meetingware for the first time and realize its potential impact on the way they work invariably have a laundry list of questions, including these:

✓ How many people need to be meeting before an EMS and/or facilitator are needed?

✓ How much time will using an EMS save?

✓ What kinds of meetings should I use an EMS for?

✓ What are the advantages of using an EMS over unfacilitated meetings?

✓ What are the disadvantages of using technology to assist meetings?

✓ Can we have meetings from our desks with this (EMS) and not have to meet in a room?

✓ Can we use an EMS to support meetings for people in different time zones and countries?

These are valid questions and like a good consultant my answer to all of them is, "It depends." Since no one (including me) likes that answer, I will try to give generic answers to the questions and clarify them with specific examples from meetings I have run for client organizations.

Guidelines for Using Meetingware and Facilitators

Size of the Meeting

How many people need to be meeting before a facilitator and/or an EMS are needed?

Usually 5 or more people need to be meeting before a facilitator or EMS is useful. In groups of 5 to 20 people turn-taking becomes problematic; a few dominant people will generally take most of the "air time" in a meeting and cliques or factions of 2 to 5 people will start to form. A facilitator (even one who is also a participant) can make sure all the voices are heard, smooth over personality clashes, and keep conflicts and debate constructive. By adding an EMS you allow anonymity, which encourages both candor and participation by those less powerful or less articulate. An EMS also provides automatic documentation of the meeting and instant feedback on votes and decisions.

The business meetings I facilitate have on average 8 to 12 participants. I have had as few as 5 and as many as 25.

Time Savings

How much time will using an EMS save?

Documented cases have shown a 50 to 90 percent savings of time for meetings during the duration of a project (University of Arizona studies on IBM and Boeing). However, I tell clients the meetings will take about the same amount of time as they had planned for an unfacilitated meeting. The technology-assisted meetings actually take less time than traditional meetings, but I say about the same amount of time they planned because most people schedule half or less of the time they would really need to cover the topics in their agendas. Most people are overly optimistic in estimating time for a group to discuss, decide, or come to consensus on a topic. I can generally estimate within 10 minutes' accuracy how long a meeting will take.

You do not have to be psychic to predict actual time needed for a meeting; two factors influence accurate estimation: planning and experience. When using an EMS, the facilitator must know exactly what the meeting initiator needs to "leave the room with" to be successful. Once a facilitator knows this, she or he works backwards to design a process using the EMS tools (brainstorming, idea organization, voting etc.) to take the group through steps leading to the desired outcome (a decision, group consensus, generation of possible solutions, discussion of pros and cons, etc.) In designing the process the facilitator can estimate fairly accurately how long each part will take from experience in previous meetings. These "parts" of the process then add up to a fairly accurate time estimate.

Another reason technology-assisted meetings are not a lot shorter than traditional meetings is that people need to feel they have "discussed" an issue; they need to literally talk about it as well as interacting via computers. My meetings are a balance between leveraging technology to provide meeting efficiency and moderating conversations to meet the psychological need for participants to interact with each other.

Leaving out the "talking" part of a meeting altogether makes participants feel the meeting was "cold, impersonal, and mechanical"; this is not beneficial to the participants or the reputation of the EMS.

So when asked about time savings, I refer instead to the increased quality and detail possible in an EMS-assisted meeting of the same length as the traditional one it supersedes.

Types of Meetings

What kinds of meetings should I use an EMS for?

In meetings of 5 to 20 people an EMS is especially useful if any of these situations exist:

✓ Sensitive issues need to be discussed which participants might be reluctant to talk about openly.

✓ There is an extreme (even violent) difference of opinions among dominant personalities.

✓ Consensus is needed before going forward.

✓ Multiple expertise or perspectives are necessary to make a good decision.

✓ There is a very limited time to collect information from a large group of people.

✓ A very complex decision, based on many criteria, must be made.

✓ The meeting content must be quickly documented and used for desired impact on the organization.

Just as important to know are the kinds of meetings you should **not** use an EMS for:

✓ One-way communication; dissemination of information (instead use E-mail, Lotus Notes, intranets, memos, or videos);

✓ Gatherings designed to showcase an individual's abilities (these are also known as "grandstanding" and are often necessary precursors to promotion); these meeting won't work with the anonymous environment an EMS provides;

✓ Sharing the blame (also known as "getting everyone in the boat with you"). When decisions have already been made and the boss wants to garner the group's approval, an anonymous environment is the last thing he or she needs; all kinds of resistance and "push back" will come out under cover of anonymity.

Advantages over Traditional Meetings

What are the advantages of using an EMS over "traditional" meetings run by the person who called them?

Vendors of EMS's will list the benefits as these:

✓ Fuller participation (with accompanying increase in morale and "buy-in").

✓ Time savings (from parallel input).

✓ More candid information (due to anonymity).

✓ More creative solutions (a function of anonymity and synergy).

✓ Complete documentation at the end of a meeting.

While these are all true, there are also other, more subtle benefits:

✓ Groups seem to go through their "forming" and "storming" developmental stages more quickly.

✓ Participants get used to high levels of participation and continue the behavior in traditional settings.

✓ Because they require detailed premeeting planning, EMS meetings are better focused, flow more smoothly, and produce higher quality results.

✓ Anonymity allows a "face-saving" way for enemies to agree.

Disadvantages of an EMS

What are the disadvantages of using an EMS?

Since I offer facilitated EMS meetings for a living, I would like to think there are no disadvantages, but that's not true. Some of the drawbacks include the following:

✓ A person can leave feeling he or she was "forced" into a decision the group agreed on, but he or she didn't articulate.

✓ People who can't type often feel they have had less opportunity for input than in a traditional meeting.

✓ People who enjoy debate may feel they were denied an opportunity to argue.

✓ People who normally dominate meetings feel "unempowered" by the level playing field anonymity provides. Very fast typists have been known to key in supporting comments to their own suggestions (one person/one vote usually fixes this problem).

✓ A leader may mistakenly feel that letting a group vote on something obligates him or her to accept the decision; unfortunately the leader may have relevant information that the group didn't have that might have changed their decision.

Desktop Meetings

Can we have meetings from our desks with this (EMS) and not have to meet in a room?

Technically there's nothing to stop you from doing this and some people already are. Psychologically there are a myriad of reasons that "distributed" or "same time, different place" meetings can fail.

A lot of the communication that goes on in a room is "paralin-guistic" and "nonlinguistic." Paralinguistic communications include intonation and pauses in speech that communicate beyond the actual words (anger, sarcasm, despair, frustration).

Nonlinguistic communications include eye contact, posture, and gestures that may communicate a meaning completely different from the words being said. Missing these communication cues can change or destroy the meaning of messages being exchanged. These communication cues are also a reason behind having oral discussions to supplement and clarify the computer-entered comments.

There are circumstances where these missing communication cues may not be terribly important; in a group that has worked together for a long time and has a very smooth (almost choreographed) flow of ideas, there may be no problem with conversing strictly via computer interaction from different locations. However, these flawless teams are few and far between.

What about combining an EMS with a telephone conference call or a videoconferencing facility to bring back in some of those non-linguistic and paralinguistic cues? Great idea, and several groups are doing these things as well. Conferencing tools (especially videoconferencing) do address some of the missing cues in communication. However, until we have holographic videoconferencing systems that make us feel the "telepresence" of our remote counterparts, even this technology is a poor second to "being there."

Just as telephones in their 120 years of existence have not obviated the need for face-to-face discussions with associates, no distributed EMS (even with video) can replace a same-time/same-place meeting (but it can make the meeting more effective!)

Across the World Meetings

Can we use an EMS to support meetings for people in different time zones/countries?

Again our technical capabilities outstrip our knowledge of the human mind. There are EMS systems designed for WANs (wide area networks) as well as LANs (local area networks). Many tools exist, or are on the brink of debuting, that take advantage of the Internet's ubiquitous presence and inexpensive access around the world.

The drawbacks for this type of distributed use include all of the "desktop meeting" concerns with additional stumbling blocks of time zone difference, potential culture clash, and language translation, not to mention the issue of who should facilitate and from where. The complexity of communicating in this environment is staggering.

However, if time, money, and business circumstances make it impossible to be physically in the same place, arrange the situation to avoid as many of the predictable problems as you can. No doubt unpredictable problems will pop up to take their places, but you can only plan, hope, and remain flexible.

Some premeeting steps you can take include the following:

✓ Try to be sure participants have met one another at some point prior to this meeting; if this isn't possible, distribute photos and short work or personal biographies. The biographies should describe education and work experience, but also hobbies, interests, family ties, birthplace, etc. These details are exchanged in rapport-building "small talk" at meetings. While it may seem unimportant or irrelevant, it is often what fosters trust among group members and helps them be productive.

✓ Have readily available technical support and a fallback plan for technical failure at each site. If you lose network contact, can a quick phone conference call keep the group going until problems are fixed?

✓ Have a short icebreaker or some sort of warm-up of the group prior to tackling the issues at hand. This relaxes (most) businesspeople and starts communication flowing.

During the Meeting Try To:
✓ Allow ample time for input and discussion; no one likes to be rushed into a decision just because connection time is expensive.

✓ Be sure final content is available to all participants if people are entering information at different times (which is likely in different time zones).

✓ Make sure terms used have been defined—groups often use the same words when talking about different things

After the Meeting You Should:
✓ Encourage groups to maintain ongoing communication via E-mail or telephone, just as they would communicate if co-located by talking in the hallways, eating together etc.

✓ Distribute all meeting documentation of discussions, decisions, etc. for use in ongoing communications as a common reference.

Case Studies

How can we translate these general guidelines into something that relates to the meetings you will have to attend in the next few weeks? Examples go a long way in explaining ideas. These case studies describe situations commonly found in organizations and the aspects of the situation that made it useful to use an EMS and facilitator.

Case 1: FedEx Defines Future IT Employees

Task: Envisioning the future

Situation: The FedEx IT organization (about 3,000 people) was working with the corporate HR department to define the technical skills and personal characteristics needed in IT employees three years in the future.

The situation exhibited these characteristics which made it conducive to the use of an EMS:

✓ Sensitive issues participants were reluctant to talk openly about.

✓ Multiple perspectives/expertise were needed to reach a good decision.

✓ There was limited time to gather information from a large group.

✓ The meeting information needed to be quickly documented and used in order to have the desired impact on the organization.

Process: Brainstorm three-years-from-now headlines in *ComputerWorld* regarding the FedEx IT organization

Define the group's Vision of the FedEx IT organization as it would exist three years in the future in terms of:

1. Goals of IT
2. Work Environment
3. Services Provided
4. People

Specify and prioritize the technical skills and personal characteristics of the IT employees in the Vision.

Results:

The headlines the group came up with indicated several things:

✓ The group was optimistic about its success in the next three years.

✓ The group felt FedEx was "special" when compared to its peers.

✓ They anticipated specific problems and pitfalls for their group over the next three years.

The 25-person group (representing all sections and levels of IT) broke into 4 teams to define their vision of IT. With this collective vision of the future defined, the group proceeded to identify and prioritize (on a 10-point scale) 60 skills and characteristics for the Programmer Job Family and the Business Analyst Job Family.

The group accomplished this work beginning to end in approximately 3 hours using an electronic meeting system. There were discussions but no heated arguments.

When asked what they thought of using an EMS in this process (it was the groups' first use of the technology), their responses included the following:

✓ Liked anonymity.

✓ Nonthreatening.

✓ Good for touchy subjects.

✓ Effective means of gathering opinions.

✓ Working in parallel beats working sequentially.

✓ People not likely to respond in large groups feel free to contribute.

✓ Ability to view and comment on others' thoughts ... provides validity or counterargument.

✓ Effective use of technology.

Case 2: Maybelline Screens New Product Ideas

Task: Make a series of complex decisions about potential new products

Situation: Maybelline has to create the future continually by predicting future fashions, trends, and needs. They use their "envisioned future" to select product ideas for consumer testing and launching. After defining 40 or 50 new product ideas, how do you narrow the field to the right 15 or 20 for which to fund further market research and development?

The situation involved these aspects conducive to using an EMS:

✓ Consensus is needed before going forward.

✓ Multiple expertise/perspectives are needed (manufacturing, sales, etc.) to make a good decision.

✓ There is limited time to gather information from a large group.

✓ A very complex decision, based on numerous criteria, must be made.

Process:

Maybelline developed, through interviewing and discussion, 14 criteria they felt would accurately predict the success of a new product. They assigned weights to these criteria to factor in their relative importance in the product's success.

They gathered about 30 people from Marketing, Market Research, Business Development, R & D, Sales, and Advertising. These people evaluated the products across all of the criteria and added comments or suggestions about each product. The process was done in three half-day sessions, held twice a year (each person attended only one of the half-day sessions).

Results:

During these meetings the mood was upbeat and humorous. Some people ridiculed product ideas while others supported them. The process gave them a way to provide both quantitative and qualitative feedback on the products; it also provided a venue for self-criticism. Consistent low ratings across all products in certain areas let management know they needed more advertising to succeed and kept them from entering markets where they had no expertise and little hope of success.

Case 3: Sedgwick Information Technology Listens to Field Advisory Group

Task: Improve IT's support to and relationship with field technical staff

Situation: The U.S. Sedgwick IT organization provides help-desk support as well as research, system development, network design, and application development for its 60-plus field offices. Local network administrators in the U.S. field offices do not report to IT. These "Net Admins" are the jacks-of-all-trades, doing everything from budget to training to installation and troubleshooting. At a national gathering of Net Admins sponsored by IT, the HQ IT organization found there were a lot of negative feelings and comments directed their way. To define and start correcting the problems, the Senior VP of IT formed an advisory group which represented all geographic areas and the variety of different-sized offices. The Net Admins could only afford to be absent from their offices for two days.

The situation involved these aspects conducive to use of an EMS:

1. Extreme difference of opinions among dominant personalities.
2. Multiple expertise/perspectives are necessary to make a good decision.
3. Limited time to gather information.
4. Meeting content must be quickly documented and used for desired impact on the organization.
5. Emotional conflicts among participants could derail constructive discussions.

Process:

At the initial gathering of the advisory group (seven Net Admins and three corporate IT staff attended, including the Senior VP) the stated objective of the meeting was:

To gather information and insights from IT coordinators in order to:

✓ increase the advantage Sedgwick gains from technology;

✓ improve communications between corporate and the field;

✓ set the IT direction to best meet the needs of the field.

Corporate staff were observers and answer-providers, not contributing participants. Participants were asked to list their "top three" IT issues. This list was consolidated to 16 items which were then prioritized by the group. Further consolidation narrowed the list to ten critical topic areas, the top seven of which the group had time to address in more detail. For each of the critical areas the Net Admins listed: 1) what was good, 2) problems, and 3) anything "missing" in that area (e.g., services, support, products, resources, procedures, etc.)

The group prioritized the problems and missing items. This gave IT a "hot list" of needs and problems to resolve in each area. The "good" items listed in each area served two purposes:

✓ They let IT know what kind of support and resources the field found useful.

✓ They softened the "sting" of criticisms in the area.

The group proceeded to answer a series of open-ended questions designed to find out what "directions" or trends in IT should change and what should remain. The questions included:

✓ How can we get a better return on technical investments?

✓ What is IT not doing that it should?

✓ How do we get the field more involved at headquarters?

✓ What **really** irritates you?

The second day was spent identifying actions and responsible parties to address the various issues. The second day all work was done without an EMS in face-to-face discussions between IT staff and field personnel.

Results:

The IT staff proceeded to take action on many of the issues and problems. Although not all problems had been fixed by the next meeting (three months later), the atmosphere was warmer and reflected the beginnings of trust on both sides.

IT sent only one staff member to attend the second meeting—the person responsible for the topic area being discussed. The group received her warmly and at the end of the day keyed several anonymous compliments commending her for being "open to criticism," "brave enough to spend the whole day with us," and "willing to listen and change."

While there are still problems to solve and relationships to improve, both groups are pleased with their progress.

Their comments on using an EMS for the first time included:

✓ Liked ability to cover a lot of discussion topics quickly.

✓ Easy to say what you feel without hurting feelings.

✓ Took 15 hours of work and completed it in one 8-hour session.

✓ Liked that we were not on the spot to give an answer to every topic.

✓ Only way to get corporate and field on the same page.

✓ Enjoyed the process of sharing ideas and working together to find solutions.

Internal Facilitators vs. Consultants

Now we've seen how an EMS can help certain kinds of meetings. Why an outside consultant? How about an internal facilitator?

A valid question, and much of the time an internal facilitator will work well. However, sometimes the facilitator needs to be an "outsider." Here are some situations when an "outsider" would be preferable:

1. Warring factions need a neutral party to manage discussions and decision making. Even if the facilitator is from a nonpartisan group (frequently HR is a source of facilitators), the groups may suspect him or her of secret allegiance to one side or the other. Often their suspicions are accurate. It is difficult for someone who is part of an organization not to have any opinions on internal issues and politics—even if he or she is professional enough not to express them.

2. The group is so "close to the problem" that they have lost perspective and need to be prompted to take a different approach. Often a corporate culture will promote one way of solving problems or dealing with issues. When this one method fails to work in a situation, the group often stagnates and is unable to move forward. Sometimes a fresh perspective or a new way of defining the problem will help the group become productive again. Someone outside of the corporate culture is generally needed as a catalyst.

3. The group needs focused, analytical skills to plan the meeting and draw conclusions from the information gathered. While many groups have these skills in their staff, the resources in "downsized" companies are often overutilized. Serious problems that cannot be put on a back burner require an outside consultant who can work, focused and full-time, on taking a problem from definition through resolution.

Conclusion

Electronic meeting systems can be a valuable tool to make meetings shorter and more effective, but don't mistake the tool for a solution. While using an EMS can be invaluable, the information in the minds of participants is what is of real value. The skill of the facilitator in planning and managing the meetings that use the EMS is also of paramount value.

Like any facilitation technique, electronic meeting systems can be used appropriately or inappropriately and can produce good or bad results. Simply using technology does not guarantee the quality of the meeting.

As organizations are pushed more by global competition and resource constraints, they will depend on technology more heavily to make their meetings efficient and effective. However, in the final analysis the most important issue is whether to have a meeting at all. After all, the best-planned and most efficient meeting is still a waste of time if it never needed to happen.

About the Editors

Mel Silberman, Ph.D. is president of Active Training (26 Linden Lane, Princeton, New Jersey 08540, 609-924-8157, mel@active-training.com, www.activetraining.com). He is also a professor of Adult and Organizational Development at Temple University where he specializes in instructional design and team building.

He is the author of

Active Training (Pfeiffer, 1990)
101 Ways to Make Training Active (Pfeiffer, 1995)
Active Learning (Allyn & Bacon, 1996)

He is the editor of:

20 Active Training Programs, vol. I (Pfeiffer, 1992)
20 Active Training Programs, vol. II (Pfeiffer, 1994)
20 Active Training Programs, vol. III (Pfeiffer, 1997)
The 1996 and 1997 McGraw-Hill Training and Performance Sourcebooks
The 1996 and 1997 McGraw-Hill Team and Organization Development Sourcebooks

Mel has consulted for hundreds of corporate, governmental, educational, and human service organizations worldwide. Among his recent clients have been:

AT&T International
Merrill Lynch
Automated Data Processing
Bristol Myers-Squibb
Devereux Foundation
Hoffman-LaRoche
Bell Atlantic
ARCO Chemical

The World Bank
Texas Instruments
Meridian Bank
Franklin Quest
J. P. Morgan, Inc.
Naval Center for Acquisition Training
Hospital of the University of PA
Penn State University

He is also a popular speaker at professional conferences.

Patricia Philips is president of Philips Consulting Inc. (514 Radnor Ave., Pine Beach, NJ 08741, 732-505-0689, Patricia.Philips-@ASTD.Noli.com), a training and development company that provides training, developmental, and administrative services to small and medium-sized companies. A former corporate trainer, Pat has over 20 years of experience writing and presenting technical and management programs. She is a member of the New Jersey Association of Women Business Owners, the Society of Insurance Trainers and Educators, and a former Board Member of the Central Jersey Chapter of ASTD. Pat was also a contributor to *The 1997 McGraw-Hill Team and Organization Development Sourcebook* and has had articles published in *Chemical Engineering Progress.*

Are you interested in being a contributor to *The 1999 Training and Performance Sourcebook?*

In the course of your professional work, you have probably developed exercises, handouts, instruments, short articles, and other printed materials that could be useful to a wide audience of consultants, trainers, and performance improvement specialists. Consider your favorite piece of work for publication. The *1999 Sourcebook* will contain another 40 practical tools to improve learning and performance. Would you like to contribute one of them? Join our impressive list of contributors.

For more information, contact:

Mel Silberman, Editor
The Training and Performance Sourcebook
c/o Active Training
26 Linden Lane
Princeton, NJ 08540
609-924-8157
609-924-4250 fax
mel@activetraining.com

THE DEFINITIVE RESOURCE FOR CREATING WINNING TEAMS AND ORGANIZATIONS

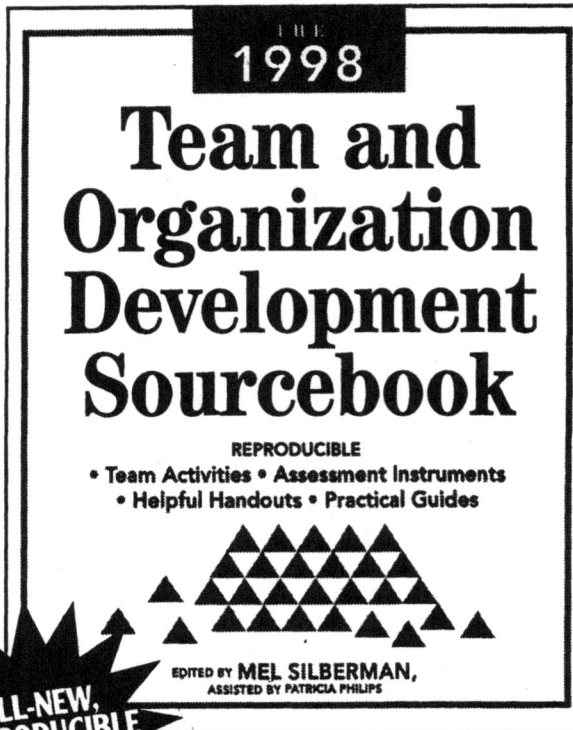

1998

Team and Organization Development Sourcebook

REPRODUCIBLE
- Team Activities • Assessment Instruments
- Helpful Handouts • Practical Guides

EDITED BY **MEL SILBERMAN,**
ASSISTED BY PATRICIA PHILIPS

ALL-NEW, REPRODUCIBLE & READY TO USE

The 1998 Team & Organization Development Sourcebook
Edited by Mel Silberman, Assisted by Patricia Philips

0-07-058002-2 • $34.95 (Paperback)
0-07-058001-4 • $79.95 (Looseleaf)
336 pages • 8 1/2" x 11"

Here is the third annual edition of the popular sourcebook that gives you direct, at-a-glance access to the right tools for building more cohesive and productive teams. With 40 reproducible activities, questionnaires, job aids, handouts, and "how-to" articles, it's sure to spark your thinking and facilitate your materials development time. Assessment of team and organizational functioning, facilitating teams, and managing and leading change are among the vital topics covered.

TOPICAL INDEX • Preface • *Team Activities* • 1. Square Wheels: A Powerful Discussion Tool on Organizational Change, Scott Simmerman • 2. Towers of Baballoon: Resolving Team Conflicts, Bill Matthews • 3. Operation Marbles: A Team-Solving Exercise, Ed Rose • 4. Stretcher Organization: A Simulation about Working Together, Stephen Hobbs • 5. Building Ground Rules for Successful Teamwork: A Consensus Activity, Harriette Mishkin • 6. The Empty Box: An Exercise in Designing Change, Lewis Welzel and Catherine Penna • 7. Coffee Break: A Case Study Exercise on Customer Service, Maxine Kamin and Donna Goldstein • 8. Climbing and Tumbling Towers: Demonstrating the Effects of Organizational Culture, Emily Schultheiss • 9. What's Wrong with This Picture? An Exercise in Team Goal Setting, Pat Kelley • 10. Fostering Creative Problem-Solving Skills within the Organization: The I-Search Technique, Tom Smith and David Price • 11. Home Page: Setting Mutual Expectations in Cross-Functional Teams, Rick Herbert • 12. Advertising Contest: A Demonstration of Hierarchical and Team Structures, Gary Topchik • 13. 7 & 7: A Team Cohesion and Trust-Building Activity, Rod Napier 14. Rules of Engagement: An Essential Team Effectiveness Tool, Ed Betof and Raymond Harrison • 15. Kaleidoscopic Thinking in Teams: A Four-Part Process, Bill Matthews • *Assessment Instruments* • 16. How Effective Is Your Work Team?, Scott Parry • 17. Is Your Team in Conflict?, Hank Karp • 18. Is Your Company a Learning Organization?, Michael Marquardt • 19. How Well Does Your Organization Manage Change?, Peter Garber • 20. What Is Your Organization's Quality Management Culture?, Roger Kaufman, Ryan Watkins, and Douglas Leigh • 21. Does Your Strategy "Make Sense" in Today's Environment?, Gina Vega • 22. How Well Are Your Managers Learning during Organizational Change?, Michaeline Skiba • 23. How Well Is Your Work Team Functioning?, Bob Preziosi • *Helpful Handouts* • 24. Tips for Building Group Consensus, Bob Guns • 25. A Quick Guide to Effective Meetings, Laura Bierema • 26. Communication: The Quality Link, Dianna Booher • 27. Ten Tips for Successful Goal Setting, Pat Kelley • 28. Ten Team Lightbulbs, Barbara Pate Glacel and Emile Robert, Jr. • 29. Six Questions to Assess Your Team's Vision, Michael Murphy • 30. The Ten Commandments for Better Team Meetings, Cynthia Solomon • 31. Eight Steps for Building a Learning Organization, Harriette Mishkin • *Practical Guides* • 32. How to Hold Your Own in Meetings, but Work as a Team, Dianna Booher • 33. How to Get Your Entire Organization to Use and Benefit from the Internet, Brian Pomeroy • 34. How to Use a Talking Stick for Group Discussions, Decisions, and Conflict Resolution, Cindy Lindsay and Janis Pasquali • 35. How to Use the Nominal Group Process to Solve Problems, Theresa Musser • 36. How to Develop Strategic Plans Based on Strategic Vision, Marlene Caroselli • 37. How to Cope with Resistance to Technology-Related Change, Jana Markowitz • 38. How to Achieve Reengineering Objectives with Results Assessment, Hal Arney • 39. How to Perform a Process Audit in the Small Business Environment, Gina Vega • 40. How to Coach Employees through Change, Nancy Jackson

McGraw Hill

A Division of The McGraw-Hill Companies